FOR LOVE OF THE GAME

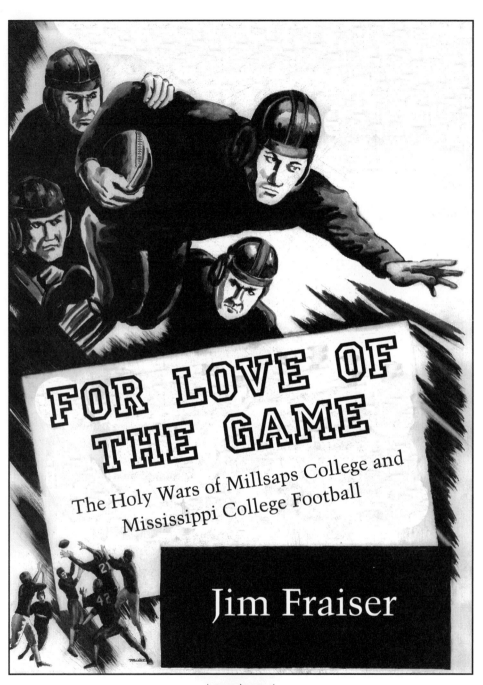

FOR LOVE OF THE GAME

The Holy Wars of Millsaps College and Mississippi College Football

Jim Fraiser

SPORTS COUNCIL

Other books by Jim Fraiser:
M Is for Mississippi: An Irreverent Guide to the Magnolia State
    (Persimmon Press, Jackson; 1991)
Shadow Seed (Black Belt Press, Montgomery; 1997)
Mississippi River Country Tales (Pelican Publishing, New Orleans; 2000)

Library of Congress Control Number: 00-136222

Photographs courtesy of the Millsaps Archives, the Bobashela, the
Tribesman, and the Special Collection, Mississippi College

Published by The Mississippi Sports Council, Inc.
Jackson, Mississippi

In memory of my aunt, Martha Gerald (1919-1997)

During the four years I spent as a student at Millsaps College during the early 70s, the only images I had of the once great gridiron rivalry between Mississippi College and my alma mater were a tattered football and a few old black and white photographs ensconced in a trophy case in the Student Union. At the time it seemed that the rivalry between MC and Millsaps was just a thing of the past—treasured memories for all the MC and Millsaps alumni long before me, but, regrettably, memories I would never experience firsthand.

Fortunately, however, the Salvation Army College Football Classic revived this famous rivalry by including Millsaps and MC in its twin bill. After a forty-year hiatus the MC-Millsaps rivalry was finally renewed. For all the alumni at both schools who missed out on being part of such a great tradition, we now have a second chance to enjoy the experience firsthand. Now those old photographs and worn football in the trophy case at Millsaps will take on new meaning to me and undoubtedly to my counterparts at Mississippi College.

Salomon Smith Barney is pleased to sponsor the publication of *For Love of the Game* and help bring the many stories surrounding the making of the rich football tradition between these two outstanding institutions to thousands of readers who will enjoy Jim Fraiser's book. If you love football, Millsaps, or Mississippi College, you are going to love this book.

Greg Frascogna
Millsaps College '74,'82

CONTENTS

ACKNOWLEDGMENTS

Having so greatly enjoyed working on this project, I must begin by thanking the Mississippi Sports Council and their attorney, Mike Frascogna, for allowing me to be a part of this wonderful Millsaps/Mississippi College football renewal. It has been a one-in-a-million experience.

Once begun, this book would never have been completed without the extraordinary guidance, aid and assistance of Millsaps College Archivist Debra McIntosh, her student staff, Betsy Perkins and Jennifer Roth, and the Special Collection Librarian for Mississippi College, Rachel Pyron, and her part-time assistant, Ann Bryant. Whether locating arcane faculty papers or digging up century-old photographs, these ladies knew where this story was hidden. Rarely have so few contributed so much!

I am also deeply indebted to the staffs of the Eudora Welty Library, the Leland Speed Mississippi College Library, the Millsaps-Wilson Library, and the Mississippi Department of Archives and History. Their willingness to "drop everything" on a moment's notice to rescue a wayward author from the depths of desperation should be an inspiration to writers across the Magnolia State!

No acknowledgment on this project would be complete without a heartfelt word of thanks to Millsaps Athletic Director Ron Jurney and Public Relations Director Kevin Russell; Mississippi College Athletic Directors Terry McMillan and Mike Jones and Public Relations Director Patty Welch; as well as "M" Club Presidents Wayne Ferrell and Gene Allen. I also thank Dr. T. W. Lewis, Dr. Van Quick, Coach Hartwell McPhail, Coach Harper Davis, Coach John Smith, Reverend Joe Whitwell, Alison Orr, Floy Holloman, Marty Frascogna and Payton Perrett for helping to make this one of the most delightful writing experiences I have ever known.

As always, I thank my wife Carole and my daughters Lucy and

Mary Adelyn, for their love, companionship and support, without which I would never ever accomplish a single worthwhile thing.

INTRODUCTION

When the Mississippi Sports Council, through their attorney, Mike Frascogna, first approached me about launching this book project, I wasn't at all certain that they had found the right man. Like most Mississippians, I was very familiar with the fine academic reputations of Millsaps College and Mississippi College, but I had never associated either church-supported, Jackson-area, private college with the concept of "big-time football." And when Mike informed me that the MC/Millsaps football rivalry had at one time been infinitely more intense than either of the Ole Miss/Mississippi State or Alabama/Auburn feuds, I didn't hesitate to argue the point.

After all, as an Ole Miss graduate, I had personally experienced the madness of the Rebel/Bulldog rivalry for the past twenty-five years, and my wife Carole, an Alabama graduate, had shown me firsthand the extent of the November madness which prevailed in Alabama every football season. That the Millsaps Majors and Mississippi College Choctaws had waged the Deep South's most heated rivalry of all time seemed more the stuff of fantasy than reality to me. But a few days of research and the first few interviews I conducted convinced me that I was in for an unexpected revelation!

To begin with, Mississippi College and Millsaps have both enjoyed a long and storied football history. From 1900 to the mid-1940s, both schools were regular gridiron opponents of Ole Miss, Mississippi State, Alabama, L.S.U., Florida, Miami, then-national powerhouse Tulane, Memphis State, Southern Mississippi, and Louisiana Tech. As late as the 1950s they were still competing against the likes of Florida State, Tampa and Central Florida!

In addition to winning a Division II National Championship and producing numerous professional football players such as Fred McAfee, Robert Fulton, and the early '80s backfield of Major Everette, Michael Williams and Darrell Posey, Mississippi College

also gave America one of its all-time greatest football stars—
Edwin "Goat" Hale. A consensus All-South halfback, Hale was
dubbed "The Red Grange of the South" by national sportswriters
and was eventually voted to the NFL Hall of Fame in 1963.

Although Millsaps football has garnered five conference championships and produced more than a dozen Kodak Little All-
Americans, many Millsaps *coaches* also gained renown during
their playing careers. The venerable "Goat" Hale led the Majors
to their first back-to-back winning seasons in the late '20s and
early '30s. "Doby" Bartling quarterbacked Ole Miss's 1936 Orange
Bowl squad before becoming one of the Majors' most successful
mentors in the '40s, and Harper Davis made All-SEC halfback at
Mississippi State before guiding Millsaps to '70s gridiron glory.

But nothing in either college's football history can compare to
the annual succession of take-no-prisoner battles waged on and
off the field by their players, students and alumni from 1920 to
1959. As for the gridiron series itself, whether played during October at the Jackson fairgrounds, as the schools' joint Homecoming
Game at Jackson's Memorial Stadium, or as a season-ending, on-
campus Thanksgiving Day match, it gave a whole new meaning
to the phrase "grudge match." It became so important in the
1930s that the teams played each other twice a season from 1936
to 1938. In the '40s, both schools' college newspapers spared no
venom while making weekly attacks on their cross-town rival's
coaches, players and fans. In the '50s, the MC/Millsaps rivalry
heated up to supernova level when it served as the Dixie Conference Title Game for four consecutive years.

But it was in the streets, and not in the trenches, where the
rivalry caught fire and eventually burned out of control. In the
1940s, "Militant" Millsaps ballplayers and students frequently
invaded the "Choctaw Reservation" to steal a school bell or sign
and to snatch a few MC freshmen beanies, while Choctaw "warriors" often went on the warpath to collect Major beanies, paint
the Millsaps campus red, and ransack the fraternity houses occu-
pying Jackson's "Methodist Hill." As the '50s progressed, the
rivalry grew so intense that on one occasion, two Millsaps students barely escaped serious injury after they were captured

attempting mischief within MC's "Baptist Boundaries." A few months later, 200 Mississippi College raiders engaged in a fist-fighting, chain-wielding rhubarb with a similarly-crazed gang of Millsaps defenders on the steps of Christian Center Auditorium!

By that decade's end, a conventional football rivalry between two church-supported, "small college" institutions had evolved into what Major Coach Doby Bartling described as nothing short of "Holy War!" Consequently, when a life-threatening, audito-rium-wide brawl broke out amongst the fans attending a Missis-sippi College/Millsaps basketball game in 1960, Millsaps officials felt they had no choice but to terminate all athletic competition between the two cross-town colleges. To the shock of football fans throughout the South, Mississippi's most intense football rivalry had suddenly come to a bloody, ignominious end. But as the new millennium dawned, more forgiving heads prevailed, the two rivals "smoked the peace pipe," and met each other on the grid-iron for the first time in forty long years.

But the beauty of the Millsaps/MC rivalry lies not in the inten-sity of disdain with which many of the two schools' fans have always regarded each other, but in the extraordinary respect and affection that the rivalry game's participants held for their fellow players, their coaches and even their gridiron opponents. For, although the fans occasionally lost their perspective, the players and coaches never did. During the entire course of the forty-year series, there was never a single, solitary fist fight, much less a brawl, between the warriors on the field. "We all loved the Mill-saps players," said a 1940s Mississippi College athlete, "because they were such competitors and never quit, even when we were ahead of them thirty to nothing."

This was a series played during a glorious time when, as another '40s era player put it, "We had no scholarship money, but we played hard and were loyal to our school because we loved the institution we played for and the man who coached us." It was a time when eleven young men, future doctors, lawyers, preach-ers, teachers and other leaders in their communities and churches, played both offense and defense while dressed only in leather hel-mets with no face guards and uniforms with no protective pads.

They played their hearts out for 60 minutes a game in the hundred degree, humidity-drenched Mississippi heat, not because they were paid to do so, or because they were treated like gods by the media and their fellow students, or even because they expected a free ride from fawning professors. They played solely for the love of the game, and no one hearing their stories can do anything but love them for doing it so courageously. One cannot help but envy what a wonderful experience these former gridiron gladiators enjoyed at Millsaps and Mississippi College. And in a world too often lacking in decency, integrity and goodness, it was a pleasure for me to visit with coaches Harper Davis and Hartwell McPhail and discover that today's student athletes can still make the sometimes treacherous passage to manhood under the tutelage of such competent, caring and character-instilling mentors as may be found in Division III football at Millsaps and Mississippi College.

Indeed, such leadership is a long-held tradition at both schools. In the 1950s, former MC head coach Stanley Robinson, who was athletic director at the time, loaned an impoverished freshman student $500 so he could afford to stay in school and obtain a college education, saying that if the boy couldn't ever pay him back, "he'd consider it a good investment." Nineteen-forties Millsaps head coach Doby Bartling was so loved and respected by his players at both Vanderbilt and Millsaps that they came from the far corners of this nation to attend his 1996 funeral so they could tell his seventeen-year-old grandson what a powerful impact Bartling had had upon their lives. Not even time can erase the incalculable good that has been accomplished in the name of sports at these two noble institutions.

And as I also discovered, time has done little to take the starch out of many of these former players' jerseys. "Why is an Ole Miss graduate writing a book about Millsaps and Mississippi College?" asked a former Millsaps player in mock indignation, upon discovering my "outsider" status. Satisfied with my explanation, he proceeded to spin some of the funniest sports-related yarns I have ever heard. I became so enthralled with his stories and kept laughing so loudly that my wife finally had to threaten to disconnect our telephone if I didn't tone it down right away.

Another former player, '40s Choctaw star Charley Armstrong, put my knowledge of Mississippi College football history to the test during a late-night telephone interview. "Who were Coach Stanley Robinson's selections for his All-Time Choctaw team at end, tackle and in the backfield," he asked.

Having luckily seen Coach Robby's list the day before, I proudly replied, "Joel Hitt, Archie Mathews, 'Goat' Hale and Cy Parks."

"And who was the other halfback?" Armstrong asked matter-of-factly.

I suddenly remembered that there had been another player in Robinson's backfield. "I just can't recall his name," I admitted.

"It was me!" Armstrong gleefully announced. "You don't know a thing about MC football!" And then he graciously proceeded to enlighten me. When has the writing of history ever been so much fun?

You see, it is one thing to write about ancient history; to mull over dusty, out-of-print manuscripts and to peruse yellowed, near-faded volumes. It is something else entirely to take modern history straight from the mouths of its creators and to experience the variety of human emotion that always accompanies those stories. And these former players and coaches seemed to enjoy telling their tales for posterity almost as much as I was moved by hearing what they had to say.

I say moved, because it is a rare thing in today's world to hear sports stars giving sincerely-felt credit to their teammates, their coaches and even to their cross-town archrivals. It is even rarer to hear one of them admit that his play cost his team a big game or that he took part in an activity that besmirched his alma mater's reputation. But having survived the character-building experience known as non-scholarship, small college football, these former weekend warriors never ducked their responsibility to tell it like it was.

And if at any point in your reading you find yourself wondering if their tales are more fiction than fact, or whether anything such as this could have ever taken place at two small, church-supported Mississippi colleges, I urge you to shrug off such concerns and get on with your reading. It gets more unbelievable with the turning of each page, but it really did happen, right here in Mississippi, at two renowned institutions called Millsaps and Mississippi College.

And you may find yourself wishing that it had also happened to you.

FOR LOVE OF THE GAME

PROLOGUE

August 26, 1999
Millsaps College Campus, Jackson, Mississippi
Football practice field
2:30 P.M.

The freshman quarterback turned and looked upfield just in time to see his tall, blue jersey-clad receiver plant a right foot and cut toward the sidelines. Payton Perrett cocked his arm and then heaved a perfectly spinning spiral fifteen yards downfield. Running a step ahead of the cornerback, the split end snared the ball just before his momentum carried him across the out-of-bounds stripe. "Yeah!" cheered Perrett, happy to have completed his first collegiate pass.

It hadn't mattered that it had come as part of an informal scrimmage, a "pass scale" drill involving only receivers and defensive backs. Or that he hadn't been facing the opposing team's pass rush. What mattered to the Mississippi College signal caller was that he had completed his first pass against his Choctaws' once and future archrival—the Millsaps College Majors. And, as he had heard all his life, such a completion was always cause for celebration.

But not everyone on the field shared Perrett's enthusiasm.

"Try it again, rookie," barked junior Millsaps cornerback, Marty Frascogna, as Perrett approached the new line of scrimmage. "A blind hog finds an acorn now and then."

"I'll be calling your number all day," replied Perrett cooly. "I want to look good on my first day out."

"Hope you do look good," a grinning Frascogna retorted, "so your parents will be welcome at your games."

"Hey, I'm ready for the real game to get here so I can rub your nose in it, Marty."

"Sure you are, Payton. The jock schools usually do win. But then you have to graduate."

"And not too long after that," chimed in Millsaps safety Craig Bowman, "you'll be working for us!"

"I could get you a job in the mail room," Frascogna offered, his voice dripping with faux southern charm.

"And I'll probably need a driver," added Bowman gleefully.

Before Perrett could respond, Mississippi College offensive coordinator Brad Griffin herded him back to the team's huddle. "What are you guys doing?" Griffin wanted to know. Were his charges talking trash in a half-baked little summertime scrimmage? Good Lord, he wondered, how would they act in next year's season opener when the Choctaws and Majors renewed a football rivalry that had been banned for forty years? Griffin simply couldn't believe what he was hearing.

A wide, boyish grin spread slowly across the handsome young quarterback's face. "It's okay, Coach," laughed Perrett. "Marty and I played high school ball together at Jackson Prep. We're good friends. Just having a little fun with each other today."

A glance at Marty Frascogna's All-American smile told Griffin that he had worked up a sweat for nothing. And he hadn't failed to notice how much his charges were enjoying their two hour scrimmage with the Majors, despite the humidity-drenched, ninety-five degree Mississippi heat. Even so, this was Mississippi College and Millsaps, an archrivalry viewed by many as one of the most heated in "small" college football history. One that had degenerated into such riotous behavior in the late '50s that Millsaps officials had to end the series forever. Or so they believed in the spring of 1960 when the news of the termination spread throughout both campuses. You could never be too careful, Griffin reminded himself, where young kids and that kind of a rivalry were concerned.

"All right, Payton," Griffin said, "guess there's nothing wrong with a little fun now and then. But now let's get back in there and show 'em you can do it every time!"

When later informed about the scrimmage "incident," Mississippi College defensive coach John Smith flashed a knowing smile. The Choctaws and Majors hadn't met each other on the gridiron for the past forty years, but his memories of that rivalry were as vivid as if he had played his last game against Millsaps just one week ago. *But who would believe me now if I told them,* Smith mused as he closed his playbook and laid it on his desk, *if I told them the truth about our old "blood and guts" rivalry? About the unbelievable intensity of the series? And how the craziness surrounding it brought an end to a great series that had dated all the way back to 1920...*

John Smith closed his office door, leaned back in his chair, and pondered the situation. How, he wondered, had such a clean-cut rivalry between two academically-renowned, southern, church schools spun so far out of control back in the late '50s? The 1950s, of all times—Dwight Eisenhower, Bob Hope and Pat Boone, for goodness sake! The days of drive-in theaters, chaperoned sock hops, Frostop root beer, crew cut hairdos and 100% wholesome athletics. How had the fans of these two prestigious, Jackson area-based, liberal arts colleges—the eventual political, academic and religious leaders of the very conservative state of Mississippi—gone so insane over the series that it had to be canceled in order to protect life and limb of participant and innocent spectator alike? And would history repeat itself when MC and Millsaps renewed their rivalry in a September, 2000, season opener in Jackson?

Knowing that there was little he could do about it now that the game had become an inevitability, Smith cast his worries aside and indulged himself in the luxury of a pleasant reminiscence. His mind drifted back to a more innocent time when God was in His heaven, Americans trusted their political leaders, a hard day's work was not only expected but heartily welcomed, and non-scholarship athletes played college ball not for the money, but solely because they loved the game. He harkened back to a brisk, fall evening, forty years ago...

CHAPTER ONE

THE GAME

October 24, 1959
Hinds Memorial Stadium, Jackson, Mississippi
6:35 P.M.

From his vantage on the Mississippi College sidelines, senior End John Smith, looked up at the twelve thousand loyal fans who had braved the gusty winds and chilly October evening temperatures to see him and his Choctaws do battle with their greatest rival, the Millsaps College Majors. Somewhere in that faceless mass, huddled together under a large woolen blanket, sat his mother and father, who, for the first time during his four year collegiate career, had come to see him snare passes for Mississippi College.

Although they had often made the thirty-mile drive from Byram to Clinton to see him play Choctaw baseball, they had stayed away from his football games, contests they viewed as barbaric, potentially injurious exercises. As pleased as they were that their son had chosen to attend a small, Baptist-owned college, and to participate there in the glorious American pastime of baseball, they could never bring themselves to watch him and other fine young men risk permanent injury on the gridiron.

Smith had always understood his parent's feelings about the sport which, he knew as well as anyone, was every bit the violent and potentially dangerous game they believed it to be. But small college football was far more than just a chance to get injured to him. It was also about something special; something with an almost religious quality. Something he lacked the artistry of expression to fully explain. But whatever that "something" was, it compelled him to play the game, to devote every ounce of his mind, body and soul whenever he took the field. And this was so even though Smith would never receive the scholarship money, universal adulation, media accolades, or any of the other blessings major college football players took for granted every day. And, now, his parents had finally overcome their fears and traveled to Jackson to see him play the most important game of his life. It just didn't get any better than that.

Not that John Smith needed any additional motivation to get ready to play in the annual Mississippi College/Millsaps grudge match. The series, which had begun innocently enough in 1920, had over the past thirty-nine years become one of the most heated football rivalries in the South. Which was just another way of pronouncing it one of the most heated sports rivalries in the world. For although longstanding major college pigskin rivalries such as Ole Miss vs. Mississippi State and Alabama vs. Auburn were more renowned, drew considerably more fans to their games, and produced nationally-heralded players such as consensus All-Americans Jake Gibbs, Jackie Parker, Joe Namath and Charlie Flowers, those rivalries had nothing on the annual MC/Millsaps bloodletting, at least not where hard-nosed football and emotionally-charged fan mania were concerned.

And the wide-ranging hostilities preceding this 1959 game had left little doubt in Smith's mind that the rivalry had lost nothing by way of intensity. If anything, Smith mused as he turned his gaze back toward the field and surveyed the gold-helmeted, white jersey-clad Millsaps players across the field, the rivalry had reached a boiling point among the faithful of both schools which now threatened the very existence of the annual grudge match.

The amazing thing was, the series had never been tainted by any on-the-field fistfights or bench-clearing rhubarbs, at least not during Smith's four-year tenure. True enough, there had always been sporadic incidences of barroom brawls and movie-theater fisticuffs in downtown Jackson involving players as well as students of both schools. But those incidents had led to little more than a few black eyes and an occasional bloody nose, and had done nothing to put a damper on the generally-held good spirits among the series's participants.

Unfortunately, in recent years, the off-the-field violence associated with the series had escalated from small-scale conflicts to all-out war. And the cause of much of this strife, apart from the intensity of the football rivalry, had been the participants' penchant for making trophies of the other school's freshmen headgear.

For decades, athletes and students at both schools had made a mutually-favored ritual of snatching their opponents' beanie caps—the small, round, felt caps with which the freshmen were required to cover their recently-shaved heads. And on special "M" Club initiation occasions, Millsaps football players drove the twenty miles down Highway 80 from their campus in downtown Jackson to the nearby hamlet of Clinton to snatch a few beanies from unsuspecting Mississippi College freshmen, just as carloads of Choctaw athletes frequently descended upon their opponents' campus to "scalp" oft-harried Millsaps frosh. For thirty years these beanie-snatching events had been carried out in the congenial spirit of a treasured collegiate rivalry, but in the past three years, they had taken a darker, more sadistic turn.

Some attributed the change to the mere fact of a more competitive series. After winning the first game in the series by a score of 60-0, Mississippi College had dominated the rivalry and now held an overall lead in the football series of 23 wins to 9, with six games resulting in ties. However, Millsaps had begun to turn the tide in the 1950s, winning three of four games between 1951 and 1954, and claiming moral victories in 1956 and 1958 when those matches ended deadlocked at 0-0. Closer games with conference championships resting on the outcome had raised the intensity level of this already heated rivalry to a volcanic, fever pitch. It was precisely this fact, many believed, which had led to an eruption of violence on both campuses during the late 1950s.

And John Smith had been right there in the middle of it when all-out warfare had been declared. In the fall of 1957, partially in response to a 19-0 thrashing at the hands of the Choctaws, Millsaps footballer and man-among-men, Ted Alexander, who had further distinguished himself as a Golden Gloves boxer, had issued an unusual challenge to the whole MC squad.

"Y'all bring a group of players to our campus," Alexander had said over the phone, "and we'll wrestle each other for the right to the other freshmen players' beanies." And to make it all official, Alexander had proposed, "We'll set up a bipartisan committee to decide who wins."

Never ones to ignore such a challenge, Smith and fourteen Choctaw freshmen had driven to the Millsaps campus just off State Street, several miles north of the Old State Capitol Museum in downtown Jackson. There, they had met fifteen opposing freshmen at the base of the Millsaps campus flagpole. And though they had brought another fifteen supporters with them, the Choctaw partisans soon found themselves in a decided minority, surrounded by a host of highly agitated Millsaps onlookers.

But despite this recipe for disaster, accustomed good spirits seemed to prevail as the participants met to write a new wrestling chapter in the ancient cross-town rivalry. In the bold but gentlemanly demeanor of the turn-of-the-century Old South duelist, Alexander approached the Mississippi College group and said, "I'm ready to go and I'll take on anybody who wants me." With neither just provocation nor any warning whatsoever, MC freshman footballer, Barry Landrum, struck Alexander square in the mouth! In the melee that followed, the MC boys were attacked on all sides, soundly whipped and chased from the Millsaps campus.

This proved to be the first volley of what a Millsaps coach had called the MC/Millsaps "Holy War," and the second shot was not very long in coming. A few months later, on a spring evening in 1958, a bell rang out on the Mississippi College campus which everyone recognized as a warning that miscreant Millsapsers had been sighted making a beanie raid on the Clinton campus. The two offenders, who had been scooting across campus in an MG convertible, were soon captured while afoot by the Choctaw football squad. After shaving their captives' heads, the MC boys, John Smith among them, had taken the "Saps" to the freshman girls dorm and forced them to serenade the ladies.

Hours later, when the two humiliated Millsapsers drove away from the Choctaw crowd, their car's front tire rolled across onlooker Billy "Oscar" Stevens's foot. Enraged by this painful turn of events, Stevens hopped in his car and outraced the Millsaps boys to the edge of the MC campus. As they attempted to reach the highway leading back to Jackson, Stevens blocked the roadway with his car, forcing them off the pavement and into a heavily wooded forest. The MG was practically demolished by a tree and the Millsaps boys were thrown headlong from their car. Luckily, they escaped serious injury.

When word of these events reached Mississippi College officials, they conducted an inquiry which resulted in heavy sanctions for several MC students. One of those sanctioned, Jay Higgenbotham, added further flame to the fire by defending his actions on grounds that he had simply been seeking satisfaction for having been tied to a pine tree in front of Jackson's University Medical Center and left there all night by renegade Millsaps students. Although John Smith had no way of knowing if Higgenbotham's story was true, he had, for the first time, begun to wonder if the MC/Millsaps rivalry was spiraling out of control.

But Smith was determined not to dwell on such worrisome matters as he stood beside his teammates in Hinds Memorial Stadium, preparing to play his final Millsaps/Mississippi College football game. As the kickoff drew nearer, one thought began to dominate John Smith's mind. And that thought was "whip the Millsaps Majors!"

Millsaps sophomore split end, Joe Whitwell, gazed across the field at his Mississippi College opponents. In their dark helmets and navy jerseys, the swaggering, athletic-looking Choctaws gave every impression that they agreed with the pundits who had made them near unanimous favorites to win this ballgame. Even Whitwell couldn't find fault with those predictions; not only did the Choctaws sport an impressive 4-1 record compared to the Majors' paltry 1-4 mark, they had fared considerably better against common opponents, whipping Samford and Sewanee by identical scores of 27-6, while those teams had outscored Millsaps by a combined total of 47 points to none.

But Whitwell preferred to believe what his coaches had been saying for the past few weeks—you could throw away the record book where this hotly contested, "must win" rivalry was concerned. If the prognosticators were willing to give this game to the

Choctaws on paper, he and his teammates were more than willing to take their chances settling matters on the field. And considering that this was the last contest of the decade and Homecoming for both schools, to say nothing of all the extra-curricular hoopla and controversial incidents that had occurred in the days preceding this game, he and his fellow Majors had every reason to give their all to win the contest. There was even the added motivation of recovering their ceremonial Major sword which had, for the past five years, taken up ignominious residence in a trophy case on "the Choctaw Reservation." It was long past time for Whitwell and his Majors to claim the ceremonial Choctaw tomahawk as their Homecoming Game prize.

Whitwell reckoned that if any of his fellow sophomores hadn't learned earlier in the season what this game meant to Millsaps's veteran players, students, fans and anyone remotely associated with either school, they had certainly gained a first-class education during the past few days. If a week's worth of headlines in the statewide newspaper, the *Clarion-Ledger*, hadn't gotten their attention, then the articles appearing in the two schools' newspapers certainly had. Writing for the *Mississippi Collegian*, Choctaw scribe Jack Curtis, Jr., had sarcastically noted that, "Millsaps recently fell to winless Sewanee, 21-0. It looks like the same old bunch of Saps over across town. I thought this year might be different and have them furnish a little competition. Oh, well, if we keep your sword much longer, Majors, you might as well give it to us." Hundreds of copies of that article had mysteriously appeared on the Millsaps campus little more than twenty minutes after the offending rag had left the MC presses two days earlier.

Not to be outdone, an anonymous editorialist for Millsaps's student publication, *The Purple and White*, had predicted, in bold print no less, that "THE MAJORS ARE GOING TO SLASH THE CHOCTAWS' THROAT WITH THEIR SWORD AND THEN SCALP HIM WITH HIS OWN TOMAHAWK!"

And as the *P&W* had revealed the day before the game, even the coeds had gotten into the act this year. Whitwell smiled as he remembered when his roommate and fellow ball player

"Wooky" Gray, had shown him the article. According to the story, a week before the big game, four Millsaps coeds had relieved an MC freshman of his beanie at the state fair in downtown Jackson. The girls had spotted their victim in a crowd of fair-goers, snuck up behind him, snatched his beanie and run. When the stunned young man had finally chased them down, he still couldn't recover his hat, because one of the girls had stashed it in an unapproachable region underneath her sweater. Although the MC boy had tried to force a bargain with his antagonists by grabbing the nearest girl's purse, a policeman made him return it, and the girls had slipped away in the crowd before he'd had time to demand the return of his beanie. The article had ended with a tribute hailing the girls as "heroes forever."

But another recent news report had injected a more sobering note into the relatively harmless pre-game fun. A Mississippi Collegian column entitled "Old Custom, New Spirit," had mentioned a spring 1958 automobile accident involving two Millsaps students who had been caught on the MC campus stealing freshman beanies. The article further related that as part of the Mississippi College administration's crackdown on taunting and tormenting between the two colleges, freshman football initiation had been canceled for 1959 and there had been no beating of the traditional Tom-Tom at the annual Choctaw pep rally the week before the Millsaps game. But that ban had apparently been rescinded, Whitwell realized, as the incessant sound of drumbeats arose from the MC student section and reverberated throughout Hinds Memorial Stadium. And rescinded or not, the MC administration's edict certainly hadn't prevented the all-out brawl that Whitwell and some of his fellow Millsapsers had fought with MC students the very day that article had been published.

On the Thursday night before the game, about a hundred of the MC faithful had gathered across the street from the Millsaps campus, at the bottom of a hill in front of the Christian Center Auditorium. Aware of rumors that a Mississippi College gang was coming to town to "whip some Millsaps butts," the Millsaps administration had declared a moratorium on all fighting and other violence. Nevertheless, Whitwell and about twenty-five other Majors, including the fearsome Ted Alexander, had come out that night to meet the Choctaw invaders. Finally, after a few harsh words passed between the rival gangs, the Millsaps boys had charged across the street and attacked the Mississippi College crowd.

A punch had sent Whitwell tumbling to the ground, and before he could recover, several Choctaw brawlers had pummeled him to near senselessness. As soon as he managed to escape, Whitwell had limped back to his Burton Hall dorm room clad only in his underwear, carrying one leg of his torn jeans in one hand, with the other leg draped across his shoulder. His torn clothing had served as a trophy the next day in the dorm—a sure sign that he had fought bravely against overwhelming odds in a holy crusade to slay the Mississippi College "dragon."

But that had been two days ago; ancient history as far as Joe Whitwell was concerned. Nothing mattered to him right now except the big game he was about to play. He glanced down the sideline at his fellow Majors anxiously awaiting the whistle which would signal the contest's beginning. An unexpected sense of pride suddenly welled up inside him. Despite the barroom brawls and campus fistfights he and his teammates had waged during their brief Millsaps tenure, neither they nor any of the opposing Choctaw ballplayers had ever engaged in any on-the-field taunting, cheap hits, or fistfighting. As hard-hitting as each Millsaps/MC game had been, they had all been waged decently, fairly, and honorably.

As for what had driven those same young men to violence off the field, Whitwell was at a complete loss to understand it. Perhaps there was a religious dimension to the rivalry. Mississippi College was a Baptist-owned school while Millsaps was a Methodist-supported institution, and it was simply a case of who had the biggest TRUTH, the Baptists or the Methodists. On the other hand, Whitwell's former roommate, a divinity student named Keith Tonkel, had put the "religious dimension" in more humorous, possibly more accurate terms. It was a case of Christians vs. the Lions, Tonkel had said with a grin, and the only issue to be decided was who would be the Christians and who would be the Lions!

Unfortunately, more often that not, Whitwell's Majors had played the sacrificial Christians to the Choctaws' marauding lions. But recent years had seen a reversal of that trend, and maybe the mere fact of a more competitive rivalry had driven the participants to such violent, off-the-field extremes. Then again, maybe the old, rural Mississippi axiom was correct after all—when two big dogs share the same pound, sooner or later they're going to have to find out which of them is the top dog. Whatever the reason, where cross-town rivals Millsaps and Mississippi College were concerned, no player ever left anything on the sideline, Whitwell knew. Every one of them gave everything he had on the battlefield, win, lose or draw.

Be it "Holy War," as a former Millsaps coach had labeled it, or Mississippi barnyard scrap, as it was popularly known, Whitwell knew that this was one game that nobody on the field could bear to lose. And everyone seated in Memorial Stadium when this game kicked off at 8:00 P.M. would discover exactly what the word 'rivalry' was all about...

THE GAME

Third Quarter
1:00 remaining
Choctaws—14, Majors—0
Choctaw ball on their own 45 yard line

John Smith stood patiently in the huddle and waited for his quarterback, Larry Therrell, to call the next play. All three Choctaw quarterbacks had been calling fullback Linus Bridges's number most of the night, and Bridges had responded by staking his team to a 14 point lead with a one-yard scoring dive in the second quarter and a five yard TD scamper in the third. Bridges had followed up his second TD by snagging a pass in the end zone from Choc QB Milton Thomas for a two point conversion.

But the determined expressions on the faces of their Millsaps opponents had convinced Smith and his teammates that a 14-point cushion was not a sufficient margin to warrant even a moment's let down. What they needed now was a game-icing, knockout blow.

For once, Therrell ignored the trap-blocking play which had opened huge holes for Bridges to run through all night, and called for an unexpected long pass—the "bomb" to John Smith. Therrell looked his receiver in the eye, as if to ask, "Do you think you can do it?" The unspoken answer clearly evident in Smith's eyes—"You get me the ball, and I'll get us six"—was all Therrell needed to see. "Ready. . . Break!" barked Therrell as he led his team to the line of scrimmage.

At the snap of the ball, Smith raced downfield, looking back for the pass only after he had crossed the Majors' forty yard line. He snagged the perfectly thrown ball at the Millsaps 35 and raced untouched into the end zone for the score!

Smith handed the ball to the referee and jogged back toward his bench where his teammates were waiting to shake his hand. . .

Fourth Quarter
10:52 remaining
Choctaws–26, Millsaps–0

"Good run, Bean Pole," said Joe Whitwell to his tall, gangly quarterback, Larry Marett, who had just made an electrifying twenty-five yard dash from Millsaps territory to the Choctaw 46 yard line. And though Whitwell bravely tried to put a good face on the moment, everyone in the huddle knew that, with the Choctaws leading by twenty-six points and in complete control of the game, there was no chance of mounting a comeback with less than eleven minutes left to play. Even worse for Whitwell, his costly fumble in the opening minutes of the second quarter at his own 28 yard line had enabled the Choctaws to break a hard-fought, scoreless tie with their first touchdown of the game. His mistake had proved the turning point of the game, but he knew that this was no time to wallow in self-recrimination. He still had important work to do.

Getting skunked by their greatest rival on Homecoming night in front of the largest crowd to ever see a MC/Millsaps game was something no red-blooded ballplayer could stomach. It was one thing to lose to a clearly superior team; it was something else entirely to suffer a shutout at the hands of their archrival.

Fortunately, the Millsaps signal caller had worked out a good plan to avoid that ultimate humiliation. Marett took control of the huddle and then focused his one good eye on his favorite receiver. "Get open, Joe," was all he said. Whitwell nodded enthusiastically. The down and out pattern had been their most successful combination all night. Now was the perfect time to turn it upfield for a score.

At the snap of the ball, Whitwell loped fifteen yards downfield, then cut towards the sideline to sell Marett's pump fake. Planting his right foot on the turf, Whitwell suddenly turned and flew past a surprised Choctaw cornerback just as Marett released the ball.

Whitwell snared the perfectly thrown pass practically in midstride and then raced towards pay dirt. Choctaw safety Milton Thomas made the most of a good angle and caught up to the receiver at the MC ten yard line, but Whitwell shook off the intended tackle and lunged forward into the end zone for the game's final score.

Twenty-six to six wasn't what I wanted, Whitwell told himself as he hustled unceremoniously towards the Millsaps sideline, *but it sure as heck beats a whitewashing.* And the touchdown had gone a long way towards making up for his earlier mistake. *And after all,* Whitwell reminded himself, *I'm only a sophomore. I've still got two more shots at them. . . .*

THE BRAWL

February 16, 1960
Municipal Auditorium, downtown Jackson
Millsaps/Mississippi College basketball game
7:44 P.M.

Nestled comfortably in the theater-style seating of the wooden grandstands in the sold-out 3000-capacity Municipal Auditorium, John Smith and his fellow Choctaw supporters were enjoying every minute of a rough and tumble basketball game with the

Millsaps cagers. The only thing better than taking your licks while whipping your biggest rival, Smith mused, was watching someone else take their licks while whipping your biggest rival. And despite owning a commanding first period lead, the "Baptist Braves" were certainly taking their licks on the basketball court this night.

With less than ten minutes gone in the first half, the Mississippi College squad had already been whistled for eighteen fouls, most of them incurred while unsuccessfully trying to take the ball away from their game-freezing opponents. And although Mississippi College's roundballers had come into the Millsaps game leading the nation in scoring with a 113 points-per-game average, the Majors, led by their lone effective shooter, Larry Marett, had effectively put on the freeze and held the Chocs to a point total that was far short of their first period average. Never mind that the Majors seemed not to care whether they scored very many points; just putting the skids to Little All America candidate Tommy Covington and his high-powered MC offense was what motivated their players this evening.

As the Choctaws pulled away with a 30 point, 54-24 lead at the fifteen minute mark, the MC student section began mercilessly taunting their hapless rivals. Two rows above Smith, Choctaw linebacker Barry Lambert held aloft a flag that MC student Chuck Brandon had recently stolen from Millsaps's Kappa Sigma Fraternity house during an otherwise unsuccessful beanie raid. When Smith realized that two of Millsaps's Kappa Sig football players, rugged defensive tackle John Woods, and the fearsome, 6'3", 230 pound, offensive lineman, Wooky Gray, had spied their sign in Lambert's hands, he knew that trouble was headed his way.

When he saw Gray and Woods leave the auditorium, Smith felt certain they would return moments later fully reinforced. Shortly before halftime, they proved Smith right by marching back into the arena with their numbers greatly increased and heading straight for the MC student section. As Gray and his cohorts made the trek up the perilously steep bleachers, undaunted as they were by a sea of hostile Choctaw faces, Lambert placed the Kappa Sigma banner underneath Smith's chair. Also just arriving from a nearby row, Jerry Napier and Ray McPhail closed ranks in support of their fellow MC classmates.

Gray pushed his way through the heavily partisan MC crowd and confronted Lambert man to man. "We don't want any trouble," Gray somberly declared. "We just want our sign back." Spying the sign underneath Smith's seat, Gray reached down to retrieve it. But before he could grab it, Lambert cold-cocked him with a right hook to the jaw. Bedlam immediately erupted throughout the stands, and John Smith soon found himself swinging for his life. The fight quickly spread from the MC bleachers down to the auditorium floor, and from there several yards further into the concession area. One on one confrontations arose throughout the auditorium, and near the spot where the melee had begun, a group of MC students hoisted the fallen Wooky Gray over their shoulders, carried him to the bleacher railing, and dangled him over the edge, fifteen yards above the hardwood auditorium floor. They were eventually talked out of dropping Gray, as the fall would surely have killed or crippled him.

After Smith had successfully fended off numerous glancing blows, a blindside punch sent him sprawling on the auditorium floor. He picked himself up and backed up to a steel post to prevent any further surprise attacks. To his right, Smith saw an MC student deliver a wicked jab to Millsaps junior Gene Davenport, opening a large gash on his forehead.

On the court, where cooler heads had prevailed despite the foul-plagued, hard-nosed play, the game had been halted by the officials, leaving Choctaw guard Tom Lee stranded at the free-throw line. On the Millsaps bench, forward Tom Royals readied himself for trouble when muscular MC guard Dutch Nichols strode purposefully across the floor straight toward Royals. He breathed a sigh of relief when Nichols sat down beside him and calmly said, "Boy, it sure is a shame that our schools do this sort of thing."

The police finally moved in and broke up the fighting, and after several of the participants had been ejected from the building, and both Gray and Davenport had been rushed to the hospital, play was eventually resumed. And although Smith and the Choctaws faithful later celebrated a record-breaking 131-72 victory and a sweep of the 1960 basketball series, they soon discovered that the shameful extra-curricular activities attending the game would come back to haunt them in less than a week's time.

GROUND ZERO

The next morning
Millsaps campus

When Wooky Gray finally returned to his dorm room after his release from Baptist Hospital, his roommate, Joe Whitwell, gave him the news that was already spreading across the Millsaps campus like wildfire. School officials, Whitwell said, were already planning a meeting to discuss the possibility of discontinuing all sports contests between Millsaps and Mississippi College!

During the next four days, articles in several local newspapers confirmed their worst fears—Dr. Milton C. White, Chairman of the Millsaps Faculty Athletic Committee, had written a terse letter to Mississippi College officials terminating all intercollegiate sports competition between the two schools, citing as his reason the "bad feelings between the two schools when their student bodies get together" for ballgames. Surprisingly, the Jackson press corps were almost unanimous in their support of White's decision. This was certainly true of the *Purple & White*, which hailed the decision as "wise" in light of the "difference in attitude [and] conduct" of the two schools where athletic events were concerned.

In his weekly *State Times* column, sportswriter Jimmie McDowell wrote that

> continued shabby, unsportsmanlike conduct by [Mississippi College] students at these athletic contests is simply going to take away some of the luster from the team. By ridiculing outclassed opponents, MC students certainly displayed none of that Choctaw spirit which helped make the college great. There was no move by a Mississippi College official to halt the brawl.

In a February 1960 *Clarion-Ledger* column entitled "Walters's Shavin's," Carl Walters labeled Millsaps's decision as "regrettable—but wise." He characterized the prevailing atmosphere at MC/Millsaps games as "unwholesome," and pointed out that the only school with which Millsaps had any such troubles was their main rival, Mississippi College. Rebutting another pundit's opinion that the Majors had quit playing the Choctaws because "they couldn't take it when they get their brains beat out," Walters opined that Millsaps, with its meager athletic budget, prohibition against athletic scholarships, and "low pressure," "play for fun" attitude, had for years been "taking it from just about every athletic opponent they have met," while Mississippi College was pursuing a "more comprehensive and ambitious athletic program."

"It is best that they go their separate ways," Walters concluded. "Athletically speaking, their policies are so different that they have little in common."

Joe Whitwell shook his head as he laid the Walters column on his dorm room desk. He knew that Millsaps had broken off basketball competition with MC several years earlier when the Choctaws had run afoul of Dixie Conference prohibitions against athletic scholarships and been placed on NCAA probation, but that the two schools had resumed cage play only two seasons later. The rift was far more serious this time. Dr. White's letter had the ring of finality to it, and it appeared that neither Whitwell nor any other Major would ever get the chance to win back Millsaps's ceremonial sword from the Choctaws. Or to avenge the 1959 loss that would haunt him and his teammates forever. . .

CHAPTER TWO

BACK TO THE BEGINNING
1798-1900

Mississippi College

Shortly after falling into American hands in 1798, the Mississippi Territory, which included most of present-day Mississippi and Alabama, became known throughout the United States as an unimaginably wild frontier where legendary events were as common as water moccasins. Territorial news reports carried daily accounts of sandbar duels-to-the-death, world famous Mississippi River steamboat races, extravagant floating casino palaces with infamous riverboat gamblers, daily hold-ups on the Natchez Trace by merciless land pirates, and brawling 'Kaintock' flatboatmen and women who claimed kinship with alligators and bears. There were rampaging Chickasaw Indians, flamboyant backwoods politicians, brazen flophouse prostitutes, bizarre voodoo practitioners, hell-raising itinerant preachers, nationally-renowned actors, half-baked frontier sawbones and shysters, and the ineffable stuff of which legends are made. These were the days of Andrew Jackson, Jim Bowie, Jean Lafitte, Meriwether Lewis, Aaron Burr, Chief Pushmataha, Chief Greenwood Leflore, riverboat fighter Annie Christmas, Trace robber Wiley Harpe, Rev. "Crazy" Lorenzo Dow and renowned British actor Tyrone Power.

But after Mississippi became the burgeoning American nation's twentieth state in 1817, the frontier slowly gave way to the inexorable rise of civilization. Within a few scant years, Mississippians decided that the time had come to bring the amenities of higher education to a largely illiterate populace. Toward that end, the citizens of a small central Mississippi village called Mount

Salus founded Hampstead Academy in order to educate their children. Then, in early 1827, eight prominent local landowners helped the new academy gain the state legislature's approval as well as the right to raise $25,000 via a lottery for its support. The legislature promptly adopted a new name for the school—Mississippi Academy—and granted it the further support of five years' income from thirty-six sections of timber and farm land. In addition to receiving this legislative assistance, the school also sold scholarships at a premium of $500 each.

In April of 1827, Gideon Fitz, the first President of the Academy's Board of Trustees, notified prospective students that the English Department would offer grammar, geography and history, while the Classical Department would teach Latin and Greek languages, mathematics, natural philosophy, chemistry, astronomy and rhetoric. Tuition fees would be "$7.50 for an English student and $10 for a classical." He also published the school's conduct guidelines, which declared that students would be punished for "lying, drunkenness, profaneness, uncleanliness, and playing at unlawful games." The rules also prohibited "loud talking, hallooing, whistling and jumping...," recommended that parents be "moderate in their supplies of monies" to their attending children, required regular Sunday worship and maintenance of the "sanctification of the Sabbath," and barred students from visiting any "barroom or a tavern, tippling house or ballroom, *without the permission of the President.*"

In 1829, city fathers changed the town's name from Mt. Salus to Clinton in honor of much-admired New York Governor DeWitt Clinton. Later that year, Clinton lost a bid to become the Hinds County seat to nearby Raymond. The town's ambitious leadership next attempted to lure the state capital to Clinton from Jackson by offering the Academy's buildings for governmental use, but a close legislative vote made Clinton a bridesmaid once more. The hotly contested "Capital" affair led to a duel between one of the board's trustees, Judge Isaac Caldwell, and Raymond Judge John R. Peyton, in which both parties suffered only minor injuries. Caldwell died of injuries sustained in another duel fought six years later.

Even though Clinton had lost its bids to be the state capital and county seat, it was nevertheless considered by some to be a finer town than Mississippi's capital city. One Col. T. J. Wharton, who visited both towns in the late 1830s, wrote that, "Disappointed, disheartened and disgusted [with the city of Jackson]. . . I went to Clinton. There I found a town very much larger. . . I mean in population. Everything denoted thrift, prosperity and enterprise." Wharton noted that the town boasted "over twenty dry goods stores" and "ten or twelve lawyers, among them Henry S. Foote. . ." Wharton also added that "Mississippi College was in full and successful operation," and that the "streets were filled with wagons of cotton bound for Vicksburg." A "more refined, cultured and hospitable society," Wharton concluded, "could not be found in any city or town in the United States."

After Clinton's Academy boasted an enrollment of ninety students in 1829, the state legislature authorized a loan of $5000 to the school, which, on December 16, 1830, changed its name to Mississippi College. The institution promptly offered "such degrees in the arts, sciences, and languages, as are usually conferred in most respectable colleges in the United States" and students were given the option of boarding in the homes of prominent Clintonians. One hundred and forty students enrolled for the 1831 session, but graduations were rare, especially among the male students. Augustus M. Foote, Jr., didn't become the first male to graduate until July 31, 1845, thirteen years after Mississippi College became the United States's first coeducational college to grant a degree to a woman. On June 13, 1832, two young women, Alice M. Robinson and Catherine Hall, were awarded diplomas and gold medals on the event of their graduation from Mississippi College.

Although the new institution failed in its 1837 bid to become the official state-supported university, a Clinton *Gazette* article nevertheless touted it as having a "reputation and an influence, which is to be felt in all this southwestern [U.S.] country." Still, the college needed funds, and a further attempt to garner much needed financial support from the Methodist Church failed. In 1841, the Presbyterian Church took over operation of the school.

Unfortunately, a schism in that church soon lessened its ability to support the struggling college; era records indicate that a newly-hired professor was paid a mere $50 per annum in 1844 and that the President received a meager salary of $1000 in 1845.

The schismatic controversy arose over two key issues, namely, should Presbyterians support the Mississippi Colonization Society's efforts to return blacks to Africa and whether or not slavery was a positive good. During the years of 1843 to 1848, the more liberal view of this second issue prevailed among the Clinton Presbyterians, but such controversies seriously interfered with the Presbyterian Church's ability to manage the College. In 1850, the Presbyterians were forced to return Mississippi College to the people of Clinton.

Although Clinton was at the time a prosperous town of 5,000, with numerous productive plantations and a "cotton express" railroad line to Vicksburg, the College trustees realized that the town simply could not support their institution absent outside financial aid. When the college lost out to the University of Mississippi to become Mississippi's flagship, state-supported university in 1848, Methodist minister Rev. Thomas Ford suggested that the trustees look to the Baptist Church for their salvation. Although the Baptists first met the suggestion with skepticism, when one of the state's wealthiest men, Benjamin Whitfield, a co-founder of the Mississippi Baptist Convention, was elected as a Mississippi College trustee, the Baptists opened serious negotiations with the struggling institution. Unfortunately, the nearby town of Raymond was also bidding for the Baptists' support of its own proposed institution of higher learning. However, with the understanding that Mississippi College would relinquish "the entire property (then valued at $11,000) and control of the college" to the Mississippi Baptist State Convention, the Clinton school succeeded in gaining the "cordial sympathies, and liberal patronage" of the Mississippi Baptist Church on November 30, 1850.

G. G. Banks, the school's first President, brought Mississippi College to new heights of prosperity with sound financial government, but the school's greatest early guiding light was Whitfield, who served as President from 1851 to 1861, and who helped hold the institution together during the devastation wrought by the War Between the States. While serving as a trustee in later years, Whitfield would eventually live to see the total elimination of the heavy debt (about $8,000) the college had incurred during the war years.

But before the Civil War broke out, Mississippi College became Mississippi's leading institution of higher learning. The school's pre-war entry requirements included English, Latin and Greek Grammar, courses in Caesar's writings and Cicero's orations, familiarity with Greek literature and Xenophon's Anabasis, and studies in Geography, History, Arithmetic, and Algebra. The courses offered for study during the Freshman year included Xenophon, Homer, Livy, Horace, Greek and Roman mythology, Algebra, Plane Geometry, English Composition and Declamation, and Biblical Antiquities.

A subject soon eliminated from the curriculum was Wayland's Moral Science. The Board of Trustees discontinued the use of this textbook, giving as its reason that "the attempt of Dr. Wayland to place the Negro race on a social and political equality with the white race is fraught with danger to the people of the United States and especially to those of the Southern states. . . and [Wayland is] an unfit teacher of the youth of your country." The Board sent a copy of its resolution to numerous other southern colleges and Baptist publications.

The number of instructors soon grew from one to six, and by 1858, enrollment had increased to 130 students, and rose to 200 by 1860. Graduations were still the exception; only eleven students earned their diplomas in 1860. Nevertheless, at that time, Mississippi College boasted the largest enrollment of Mississippi's several colleges and universities, and was fourth largest among the nation's twenty-one Baptist institutions of higher learning. The first to graduate under Baptist patronage, G. C. Granberry, received his degree in 1853. There were no more female graduates until special student Anna Ward Aven, a professor's daughter, received a diploma in 1905, and then only after extended debate by the Board of Trustees. A trustee's motion to promote regular coeducation was hotly-contested and ultimately met with defeat.

The most impressive antebellum building on the campus was easily the chapel. Opened in 1860, the chapel was a three-story brick structure with a Corinthian front and upstairs galleries and could accommodate two thousand worshipers at a time. It cost around $35,000 to construct, with almost $5000 coming from pledges made by members of the Clinton Baptist Church.

During this era, the legislature helped provide moral direction to the students by passing a law which banned the sale of "spiritous liquors" within five miles of the campus, and another which forbade merchants from selling suits, shoes, horses, carriages or even fancy desserts to students without written authority from their parents or guardians. These edicts were in keeping with the day's prevailing "old-time college" philosophy of higher education, namely that the proper development of young minds was best accomplished through mental discipline and training. This "discipline" included rigorous moral guidance and a curriculum heavy on Latin and Greek languages, classical history and literature, and philosophy. This discipline, together with Christianity, was, in old time educators' minds, "the substance of western civilization."

Unfortunately, the Civil War's outbreak brought unavoidable hardship to Mississippi College, which produced a mere two graduates in 1862 and accepted the resignations of all but one faculty member. I. N. Urner remained on staff to teach such students as appeared on the scene and to safeguard the college's property. As temporary President of Mississippi College, Urner served four years without pay and ultimately had to sue the college to recover the $6681.50 owed him. Three teachers, J. H. York, E. G. Banks, and M. J. Thigpen, formed a Confederate company called the Mississippi College Rifles, which was commanded by then-trustee Capt. J. W. Welborn.

After the war, Walter Hillman was chosen President and Capt. W. T. Ratliff was appointed President of the Board of Trustees, and their leadership brought Mississippi College back from the brink of extinction. Under their tenure, enrollment increased from 29 in 1869 to 190 in 1872. An article in the *Tennessee Baptist* newspaper noted that, with an 1874 enrollment of 145 students and a tuition fee of $50, Mississippi College charged lower fees and was better attended than most other Baptist-supported colleges in the United States, including such prominent schools as Wake Forest, Howard and Baylor. The article also noted, with pointed chagrin, that of the 90,572 Mississippi youth in the college-eligible age group, only 286 boys and 586 women attended college in 1873.

The school next faced an 1893 effort from Baptist Convention members to uproot it from its Clinton home. The *Baptist Record* reported several heated debates, including one in which a participant suggested that those in favor of the move either "get sick and stay home" during deliberations, go on a fishing trip or "go visit their mothers-in-law." Another member suggested the healing power of prayer as a tonic to the tumult and asked his fellow Baptists to allow the Holy Spirit to "subdue the passions, mellow the spirit and make lovely the speech of his people." The proposal to move the college failed, and it remained happily ensconced in Clinton.

Mississippi College came into its own when Dr. J. W. Provine succeeded to the Presidency in 1895. He was Mississippi's first college President with a Ph.D. degree and the first college teacher to sport a Ph.D. that had been granted by a European university. During his thirty-seven-year tenure, Dr. Provine spearheaded a building program which garnered an $80,000 dormitory, a $45,000 science hall, a $75,000 administration building, $25,000 library, and a $15,000 gymnasium. He also sought and received a $100,000 endowment from the Baptist Convention's General Education Board, which was in turn matched by $200,000 in gifts from other patrons.

The only thing that Mississippi College lacked now, many believed at the turn-of-the-century, was a rip-roaring football team to carry the school's standard into battle. This new game's devotees would soon see their dreams come true. . .

Millsaps College

After the Civil War, Jackson, Mississippi, struggled desperately to recover from the near-total devastation it had suffered at the hands of marauding Union forces. The downtown area had been razed by General Sherman, and its haunting skyline of lone-standing blackened chimneys had earned it the cruel but appropriate sobriquet, "Chimneyville." But by the late 1880s, the state capital was a fully-recovered, bustling town of 9000 citizens, served by twelve daily passenger trains and graced with shady, winding streets distinguished by the occasional stately antebellum mansion.

Although mule-drawn trolley car service had come to Jackson on October 20, 1871 (electric trolley cars didn't arrive until 1899), the mule-wagon remained the favorite mode of public transportation of the day. Downtown mule driver Norris Morgan was a favorite with the ladies on State and Fortification Streets, taking their shopping orders along his route and making their purchases on Capitol Street before returning on his northerly route. Telephone service had become available in 1882, but was for years rarely utilized. A newspaper called *The Eastern Clarion*, which had moved to Jackson from Meridian, was gaining preeminence over established papers such as *The Mississippian*, *The Pearl River Gazette*, and *The State Register*. Although electricity arrived in 1889, most of the better homes still used candles, kerosene lamps and gas-lighted chandeliers. Municipal services included a post office and a seven-man police force, six of whom were black.

Malaria, typhoid, and yellow fever were the bane of the population, which sought diversion through open-house calling on Sunday evenings, romantic, carriage rides for the newly betrothed, formal cotillion balls highlighted by elegant ladies clad in Watteau gowns, and informal parties replete with the chafing dish, family album, and newfangled stereoscope. Viewing legislators' speeches from the upper galleries of the state capitol building at the east end of Capitol Street proved a popular spectator sport, but the less-than-civilized displays of disapproval by a few onlookers prompted one offended lawmaker to propose a bill that would make spitting tobacco on legislators' heads a felony offense!

Understandably desirous of making a grand entrance into the twentieth century, and keenly aware of the great educational strides being taken by Mississippi College President J. W. Provine just ten miles to the west in neighboring Clinton, the local citizenry decided to establish their own college in or near the capital city. They sought aid from the Methodist Church which, in 1886, had become the first denomination to produce multiple congregations in Jackson.

The Jackson initiative found immediate support in both the Northern and Southern conferences of Mississippi Methodism. Acting on a suggestion from Dr. T. A. S. Adams, both conferences voted to endorse a young men's Christian college in December of 1888. They established a joint commission chaired by the Rev. J. J. Wheat which met in Jackson in early 1889. This commission, which included influential laymen and clergy, most notably Major Reuben Webster Millsaps and Bishop Charles Betts Galloway, immediately set about the business of funding a Methodist-supported college.

On February 14, 1889, in a meeting held at the Jackson Y.M.C.A., Millsaps, a graduate of DePauw University and Harvard Law School who had risen to the rank of Major in the Confederacy, offered to give $50,000 to endow the institution, so long as the Mississippi Methodists came up with matching endowment funds. This suggestion was heartily approved by the joint committee, and Bishop Galloway set out on an ambitious campaign to enlarge the fund.

While these monies were being sought, the joint committee, on January 10, 1890, approved a motion made by Rev. W. C. Black to name the proposed institution "Millsaps College." They chose Galloway, a Kosciusko native and University of Mississippi graduate, as the college's first President of the Board of Trustees, and then selected a Board of Trustees from prominent clergy and civic leaders. After the legislature enacted the college's charter on February 21, 1890, the new Board officially met for the first time on June 25, 1890, and approved the charter.

The Board's next consideration was to select a location for the new college. Several towns made reasonable offers, including Holly Springs, Grenada, Canton, Brandon, and Clinton, but Jackson's offer of $21,000 cash and an extension of water and electric service to the site was accepted on March 18, 1891. Major Millsaps added another $15,000 to help pay for building construction. The city of Jackson also offered a choice of two locations, the Hemingway place north of city limits and the Hamilton country place to the east. The former was approved during a May 20, 1891, meeting, largely because it contained eighty acres of land and one attractive building, set some distance back from North West Street.

In addition to the former Hemingway residence, an on-campus dormitory was constructed to house students, and a few shacks on North West Street, and the Echols house on North State Street housed several more. On April 27, 1892, the Board hired a faculty at wages of $1500 per year for the President and $1200 per annum for the professors. The first staff included Dr. William Belton Murrah as President, with N. A. Patillo elected Professor of Math, W. L. Weber as Professor of English Language and Literature, G. C. Swearingen as Professor of Latin and Greek, and Murrah as Professor of Mental and Moral Philosophy. Rev. M. M. Black served as Principal of the Preparatory Department, a division designed to give poorly-trained high school students a fighting chance of passing college-level courses.

After learning of the new college from pastor's sermons, articles in the *Methodist Register,* editorials in church newspapers, and word-of-mouth, one hundred and forty-nine students, including three young women, Hallie and Willie Galloway, and Annie Hemingway, enrolled for the first session. The doors officially opened at Millsaps College at 11:00 a.m., on Thursday, September 29, 1892.

A member of that first class, L. E. Alford, who later became the first minister to graduate Millsaps, described the fruits of that 1892 registration:

> We came from every section of the state. Many of us had never been given an examination in school. The faculty simply

asked us a few questions and then took us in on trial. There were fifty of us taken into the Freshman Class in English and Mathematics. But most of us had to start from the beginning in Latin and Greek. Of that fifty that started in the Freshman Class, half were unable to pass the mid-term Examination, hence were left behind. Almost half of that half failed in the final examination. Only fifteen were eligible for the Sophomore Class. A number of these failed and one or two did not return. Only eight entered the Junior Class. One died, and I dropped out on account of sickness for one year.

Two others failed to return for the Senior year. So in the graduating class of 1896 only three boys who started in the first freshman class of fifty finished the course, the 4th of the boys coming [from] the Sophomore [class]. I returned and finished with the Class of '97.

The first student enrolled in 1892 was Henry Anderson Gatlin, a preacher from Summit, Mississippi, but Francis Marion Austin was the first to graduate with a B.A. in 1895, and was also awarded a Millsaps law degree in 1897. Annie Hemingway was the first female student enrolled, although only as a "special student," i.e., either the daughter of a major contributor or a professor. Mary Letitia Hollman Scott was the first female to graduate Millsaps College with a B.A. in 1901. The school yearbook, the *Bobashela*, was begun in 1905, and the student newspaper, the *Purple and White*, was founded in 1909.

President Murrah, known as "old Doc" to his students, quickly established "gentlemanly conduct" as the prevailing standard of the day. Students were not allowed to leave town except with Murrah's permission, and could not visit downtown Jackson without faculty approval. All students were required to attend church every Sunday, to keep the Sabbath holy, and prohibited from ever attending theaters. Room and board was inexpensive and tuition was free, although students were charged a $25 Matriculation fee and a $5 Incidental fee, except for young preachers' or ministers' sons, who were exempt from all such fees. Over 160 students were enrolled for the second session, the college's endowment had risen to a respectable $100,000, and the value of the buildings and grounds had been assessed at $50,000. The Board finally instituted tuition fees in 1898, at a very reasonable $30 per session.

The early professors were a unique lot, none more so than George C. Swearingen, the classical educator who, in his spare time, bested students at tennis in his backyard, in the shade of his chinaberry and locust trees. Gentlemanly geology professor Robert S. Ricketts was considered a "man-among men," having been captured by Yankees at Vicksburg while serving with the Confederacy. His fame lay in the fact that his captors discovered, much to their dismay, that the young Rebel had cracked their "unbreakable" signal code all by himself.

But perhaps the most unusual member of the faculty was the Professor of Chemistry and Physics, James Magruder Sullivan. Apart from his national reputation as a scientist, Sullivan was much celebrated for his humorous exchanges with students—

> **Dr. Sullivan:** What are concave mirrors?
> **Kennedy:** Why, er—they are mirrors that are concave.
> **Dr. Sullivan:** Well, then, tell me what you mean by "concave."
> **Kennedy:** Why, Doctor, a professor is expected to know something about the English language.

and

> **Dr. Sullivan:** Mr. Moore, how are your Biology experiments going?
> **Moore:** The rats got them, Doc.
> **Dr. Sullivan:** Yes. . . And the rats are going to get your grades.

Fond students often asked Sullivan to make impromptu speeches from the front gallery of his home, and he always complied, often making presentations in wordless pantomime. In response to one of Sullivan's spoken speeches, the *Purple and White* declared that "if hot air were music, Dr. Sullivan would be a brass band."

But flamboyant professors aside, the Big Three Founders, Millsaps, Galloway, and Murrah, were the driving force behind the new Millsaps College. Major Millsaps believed in "the dignity of labor, the wisdom of personal supervision of one's assignment in life, the wisdom of thrift, [and] a respect for other peoples and other religions." Millsaps's beliefs became the cornerstone philosophies of the new college. Major Millsaps also supported other academic enterprises, including the all-black Piney Woods School twenty miles south of Jackson. In 1910, he gave $1000 to help rebuild a recently burned Presbyterian school for girls, Belhaven College, which was located a few miles east of Millsaps.

Dr. Murrah was not only the first President, he was also professor of religion, philosophy, psychology and every other subject offered but not taught by the other professors. Although he was the school's disciplinarian during its early years, Murrah also gained a reputation for having a big heart. Once, in the winter of 1901, when advised that a poor, doomed North Mississippi student was suffering from pneumonia, Murrah hired the city's best physicians, knelt at the sick boy's bedside, and tearfully prayed for his recovery.

In addition to being an esteemed churchman and educator, Bishop Galloway also expressed support for the education of Southern blacks, and suffered severe criticism for preaching the commencement sermon at the Tuskegee Institute in Alabama. When accused by a politician of being "a greater traitor to the South than Benedict Arnold was to the Colonies," Galloway boldly declared, "If it be treason to preach the Gospel to the Negroes then I am a traitor and not ashamed of it."

While addressing a convention in London, Galloway once gave a speech which received worldwide acclaim during the great controversy over Darwin's Theory of Organic Evolution. Keenly aware that he risked censure for addressing this controversial topic before the world press, but determined to defend the very foundations of free thought, Galloway said, "Christianity is a Declaration. Yes, that is the answer. Christianity is a declaration of faith in a way of life and of salvation. You can take it or you can leave it. It does not depend upon the doctrines of science as such."

Under the wise counsel and leadership of its three founders,

Murrah, Millsaps and Galloway, Millsaps College achieved its goals of moving prosperously and efficiently into the twentieth century. And with the college's academic reputation firmly established, it wouldn't be very long before a newly forged game would capture its student body's unceasing interest. The students called their new game "football," and its day was about to dawn. . .

CHAPTER THREE

THE FIRST GAME
1900-1920

Intercollegiate "football" burst upon the American scene on November 6, 1869, when Rutgers defeated Princeton 6 to 4 in New Brunswick, New Jersey. But as many would later point out, the 1869 game was more like soccer than football, with twenty-five men squads advancing the ball with only their feet, heads and shoulders. It wasn't until 1874 that Harvard insisted upon playing its own version of football, a rugby-like game which allowed the players to traverse the field with ball in hand.

Finally, on November 23, 1876, Harvard, Rutgers, Columbia, Princeton, and a Walter Camp-led Yale formed the Intercollegiate Football Association, which by the 1880s, had shortened the field to 110 yards and narrowed it to 55 and a third yards. The IFA's game approximated many modern-day football features such as eleven man teams, a line of scrimmage, three downs to make five yards, five points for a touchdown with an opportunity for an extra point, five points for a field goal, and one for a safety.

The South first enjoyed intercollegiate football in 1887 when the Virginia Military Institute played William and Mary College. The sport finally came to Mississippi in 1893, when the University of Mississippi Flood (later the Ole Miss Rebels) played a five game schedule, which began with a 56-0 walloping of Union (Tennessee) in Oxford and concluded with a 12-4 win over Tulane in New Orleans. The University played seven games the next season, vanquishing mighty Alabama, L.S.U., and Tulane. Football fever spread like wildfire across the Magnolia State, and by 1895, Mississippi A & M College (later known as Mississippi State University) had caught a permanent case of the pigskin bug, despite losing every game that season and the next.

Although Millsaps students had formed an unofficial team to

play local Jackson squads as early as 1893, and the Millsaps Athletic Association had come into being in 1894, intercollegiate football remained an unrealized dream. In June of 1895, a large number of Millsaps students presented a petition to the Board of Trustees requesting that intercollegiate sports be allowed, but their petition was summarily denied. Finally, in 1900, the students took matters into their own hands, and led by Professor B. E. Young, President of the Athletic Association, and a coach known today only as "Abby," Millsaps played its first intercollegiate tilt against Tulane in New Orleans, losing 30 to 0. A New Orleans *Daily Picayune* article, "Tulane Feels Like a Football Team Defeating Millsaps College 35-0," gave an even-handed account of the game:

> [Millsaps] is a new team seeking experience, and obtained some excellent lessons in yesterday's game. . . At no time was Tulane in the slightest danger, although on one occasion Millsaps had the ball far down in the local territory. The Millsaps men, for a new team did remarkably well. . . As this is the first season of Millsaps in the football world, the showing they made was very fair. They were defeated in a most thorough manner, but were not disheartened.

The very next day, the Purple and White were soundly whipped, 70-0, by L.S.U. in Baton Rouge. They gained their first win shortly thereafter, downing a Greenville intramural squad by a 30-0 score.

Buoyed by their initial success, the Majors gamely took on L.S.U. once more, this time in Jackson, the results of which were memorialized by William F. Murrah's article for the *Bobashela*:

> The momentous hour came, and the two teams lined up against each other on the field while a multitude looked on with eager eyes. Millsaps made the first touchdown and successfully kicked the goal; L.S.U. made a touchdown but failed to kick the goal. From that time on the ball swayed back and forth. . . but neither team could score again. Thus ended the

greatest game ever played by Millsaps, the score being 6-5. The spectators were almost wild with delight, and the college boys uncontrollable.

The Millsaps ball players, Fielder A. Fridge, H. Fridge, Hughes, Howell, McCloud, Hall, Shields, Smith, Simpson, Thompson and Hood, and the eight other students who regularly traveled with the team, had brought intercollegiate football to Millsaps in grand, typically hard-nosed fashion. Unfortunately, the boys' celebration proved exceedingly short-lived.

Convinced that the athletic club had overstepped its bounds, the Annual Methodist Conference of 1900 passed a resolution banning intercollegiate athletics in all church-supported Mississippi colleges, and when the alumni and student body appealed the matter to the Board of Trustees, those gentlemen left the matter in the hands of the faculty. The *Register of Millsaps College for 1899-1900* perfectly summed up the faculty's views on the subject: "It has been the unvarying policy of the College to discourage intercollegiate contests. It is believed that there is in the college community sufficient incentive to activate interest in athletics." And while local football games, baseball tournaments, track and field events, and tennis matches remained available for student participation, Millsaps students and alumni continued to miss out on intercollegiate football at their alma mater.

Although intercollegiate football did not become reality at Millsaps for another twenty years, intra-collegiate sports and individual heroics continued unabated. In 1905, left halfback E. C. McGilvray lead the intramural Millsaps footballers to a rousing 10-0 victory over the Jackson Athletic Club with two thrilling, forty-yard runs. Millsaps also sent several students—including a pass-happy quarterback named Peeples—to Rushton, Louisiana, in late 1908, where, as part of a Mississippi all-star team, they won a championship football series with teams from Louisiana, Texas, and Oklahoma.

In intra-dorm baseball, The Founder's Hall Bullnecks whipped the Cooper Home Grits in one of many regular on-campus matches. As reported by the *Purple and White*, the Bullnecks won "only by. . . the masterly work of their pitcher, who yielded *only twenty-nine base hits* and [walked] only fifteen in six innings. The Grits pitcher also twirled in fine form, but the *thirty-one errors* behind him lost the game."

In the fall of 1907, the Millsaps basketball team bucked church authority and played Mississippi College in basketball, losing 19-9. Subsequent support from the *Purple & White*, the *Bobashela*, and the editors of the *Jackson Daily News* led directly to the Methodist Church's lifting of the intercollegiate ban on all sports *except* football later that year. The *P & W* editors wrote: "Of course, we would have liked to have had intercollegiate football as well, but we will have to content ourselves with what we have obtained."

Unfortunately, the *P & W* also supported free-for-all brawling between freshmen and upperclassmen, as a January 15, 1909, editorial reveals: "We are doubtful as to whether this should come under the head of 'college athletics' or not, but if so, it is a branch of athletics which should be encouraged. . . . Of course we do not mean to say that we are in favor of the knock-down and drag-out style, but we want to see spirit and enthusiasm in everything at Millsaps."

And though organized brawling did little to convince the Millsaps faculty that the rowdy game of football would do anything to advance the college's academic reputation, circumstances surrounding the game itself soon made intercollegiate athletics more palatable to church and school leaders nationwide. Back in 1905, President Theodore Roosevelt had met with college football's leaders to discuss the many injuries and deaths caused by collegiate football, and this meeting had yielded a Football Rules Committee and the Intercollegiate Athletic Association (IAA), which later outlawed dangerous plays such as hurdling, and legalized the forward pass. This organization ultimately became the NCAA in 1910, and the rule changes forged by that body essentially fashioned the game into the sport it is today—100 yard fields, 60 minute games, ten-yard-deep end zones, four plays to make ten yards, and six points for a touchdown.

Armed with safer rules and the widely-held belief that football helped establish manly character, Millsaps Athletic Association President Carl Howorth and several supportive students signed an October 19, 1919, petition requesting that the Methodist Church relinquish control of athletics to the Board of Trustees. On November 27, Professor J. M. Sullivan sent a telegram to Howorth stating that the Southern Conference had agreed to the request by an 81-54 vote, and in a subsequent telegram advised that the petition was adopted by the Northern Conference without opposition. Consequently, the Millsaps Majors, led by first-year Head Coach and Athletic Director, W. P. Bales, embarked on their first official intercollegiate season in the fall of 1920.

The Majors kicked off the 1920 football season with a win, besting Chamberlain Hunt Academy of Port Gibson, 36-0, and tying Mississippi Normal of Hattiesburg (the future University of Southern Mississippi) by a score of 7-7. Early success soon turned to mid-season disaster as Millsaps lost to Jefferson College (Louisiana) 13-0, then got manhandled by Spring Hill (Alabama) College, 62-0. It was at this juncture that the Majors began preparing for an Armistice Day game with the school that was destined to become their all-time greatest rival—the Mississippi College Collegians. . . .

Although Millsaps students fought a long and difficult battle to overcome resistance to intercollegiate athletics, Mississippi College officials were in favor of the new game almost from the very beginning. In his 1856 inaugural address, President Simeon Colton said, "Education, taken in the largest sense of the term, includes physical and intellectual culture. Physical education, or that which relates to the care of the body, comprises all that is necessary or useful, in giving strength and energy to the corporal system." Although military training, and not organized sports, was what Colton had in mind at the time, his words nevertheless exemplified the favorable view taken thereafter by school officials with regard to athletic competition.

Mississippi College students formed a tennis club in 1889, and seven years later in 1896, their school was playing intercollegiate tennis well enough to defeat the University of Mississippi for the state championship, a feat they repeated in 1897. Baseball, which had begun at MC in the 1890s, had become so important by 1904 that students were paying a dollar each year to join the school's Athletic Association. The next year, the Collegians paid their first coach, Perry Worden of New Orleans, to lead their baseball team, and he responded with a winning season. Football finally arrived on the scene when, in May, 1905, the *Mississippi College Magazine* announced that, "At a recent meeting of our Faculty they voted to have football next session, and arrangements are being made to hire a coach and put out a first class football team next session. . . . We would like to arrange several games with schools in Mississippi."

A year later, on December 6, 1907, Mississippi College played and won its first intercollegiate football game, defeating Chamberlain Hunt Academy 6-0. Coach Dale E. Chadwick's charges included boys named Rice, Grice, Farrell, Prichard, Smith, Davis, Johnson, Brown, Price, and a few substitutes whose names have been lost to posterity.

The 1908 squad also played only one game, losing to the University of Mississippi, 41-0. Fortunes improved in 1909, as the Collegians went 3-0, with a season-ending 6-5 victory over the University of Memphis. The next two seasons, they finished a disappointing 0-4 and 1-5, respectively, suffering back to back shutouts at the hands of L.S.U. (40-0 both years), Ole Miss, Tulane, and Louisiana Industrial Institution, and posting consecutive losses to Mississippi A & M. Their sole victory was a 1911, 5-0 squeaker against Southern University of Alabama. The slaughter continued in 1912, but the Collegians gained their first winning season in 1913, posting a 5-2 record highlighted by a 13-3 victory over Tulane. They also gave two valiant but losing efforts against Mississippi A & M's Maroons (14-13) and Alabama's Crimson Tide (21-3).

The situation improved in 1914 when the venerable Dana

Xenophon Bible became head coach and athletic director. During that season, the yellow-and-blue-clad Collegians went 4-2-1 and gained a victory over Mississippi Normal, 40-0, a 7-7 tie with Ole Miss, and a third consecutive victory over their Baptist rival, Howard College (later Samford), 27-6. The 1915 schedule was impressive by any standard, with games against Alabama (lost 40-0), L.S.U., Tulane, Ole Miss, and Mississippi A & M. The Collegians whipped Tulane, 20-8, and demolished Ole Miss by a whopping tally of 74-6, thanks in part to the greatest player to ever don a Mississippi College uniform. Freshman running back Edwin "Goat" Hale, who would gain induction into the National Football Hall of Fame in 1963, scored six touchdowns to lead the Collegians' rout of Ole Miss.

In 1916, the Collegians hired a new football coach, C. R. "Dudy" Noble, and as reported by a September 23, *Mississippi Collegian* editorial, enthusiasm ran high for the forthcoming football season, especially insofar as their cross-state rivalries were concerned:

> Last year we drubbed the University [of Mississippi] to our heart's content, and though they will have a much better team this year, we can see nothing but another victory in store for us this year, for barring a bad lot of disaster to our team, they can scarcely hope to build up a new team in one year that can hold the seasoned and well running team that Noble will have when Turkey day rolls around. . . . The team that we are going after this year good and proper is this bunch from [Mississippi] A & M. They have the habit of being on top when the whistle sounds, but there is a time for all things, we think this is the time for us to give them what we think they need most, and we think they need a good dressing at the hands of a Mississippi [College] team as bad as they need anything.

The *Collegian*'s optimistic predictions proved to be well founded, as Coach Noble and company brought "Mississippi" a winning season (4-3), with victories over cross-state rivals Ole Miss (36-14), Mississippi A & M (13-6; thanks largely to Rat Anderson's

90 yard kick-off return for a touchdown), and a 90-0 slaughter of Southern Mississippi, which was mercifully terminated after the third quarter ended. These victories over their Mississippi rivals brought Mississippi College the mythical but dearly-coveted 1916 State Championship. Unfortunately, the Collegians were routed by out-of-state L.S.U. (50-7), and soundly whipped by Alabama for the second consecutive year.

Collegian halfback "Goat" Hale continued his gridiron mastery, contributing three touchdown dashes in the season-opening, 32-0 rout of Marion Institute (Alabama), a seventy-yard run for his team's only score against L.S.U., three touchdowns and two extra points in the Ole Miss game, and five rushing touchdowns behind the blocking of tackle "Parsons" Tate in the home-field, 90-0, rout of Southern Mississippi.

Mississippi College didn't field a football team during the war years of 1917-1918, and the layoff proved detrimental as the 1919 Collegians went 3-5-1, losing to Ole Miss (6-0), Mississippi A & M (56-0), Tulane (59-0), and L.S.U. (24-0). The season was not a total loss however; they did edge Southern Mississippi in Hattiesburg by a score of 19-7 in the season's final contest. That game was highlighted by the pre-game and halftime performances of a number of coeds from Mississippi College for Women (later M.U.W.), which garnered a November 29, *Mississippi Collegian* headline—"Great Crowd Sees Game—Coeds Give Snake Dance."

Led by two little girls mounted on calico-colored Shetland ponies, the Columbus coeds took the field wearing caps and flowing gowns, marched down the sidelines to their seats in the east stands of Kemper Park, and seated themselves *en masse* for the game. At halftime, they, along with several coeds from MC and Southern, "rushed the field, and, with songs and cheers, staged a snake dance which was suitable 'shot' for any 'movie' camera." The *Collegian* gave the coeds' performance a favorable review, saying, "the fair damsels certainly instilled 'la esprit de corps' in their respective teams."

The football team's success added to the aura of good feeling surrounding Mississippi College, so much so that the *Collegian* ran regular columns called "Hash and Catsup" and "Corned Beef

& Cabbage," which offered snippets of the corny brand of All-American humor that reigned supreme in those days of innocence and optimism:

'19: I want some winter underclothes.
Clerk: How long?
'19: You boob. I don't want to rent 'em; I want to buy 'em.

and

"Was Jonah one of the wise men?"
"Well, he had lots of inside information!"

and

Peck Koonce: Did you ever take chloroform?
Sam Woodall: No; who teaches it?

But by 1920, the time had come to get serious about the sport, and with teams like Ole Miss, Alabama, and Mississippi A & M achieving success in the limelight of big-time college football, Mississippi College needed to establish a cross-state rivalry with a school they not only could compete with, but which could excite the Collegian faithful as much as had the annual A & M Thanksgiving Day contest. As fortune would have it, that very season gave birth to just such a rivalry.

The 1920 season had MC fans hoping for a more suitable rivalry right from the start. They suffered humiliating losses to A & M (27-0), Tulane (27-0), Alabama (52-0) and L.S.U. (41-9), with their lone touchdown in those four games coming on a 65-yard broken field run by star running back, "Goat" Hale. Hale had returned home from WWI and made a complete recovery from career-threatening shrapnel wounds.

New Head Coach Stanley L. Robinson, who had been a Colgate All-American in his playing days, led the Collegians to their first win, defeating Ouachita (Arkansas) 6-0 in a rain soaked, October 29 Homecoming game, thanks to Hale's first quarter touchdown gallop off a fake end run. The *Mississippi Collegian* account of the Ouachita game said as much about early football play-calling as it did about the weather conditions: "Several forward passes were attempted by both sides, but owing to the condition of the ball, occasioned by the condition of the field, which was in turn occasioned by the condition of the weather, *none were completed.*"

But despite that win, the Gold and Blue were still smarting from lopsided losses to in-state schools. They ardently hoped that the cure for what ailed them would be the purple-and-white-clad team due to arrive at the Clinton campus on November 13, 1920; a scrappy cross-town bunch known as the Millsaps Majors. . .

In October of 1920, at the Jackson fair grounds just west of the Old Capitol Building, Millsaps had lost to Jefferson College of Lafayette, Louisiana, by the score of 13 to 0. There was nothing unusual about the loss; Millsaps's inexperienced first year squad had expected to strike a few icebergs on its maiden gridiron voyage. The surprising aspect of the game was the extraordinary support given the Majors by a visiting group of students from Clinton. The *Purple and White* reported that the Millsaps eleven were serenaded by the Mississippi College band and cheered on by a large contingent of Collegian fans who "rent the air with a most snappy and voluminous yell." The *P & W* editorialist declared his appreciation for the support, and pledged to have a crowd of Major fans in attendance at the Collegians' next game.

The next day, another *Purple and White* editorial, entitled "The Era of Good Feeling," explained why the Millsaps fans had been so surprised by the Collegian fans's support. "A violently antagonistic spirit" had prevailed between the fans of the two colleges, the editorial revealed, ever since the big "fistic encounter" which had broken out on Capitol Street following a Millsaps/MC baseball game in the spring of 1918. This "cave man act" had resulted in numerous "black eyes and broken noses" and led directly to a year's ban on athletic contests between the two schools. They had resumed baseball competition in 1919, and after that year's games were played "as cleanly and squarely as any game could be played," and after the Mississippi College fans supported Millsaps so strongly during the Jefferson College game, officials at both schools had relaxed their ban on MC/Millsaps athletic competition. All of the antagonism between the two schools was "done away with forever," the *P & W* declared, and the two student bodies enjoyed "a complete burial of the hatchet. . . May friendship continue to grow and blossom," concluded the optimistic writer, "so that this era of good feeling will know no end."

Ironically, the tumultuous football rivalry between these two Jackson-area colleges, which would one day become one of the most heated series in America, had its stormy beginnings in hard feelings generated by conflicts that predated the football series! But in the days immediately preceding that first MC/Millsaps football game, the students at both institutions reveled in a feeling of camaraderie generally reflective of the post-WWI era.

As the *Mississippi Collegian* had done with its "Hash and Catsup" section, the *Purple and White* published a column entitled "Jokes," which perfectly captured the innocent, corn-ball, happy-go-lucky spirit of the times:

Lady: Oh, Mister, I have lost my dog!
Man: What are you looking at me for?

The good-looking coeds dye young.

She: I got my complexion from my father.
He: He must have been a druggist.

and

Edd: Prof. White is a self-made man.
Coed: Then why didn't he put some more hair on his head?

The paper also ran a daily joke based upon the purported sayings of well-loved philosophy professor, J. Reese "Ducky" Lin:

Ducky might have said: "A lot of fish would starve if it weren't for a lot of people trying to catch them."

Ducky might have said: "A little learning is the usual thing."

With the German menace ended and the specter of European Communism too ephemeral to warrant serious consideration, youthful enthusiasm in the guise of "the old college spirit" ran rampant across every American campus. During football games, students frequently performed in-unison cheers known as "yells," and the Millsaps faithful came up with two such cheers just for the 1920 season:

Rap, Rap, Rap, Tap, Tap;
Rap, Rap, Rap, Tap, Tap;
Millsaps, Millsaps, Rap, Tap, Tap;
Boom-la, Boom-la Saps;
Boom-la, Boom-la, Play Millsaps.

and

Rock-a, Chick-a Boom. Rock-a, Chick-a Boom,
Wah-Who-Rah, Wha-Who-Rah,
Millsaps, Millsaps, Rah, Rah, Rah!

Football songs were also popular, including this optimistic ditty sung to the tune of "Laddies Who Fought & Won":

When the whistle blows and the game is on,
And the Purple team has charged,
When the lines are crashing and the ends are smashing,
And Millsaps yells—Rah, Rah:
When the halfback goes around the end,
And the fullback hits 'em low,
Then the game will be a victory for the Majors,
So, Purple and White, Let's go!

Glee clubs, pep squads, cheerleaders, dancing girls, and marching bands playing songs like "How Dry I Am" and "A Hot Time in the Old Town Tonight" added to the pomp and circumstance of Friday and Saturday afternoon Millsaps football games on the bustling Mississippi fair grounds.

But while the Majors were reveling in the color, music and pageantry of '20s college football, their cross-town rivals at Mississippi College were devising a fail-safe scheme for winning the upcoming ball game. The plan mainly called for handing the ball off to their team captain, bruising Right Halfback Griff Lee, or to their fleet Left Halfback, All-American "Goat" Hale.

Although L.S.U., Ole Miss and Mississippi A & M had invited Hale to join their squads after the war, "Goat" had rejoined the Collegians in order to be close to his mother, whom he could visit in Jackson every weekend by taking a "quarter [of a dollar] taxi ride there and a quarter taxi ride back." Two years of military service and a year of wandering while recuperating from war wounds hadn't slowed the mercurial Hale, and he returned to Mississippi College the same game-breaking star he had been in the '15 & '16 seasons. The college yearbook, *The L'Allegro*, perhaps said it best: "Speedy, shifty and elusive, [Hale's] broken field runs have bewildered his opponents and amazed the stands. He is one of the best ground gainers in Dixie and he scores on 'em all."

But if Hale was Mississippi College's most gifted athlete, he was far from reigning as her most accomplished student. An anecdotal tale about the football star's academic "prowess" has been handed down to posterity by Hale's fellow '20s student, the late Mississippi Governor Ross Barnett. According to Governor Barnett's son, Jackson attorney Ross Barnett, Jr., his father often recounted the story of how Hale's history professor contacted President Provine and informed him that Hale would not be participating in a 1921 game against national powerhouse Tulane.

"What's the matter," asked a concerned Provine. "Is Mr. Hale sick?"

"Oh, no," replied the professor. "He's failing my class, and you know we have a 'no pass/no play' policy."

"You bring him to my office this afternoon," the deeply concerned president demanded, "and we'll see about this."

When Hale and his professor met with Dr. Provine later that

day, Hale was informed that he would be given a test to determine whether he could play on Saturday afternoon. "I'm going to give you an oral exam," said Provine, "to determine whether you have a passing grade."

After everyone agreed to the terms, Provine said, "Very well, Edwin, I'm going to ask you one question: What is the capital of Mississippi?"

After pondering the matter with furrowed brow for several minutes, Hale tentatively replied, "Clinton?"

As the story goes, Dr. Provine shook his head, turned to the professor, and said, "Well, Clinton is ten miles from Jackson, so I'm going to give him a 90. Mr. Hale is cleared to play!"

And play he did. He led his teammates to a 14-0 victory over the nationally ranked Green Wave, rushing for 257 yards and two touchdowns, and even kicking two extra points! But that was in 1921, and before Hale led Mississippi College to its best season ever in 1921, he had to find a way to whip Millsaps College to salvage his Collegian's dismal 1920 season.

A November 19, 1920, *Purple and White* article renders the details of how Hale and Co., accomplished that task against the Majors, with "Goat Hale and Griff Lee furnish[ing] the thrills of the game, both men repeatedly making end runs for 40 and 60 yards. In spite of the fact that *Hale had a broken collar bone*, he lived up to his reputation and performed some of the best broken field running ever witnessed in Jackson."

Mississippi College's 60-0 rout of Millsaps not only made for a one-sided beginning to a much-anticipated series, it also set the tone for MC success and Millsaps frustration for many years to come. Even though the Collegians ended their season with a 20-21 loss to Spring Hill, their meager 3-5 record failed to dampen their enthusiasm. With a rampaging "Goat" in their backfield and an able sideline helmsman in Coach Stanley Robinson, the Gold and Blue knew better days were waiting on the horizon.

As for the vanquished Majors, even a year-ending rout at the hands of the Howard College Bulldogs (42-0) and a 1-4-1 losing season couldn't make them hang their heads for long. As the *Bobashela* declared after the 1920 season, "The arrival of Millsaps in the football world was not heralded by any brilliant success on the gridiron, but no such thing was expected as this was our first year and the majority of the team was raw material."

Although the *Purple and White* did glumly ask where Millsaps would "be today in the football world if we had been allowed to continue intercollegiate football" in 1909, it concluded its post-season wrap-up on an optimistic note. "Twenty years from now," the editorial predicted, "Millsaps will be paying back this valuable experience. We hope so anyway."

And though the Majors would have to wait another five years to gain their first measure of gridiron satisfaction against their cross-town archrival, they could at least take pride in having given themselves an annual opportunity to play a meaningful rivalry game. The earlier rift between the schools had been mended for good, or so it seemed to everyone at the time. The *Purple and White* expressed everyone's feelings about the new football series in a November 19 editorial, noting that, despite the bad blood between the two schools in recent years, the Armistice Day game was carried off by both teams and student bodies in "an admirable spirit of fair play and friendship." The time of antagonism was past, the editorial boldly declared, and both schools had ended "once for always that unsavory reputation" which had hung over their athletic meetings like a black cloud since 1918.

Although "once for always" would ultimately be proven false forty years later, the Millsaps/Mississippi College football series would eventually become more than just another of America's most hotly contested football rivalries. This annual contest between small college, church-supported Mississippi schools would eventually escalate into something far more intriguing. And the only words to describe it would be "Holy War!"

CHAPTER FOUR

THE SERIES
1921-1929

Football in the roaring '20s was a very different game than the one played today. During the post-WWI era, the players didn't stay in shape by working out in million dollar practice facilities with state-of-the-art weight machines, tension-relieving whirlpool baths, and a cabinet full of pain-killing narcotics. Old time players spent their summers, and many hours during school semesters, bailing hay, driving sledge hammers, picking cotton, punching cows, digging holes and engaging in various other forms of physical labor which both paid their tuition and kept them in top physical condition.

And 1920s football players needed to be in good shape. They played both offense and defense, whether in the backfield or on the line, and a starting eleven expected to play a full sixty minutes in every close game. They rarely sat down when injured, as evidenced by "Goat" Hale's game-winning performance with a broken collarbone in the 1920 Millsaps tilt. But the most inhospitable aspect of the early game must surely have been the uniforms.

While today's contestants enjoy the healthy advantages of shatter-proof plastic helmets and thick, plastic pads covering their necks, backs, shoulders, thighs and knees, pre-WWII football players persevered not because of the armor covering their bodies, but because of the fortitude harbored in their hearts. The old time uniform, which was far from uniform in its design, consisted of a thin leather helmet (optional) with no chin strap or face guard, an unpadded rugby-type shirt (with white stripes optional), plain, knicker-style pants (with knee pads optional), knee-high socks, and soft-covered, metal-cleated shoes. The uniforms weren't very rugged, but the young men who wore them were.

Fortunately, the difficult conditions that the ballplayers endured never dulled their sense of camaraderie. As early 1920s college yearbooks reveal, footballers saddled their own teammates with a variety of colorful nicknames. For example, Millsaps's 1922 *Bobashela* records a bevy of intriguing Major sobriquets— "Breezie" Reeves, "Red" Carr, "Lightening" Davenport, "Pardner" Honeycutt, "Mussell" Mussellwhite, "Snow" Stovall, "Scrap Iron" Young, and "Dud" Culley. In the same spirit, Mississippi College's *1921 L'Allegro* leaves these interesting Collegian nicknames to posterity— "Goat" Hale, "Wop" Bailey, "Spigot" Stuart, "Pinch" Hudson, "Alabama" Caylor, "Salty" Everett, "Aunt" Stuart, and "Ponce" Gulley.

Even the Mississippi College team acquired a new nickname for the 1921 season, dropping the mundane "Collegians" for the more interesting and historically accurate "Choctaws." The student body chose between several names, including the "Dutchies," in honor of popular school President "Dutchie" Provine, and the aggressive-sounding, "Hornets." Before the vote, Raleigh preacher Monte Davis gave a rousing oration to the effect that Mississippi College should name its team after the Choctaw Indian braves, who were courageous, friendly and honest. His words swayed the voters, and "Choctaws" won the day.

The new name was also historically accurate in that, as late as the early 1800s, the land upon which Hampton Academy (later Mississippi College) would one day rest had served as the ancient hunting grounds of the Choctaw Indians. The Choctaws had finally sold their remaining holdings to the state of Mississippi in the 1830 Treaty of Dancing Rabbit Creek, and left for Oklahoma reservations on the sorrow-filled Trail of Tears. The MC student body chose to honor Mississippi's Native American heritage by going all out with the "Choctaw" motif, referring to their campus as the "Reservation," beating tom-tom drums at pep rallies and sporting events, crowning their homecoming queen with an Indian war-bonnet, fashioning a ceremonial tomahawk as the symbol of their athletic prowess, and declaring their intentions to "scalp" their pigskin opponents, most especially, the Millsaps Majors.

Led by a rampaging "Goat" Hale, the Choctaws did indeed scalp most of their 1921 opponents en route to their best ever record at 7-2-1. After Hale passed his "history exam," he led them to their opening 14-0 victory over Tulane by gaining 257 yards, scoring both MC touchdowns, and kicking two extra points. A New Orleans *Times Picayune* article declared that, it neither rained nor snowed that day, but it most certainly "Haled!" The "Goat" rushed for 273 yards and scored four touchdowns in the Choctaws' 68-0 rout of Louisiana College (Pineville) on MC's newly-christened Provine Field, but was held to a mere 160 yards and two touchdowns (on a fifty-yard run and a twenty-yard pass reception) in a 13-14 heartbreaking loss to Mississippi A & M. Hale's rare, failed second extra point attempt handed the Maroons a hard fought victory at the Jackson fairgrounds.

Hale and Co., quickly rebounded with easy victories over Union University (Jackson, Tennessee) (35-0), and Birmingham Southern (27-6), with Hale picking up 317 yards and four scores against the Alabama opponent. "Goat" ran wild against Ole Miss the next week, rushing for 350 yards in a 27-7 win, and the Choctaws immediately began looking forward to their upcoming November 11th Armistice Day match with Millsaps College.

The Chocs were optimistic about beating their cross-town rivals, considering the Majors' unimpressive mid-season record of 1-1-2. Not only had Millsaps lost to MC victim Ole Miss by a score of 49-0, they had barely managed a tie with Birmingham Southern, a team the Choctaws had destroyed earlier in the season. The Majors' sole victory had come during the School and College Day at the Mississippi State Fair, when Millsaps coach E. Y. "Big-Un" Freeland's charges, led by the ten-for-twelve passing of halfback Ben Galloway, had thumped the lowly Southern Mississippi Yellow Jackets (later Confederates, Southerners, and finally Golden Eagles), by a score of 29-0.

The size factor was another key consideration in building Mississippi College confidence. The Choctaws were well aware of the *Purple and White* account of Millsaps's, 0-45, loss to Howard in their 1921 season opener. The *P & W* had noted that the Birmingham contest had been a case of "Terrier vs. Elephant," with the

Howard eleven averaging 198 pounds per man, a 45 lb. per man weight advantage over the Majors. The matchup with Mississippi College would feature a similar disadvantage for Millsaps.

On the other hand, the Majors not only refused to be intimidated by their rivals, they seemed incapable of admitting defeat under any circumstances. In an October 21, 1921, article, the *Purple and White* declared the Majors' lopsided loss to Ole Miss a "victory" on grounds that "there was not a minute during the game that the Purple and White lightweights were not fighting with a blooming stout heart and that Ole Miss was not worried." Notwithstanding those bold words of encouragement, the paper's account of the game's second quarter revealed how lightly such braggadocio should be taken. Noting that Millsaps "cut loose with a barrage of forward passes (completing ten) and fake plays, which had the Ole Miss team looking like a bunch of school boys," the paper explained that only a *"lucky"* Ole Miss interception prevented a Millsaps touchdown, but then admitted that Ole Miss continued to score with ease even after putting in its reserves.

Despite this lone admission against interest, the *Purple and White* continued its bluster right up to the day of the Mississippi College game. In a Friday, November 11th article discussing the day's forthcoming MC/Millsaps match, the *P & W* began by conceding that the Choctaws had "a great team," that no one had "gotten their 'Goat' yet," that "team captain Hale [was] one of the greatest football players in the South," and that "last year they piled up a sixty to nothing score against us," but then boldly declared that "this year it is not going to be so easy [because] we have a team that will scrap, a team that has been well coached, and a student body that will support the team to the last. Yes it is going to be a great fight," the story concluded. Although the article fell short of predicting a Millsaps victory, it did hint at the Majors' strategy for pulling the day's upset "owing to the fact that we are *Methodists*, it is thought that we shall try an overhead attack, i.e., *sprinkle* them with passes."

But the *Purple and White's* optimism proved unwarranted as the Baptists dunked the Majors, 56-0. *The Mississippi Collegian* reported that the Choctaws played the first three quarters with their *second string squad*, during which time they ran up a 28-0 advantage. After Hale entered the game in the fourth quarter, he promptly scored 21 points in 12 minutes. The Choctaw running game was so effective, the *Collegian* noted, that the team only attempted one pass, completing it for eight yards. "Mississippi" amassed 22 first downs on the ground, the paper related, by "plowing the line or circling the terminals, which they did apparently without difficulty." *The Collegian* also pointed out that the Majors' pass-happy strategy paid few dividends, with only six completions in twenty-three attempts netting a total of 48 yards and all three of the Majors' first downs.

In a rare admission of Major ineptitude, the *Purple and White* editors declared, "Everyone realized before the game that Millsaps had not a ghost of a chance against our rivals. . . " The Majors, the article explained, were "outweighed and outclassed in every department, except the spirit to play hard and fair no matter how great the odds."

Millsaps finished the 1921 season with losses to Centenary College (21-7) in Baton Rouge and a final Thanksgiving Day home loss to the University of Tennessee Doctors (0-14). But despite the 1-1-5 record, the *Bobashela* announced that, "Millsaps did well in football. . . when everything was taken into consideration." An inexperienced team under a new coach had won one game and tied another, the yearbook editor declared, and "the main thing is that the team made progress" by holding UT to such a close score in the season's final contest.

On the far end of the winning/losing scale, Mississippi College finished with its best season ever in 1921, whipping Spring Hill College, 28-7, and tying the University of Florida, 7-7, before succumbing to the Baylor Bears, 24-0, in Dallas. "Goat" Hale, who scored 24 touchdowns, kicked 21 extra points and two field goals, and gained 2304 rushing yards for the season, garnered numerous post-season honors, among them selection as Halfback for the All-Southern team alongside Georgia Tech's famous backs, Red Barron and Judy Harlan. The national press even gave Hale a second nickname—"The Red Grange of the South." After graduating in 1921, Hale eventually gained election to the National Football Foundation's Hall of Fame in 1963. He also coached several Mississippi schools, including his alma mater from 1925–28, and even Millsaps College from 1929–30. He later served as an assistant coach for Ole Miss, Mississippi State, and Southern Mississippi, before organizing Hale & Jones Sporting Goods Co. in 1952.

At his death in 1983 at the age of 87, fellow players and coaches fondly remembered Edwin Hale as a "fellow who always insisted upon having a prayer before the game," and who "was a true gentleman in every sense of the word." Although famous for his gentleness away from the game, when Hale took the field, he was all business. "I was the captain of that [1921] ballclub, I guarantee you that," Hale told a reporter in his later years. "They were just as scared of me as they were of the coach. They knew I wanted them to stay in shape and play hard. [A team with players] that had heart and could tackle hard," Hale added, "would never embarrass the coach or themselves."

Despite the contrasting levels of success achieved by the Choctaws and Majors in 1921, the student leaders at both schools took unabashed pride in their classmates' efforts to avoid fisticuffs and riotous behavior when their teams clashed on the gridiron. Millsaps Lamar Literary Society President Mack Swearingen gave an oration on how the delicate relations with Mississippi College were being solved by the "fairness and sensibility of the student bodies of both institutions."

Other articles in both schools' newspapers also indicated the extent to which serious-minded Millsaps and MC students took an interest in other key social issues of the early 1920s. The *Collegian* revealed that the Philomatheans, an MC oratorical society, had debated whether too much emphasis was being placed upon their school's athletic programs, a question which they eventually answered in the affirmative. In a more serious matter, the *Purple and White* reported that Millsaps's Lamar Literary Society had debated the issue of whether the Ku Klux Klan should be dissolved, and had ultimately voted yes to the question, citing the "utter uselessness of the organization and the evils" arising from it. In so deciding, the Society rejected the pro-Klan position taken earlier by the *New York World*, and labeled that publication's viewpoint "absolutely unreliable and prejudiced." The debate may have been prompted in part by the *Daily Clarion-Ledger* coverage of several recent lynchings of black citizens by the Mississippi Klan.

But although the horrors occasioned by the recent world war had inculcated a greater sense of solemnity upon many college students, the times did little to diminish their fervor for the rowdy game of football. This was especially so at Millsaps and Mississippi College during the 1920s, when both schools experienced unprecedented gridiron success as members of the Southern Independent Athletic Association (S.I.A.A.).

In 1922, the Choctaws scalped Louisiana College, 22-0, for an opening day win on the way to an impressive 6-3 record. Although they suffered lopsided losses at the hands of Tulane, Baylor and Florida, the "Baptists" defeated all their small college opponents. Those wins included a thrilling, Friday the thirteenth defeat of Henderson (Arkansas), 3-0, on the strength of a drop-kick field goal, scoring dashes by halfback Tom "Ponce" Gulley and quarterback Bob Lambright in a 13-7 defeat of archrival Millsaps, and a 28-0 rout of fellow Baptist college Howard before a crowd of 6000 partisans at the State Fair. All year long, Choctaw assistant coach "Goat" Hale enjoyed watching his replacement, Tom Gulley, run wild over the opposition.

The Chocs enjoyed a banner 5-1-2 season in 1923, which included a memorable 6-0 victory over Ole Miss, gained on the strength of a touchdown dive by Little All American quarterback Cy Parks. The low point proved to be a season ending, 0-0, tie with Millsaps. This "humiliation" was Coach Stanley Robinson's last game as head coach, although he stayed on as athletic director for years to come. "Coach Robby" was replaced by John M. King for one season, who was himself replaced by George M. Bohler in 1925. Bohler's three year, .648 win percentage would not be exceeded by any other Mississippi College football coach until the 1980s.

Millsaps's fortunes appeared to be on the rise as the Majors began the '22 season with their first honest-to-God rout, a 39-0 trouncing of tiny Clarke Memorial College. The Major defense allowed Clarke only two first downs and no completed passes, and the *Purple and White* reported that the players were ready to follow new Head Coach H. F. "Zimmie" Zimoski "to the end of the earth." Caught up in the frenzy occasioned by winning, the paper demanded better fan support for the team—"BE AT THE [NEXT] GAME SATURDAY AND BE READY TO YELL ALL THE TIME. IF YOU CAN'T YELL YOURSELF, BRING SOMEONE WITH YOU WHO CAN!" Unfortunately, a new, experimental S.I.A.A. rule forbade freshmen from competing with the varsity, substantially weakening the Majors' team. Consequently, they finished with a 3-4 mark after losing 13-7 to the Choctaws.

Oddly, Millsaps fans celebrated that loss to Mississippi College as if it had been a victory. The reason for the celebration was Major quarterback William "Chick" Nelson's touchdown-scoring dive behind the blocking of "Pole" Webb and "Skinny" Oakley. In so doing, Nelson became the first Major to score a touchdown against the archrival Choctaws.

The Majors fared even worse in 1923 with a disappointing 2-7 record, although many considered the season a vast improvement after the Majors tied rival Mississippi College, 0-0. The tie, a moral victory for the Majors, was earned on the impressive Thanksgiving Day field generalship of quarterbacks "Chick" Nelson and Bascom "Bo" Holloman, and the excellent punting of the versatile Holloman.

Unfortunately, the mediocrity continued in 1924, as Millsaps finished 3-5-1 with shutout losses to Mississippi A & M, Ole Miss and Mississippi College. Five thousand fans watched the visiting Majors outgain the "Braves" 272 yards to 151, and amass 20 first downs to the homestanding Chocs' four, only to lose the game by a score of 14 to 0. Despite the team's loss to their archrivals, the *Purple and White* saluted them for battling "every minute" and always fighting "clean" games. "The finest thing that could be said of us," the editorial proclaimed, "would be—not that we won—but that every man and maiden of Millsaps College helped [their] comrades to fight that game out play by play—with a courage that never weakened—with a determination that never faltered—with an abiding faith in this college and its men. . . "

The Majors and Choctaws temporarily reversed positions in Mississippi's football hierarchy during the 1925 season. While the Chocs suffered through a deplorable 1-7-1 season which included losses to Louisiana Tech, Ole Miss, and Mississippi A & M, the Majors finally celebrated their first winning season. For the first time in team history, the Millsaps eleven were anchored by a gargantuan group of senior tackles—"Tiny" Brooks (240 lbs.), "Puny" Brooks (230 lbs.), and "Pole" Webb (250 lbs.). Although reserve tackle Wright was not so large as his mates, he carried a more impressive nickname—"Brute." Although this titanic line was still not powerful enough to handle such teams as Ole Miss and Mississippi A & M, it did wear down Louisiana Tech, 13-0, en route to an October 23rd showdown with Mississippi College.

On a miserably muddy field at the Jackson fairgrounds, Millsaps finally achieved its long-awaited goal and defeated the decade-dominant Choctaws by a score of 6-0. In a recounting which would eerily foreshadow the infamous 1959 Halloween night, 6-3, nailbiter between Ole Miss and L.S.U. which featured Billy Cannon's game winning punt return, that season's edition of the *Bobashela* told the story every Major fan was dying to hear:

> The whole Choctaw nation, including their squaws and papooses. . . pulled a big parade in a drenching rain, and that afternoon, while it was still raining, went down to the Mississippi Fair Grounds only to see Millsaps's Gaines "Windy" Crawford catch a punt on his own forty-yard line, evade the grasp of "Big Chief" Berry, and run through the mud, water and Choctaw team for a touchdown. In spite of the down pouring rain, Major Jobie Harris, the boy with the magic toe, always kicked the ball beyond the reach of the Indians; they could not bring it back for lack of canoes in which to navigate the gridiron. When the last whistle blew, and the sun went down, the purple-clad Majors trotted off the field victors by one touchdown.

With a win over their cross-town rivals finally secured, Millsaps went on to forge a respectable 5-4 season record, as Major quarterback Jimmy Francis continued to wow the faithful with his "long bomb" passes to Crawford. The strong-legged Harris also broke the state punting record with a seventy-five yard boot in a season-ending, Thanksgiving Day loss to Ole Miss. The football world regained a significant portion of its equilibrium in 1926 as Millsaps finished a miserable 2-8 and Mississippi College staged a dramatic comeback with a 7-3 record. With the Majors averaging a diminutive 160 pounds per man, the larger, rejuvenated Choctaws squashed their rivals by a score of 46-13. The Baptists gained a winning season by exercising the better part of discretion—they dumped the big colleges from their schedule. Meanwhile the Methodists paid for their undeserved optimism with lopsided losses to Alabama, Louisiana Tech, and Mississippi A & M.

In 1927, Coach Bohler lead Mississippi College to an undefeated, 8-0 season. The Chocs held every opponent scoreless except for Birmingham Southern, which managed only one touchdown and several field goals. Season highlights included a 7-0 win over Louisiana Tech, a 33-0 rout of Louisiana College, and a 12-0 pasting of Millsaps. Under the tutelage of Bohler and assistant coach "Goat" Hale, Choc quarterback Stanfield Hitt punted, passed and ran the team to unprecedented heights. In the Millsaps game, he rushed for one score and passed for another, and although the Majors blocked one of his punts and recovered it on the MC one-yard-line, the Indian defense drove the enemy back ten yards before taking over the ball on downs. Stanfield was the first of four football-playing Hitt brothers who would plague Millsaps gridders for years. And as that year's *Tribesman* yearbook declared with reference to Hitt's outstanding performance against Millsaps, "ere the day was done, another Millsaps scalp had taken its accustomed place and was dangling from the waistline of a hungry Choctaw."

The Mississippi College air attack was the main reason for the '27 team's offensive success as quarterbacks Hitt and Henry Dickerson heaved as many as twenty-five passes a game, most of them to speedy end, Burnham "Dog-Gone" Lee. After defeating Southern College (Florida), 12-0, to finish the year with an undefeated, 8-0 record, the Choctaws contended that they deserved the

S.I.A.A. national championship, but their request was not honored by the country's sportswriters.

Millsaps, by contrast, finished 2-8 in '27, although they only lost to a powerful A & M squad by a respectable six points. The Majors found a degree of redemption in being asked to play in a Florida bowl game against Miami, which they won 21-0. The success of this post-season event led directly to the founding of the Orange Bowl on the same field several years later. Of even greater importance to the Majors was their springtime success in luring "Goat" Hale away from his former Gold and Blue mates and naming him their new head coach for the upcoming season.

Both teams enjoyed success in 1928, with MC going 7-1-2, and "Goat" Hale's Millsapsers finishing with a 5-3-1 mark. Once again, the Choctaws, with Coach Stanley Robinson back at the helm, did better with a softer schedule, outscoring their opponents 216 points to 63, including an 82-0 romp over Southern Mississippi. The Majors also improved by dodging all the "big" schools except national powerhouse Tulane, and outscored their opponents 190 to 86, due in large part to a season-ending, Thanksgiving Day thrashing of Union (Tennessee), 51-0.

The Majors and Choctaws battled to a 6-6, mid-season tie on a Friday afternoon slugfest at the Jackson fairgrounds. Choctaw quarterback Dick Hitt hurdled the line for the Brave's score after they recovered a Millsaps fumble at the Majors' two-yard line, while "Eboo" Bell caught a 22-yard pass from Edwin "Little Goat" Hale, Jr., and dashed the remaining seven yards for the Majors' only touchdown. But both teams' kickers missed their extra point attempts, leaving neither team with series bragging rights for the year.

Despite the tie, Millsaps fans claimed yet another moral victory over the Chocs in 1928. In so doing, they pointed to the fact that the Choctaw offense ventured into Major territory only once, and then only on a fumble recovery at the Millsaps 2-yard line. Major fans also noted that, although their team had been generally regarded as prohibitive underdogs before the game, their ordinarily run-prone "Militants" had enjoyed far greater success through the air than had the Chocs, completing five of 12 aerials, while the vaunted MC passing attack managed only seven completions on 21 attempts. The Choctaws later silenced their rivals' "moral victory" chatter by winning three of the four MC/Millsaps basketball games played in the '28/'29 roundball season.

The decade-ending 1929 season saw "Robby's Braves" open their season with a 55-0 loss to Alabama, while "Goat" Hale's Majors crushed Clarke College, 53-12. Despite those differing fortunes, both teams' fans were, from the season's start, very excited about the prospect of playing the annual, mid-season rivalry game, which was generally predicted to be a close one that year. On the morning of October 18, the *Purple and White* declared that "both teams and students [were] on edge," and predicted that the 2:30 p.m. game at Jackson's new Fairgrounds Municipal Stadium would be "the closest and hardest-fought tilt that has taken place between the two schools." The paper also noted that the schools had wisely reconsidered their original decision to place the opposing student sections side-by-side in the stands, and had seated them on opposite sides of the stadium to avoid any potential extra-curricular misadventures.

The Majors earned their second win against the Chocs, prevailing by a score of 7 to 0 before 10,000 "raving" fairgrounds fans. Major end Bill Jacobs caught the winning touchdown pass from Carson "Little Bo" Holloman while the "Militant Methodist" defense, led by all-star tackle L. B. Jones, throttled the fabled Mississippi College passing attack. And although the Majors dropped out of the hunt for their first S.I.A.A. championship two weeks later by losing to Birmingham Southern, 20-7, their confidence remained at an all-time high, as evidenced by a November *Purple and White* editorial declaring that the Majors would "give a heavier, larger squad [whom the article rather rudely identified as the 'Starkville Cow College'] a real taste of football." The Majors backed up the paper's bravado by fighting A & M to a 0-0 draw in Starkville. They finished with a 6-3-1 record and outscored their opponents by a combined score of 165-50.

The Choctaws recovered from the Millsaps loss in time to put up a scrap against A & M, barely losing, 6-0, at the fairgrounds. They wrapped up their 4-5-1 season with a 20-7 loss to Southwestern.

Both Millsaps and Mississippi College came through the 1920s with several reasons to take pride in their gridiron accomplishments. Millsaps had achieved its primary goal of becoming competitive in the S.I.A.A., while the Choctaws had dominated the Majors by a cumulative series record of 6-2-2. The Braves had also become the state's first and the nation's second college team to play an institution in a foreign country, besting the University of Mexico by a score of 20-0 in 1929.

Both schools had also made notable improvements in other areas of athletic endeavor. Their junior varsity football teams, the Minors and Papooses, had acquired a level of fan support which rivaled that of the Majors and Choctaws. The 1927-28 Choctaw roundballers took the S.I.A.A. national championship, winning 24 of 25 games and outscoring their opponents 1,325 points to 725.

There were also significant advances in women's sports. Led by star forwards Elizabeth Setzler and Elise McCallum, the Majorettes tied the Ole Miss Coeds for the state women's basketball championship in 1925. In 1926, they claimed the coveted championship outright by winning 12 of 13 games played and outscoring their opponents 568 points to 169. In 1927 Mississippi College fielded its first women's basketball team, the Wildcats, which won six of ten games played.

While Millsaps and Mississippi College rose to a degree of athletic prominence in the 1920s, they also made strides in their attitudes toward achieving academic excellence. Reporting that the Choctaws had dismissed one of their star players in both football and baseball for being "an unsuccessful student," the *Mississippi Collegian* declared that the act was taken to uphold the school's high standards:

If athletics are to be worthwhile the standards must be high. Unfortunately, some boys, who are good athletes, come to college with no desire for an education. And some think that because they are good athletes they can participate [in sports] and ignore their studies. To their shame, some schools do tolerate such. Our faculty, and shall we not say our student body, proposed to hold the standard high for all our sports by not allowing an unsuccessful student to represent Mississippi College in an athletic contest.

In a similar spirit, a *Purple and White* editorial exhorted Millsaps freshmen to

be pleasant and courteous to everyone. Apply yourself to your studies with a good degree of diligence for Millsaps is not an easy school and we have seen many careless freshmen go by the board. Select one or two extra-curricular activities that seem suited to you and devote your spare time to them. Do not try to go out for everything, for you can't have a finger in every pie and expect to keep up your school work. . .

In January of 1924, the *P & W* reported that the Carnegie Foundation had made a $50,000 donation toward the erection of a new $100,000 library, and that Class of '22 grad Mack Swearingen had been chosen as Millsaps's second Rhodes Scholar (Frank Mitchell, '19, had been the first) and would carry his alma mater's name to Oxford, England, later that year.

Social changes were also afoot in central Mississippi's two highly regarded colleges. As the 20s began, Mississippi College professors had presented a comedy act called "Negro John" in their annual burlesque show, but they discontinued the practice, or at least it was no longer reported in the press, by the decade's end. At Millsaps, the biggest change involved attitudes toward the "fairer sex." In the paternalistic atmosphere of the early twenties, the *Purple and White* had once run a column entitled, "Birmingham Southern Game As Seen By A Coed," which displayed both the young woman's near-total non-comprehension of the game and her obsession with the "cute boys" in the stands.

Another *P & W* column offered football-watching advice to coeds: "Always ask a lot of questions in a loud tone of voice. It is enlightening to you, your partner, and the rest of the stands. It is also a source of entertainment and diversion. . . . Be sure and ask the score after the game is over. Also try and find out the name of the teams and why they played as they did. . . . Never cheer for the home team. It is very unlady-like and you're liable to catch cold in your gold teeth. . . "

A subsequent *P & W* article took an even heavier-handed tone: "The fact is that the coeds this year seem to be perhaps the best looking bunch, individually and collectively, that we've seen since we've been here. And this is said without any disparagement for the coeds of former years, either. We won't say anything else, because we're beginning to feel that we've said too much already. But we hope you coeds don't think too highly of yourselves, because the eds are never enthusiastic over you if you do. And that's that."

But by the decade's end, a Miss Theresa McDill was writing a regular *P & W* column entitled, "The Coed," which was putting those arrogant young men in their place:

Put on another coat of lipstick, girls, and gather 'round while Carrie the Coed dishes out a little dirt on "What Every Coed Should Know." The subject of the scripture reading this time will be—"Dates, Their Cause and Cure." Now dates are a species of contract entered into by two persons of the opposite sex to devote themselves to lying to each other for a stated period. For instance, if a man says, "May I come to see you at 8:30 Thursday," that's a date. But if he comes up to a Co-ed on the campus, and without saying a word, takes her books and walks her to the Grill and buys her food, that's not a date, that's an accomplishment. . . My dears, have you heard the latest?

It's a perfect scream. . . The thing to do now is to—cook. Eemagine! A Coed with an apron on her and flock of—well, utensils gathered around her. . . is the quaintest looking thing. Feed the brutes!

Bring out a pie with a demure smile and a murmured, "I made this for you," and you can fairly see yourself rising in his estimation. It works too—if you have a good cook.

The spirit of post-WWI capitalism so prevalent on Wall Street was reflected in the advertisements run by both the *Purple and White* and the *Mississippi Collegian*. Every 1920s issue of both papers contained ads which showed precisely what was on consumer-oriented students' minds and what was happening in the business-friendly Jackson/Clinton area. These ads, which often accompanied editorials requesting consideration "for our advertisers, those who make this your college paper, possible," included:

Jack Gordon—Men's Wear: We cater to the college trade.

North State Pharmacy: Fountain Drinks,
Sandwiches and Coffee

Chesterfield Cigarettes: BETTER TASTE—Such as only a
cigarette of wholesome purity and better tobaccos can have.

S. P. McRae Co.: No-name and Stetson Hats.

Baptist Book Store: We supply any book.

McCarty Holman: Wholesale Groceries.

Kolb's Cleaning & Tailoring:
We Clean 'Em—Loony Presses 'Em.

Kennington's The Men's Shop: Jackson's Best Store.

Capitol National Bank: $625,000 Capital
and Surplus Oldest Bank in Jackson

Watkins, Watkins & Eager: Attorneys & Counselors at Law
Hotel Robert E. Lee: 300 Rooms with bath.
Visit our Roof Garden where the breezes blow.

Walthall Hotel: Your Home. 250 rooms; 250 baths.

Seale-Lily Ice Cream: A Health Food—Always in Season

Elanel Beauty Shoppe No. 2:
Specializing in PERMANENT WAVING

Electric Power & Service: Helping Build Mississippi

Mullen's Tailored Clothes:
Individually Tailored Suits $25 & $35

Pittman's Billiard Hall:
Headquarters for Professional and College Men
Snooker——Pool——Drinks——Smokes

The two campus papers even ran advertisements for their own schools—

MILLSAPS COLLEGE
D. M. Key, President
A well endowed College of Liberal Arts
Southern Association of Colleges
Member: Association of American Colleges
American Council on Education
Property of Methodist Episcopal Church, South

MISSISSIPPI COLLEGE
WE EDUCATE YOU PHYSICALLY AND MENTALLY
One of the oldest and best equipped colleges in the state.
A strong faculty, best moral surroundings,
health conditions ideal.
An excellent spirit is always prevalent.
Dormitories always clean and commodius [sp].
Best location for College in the state. Send for Catalogue.
J. W. Provine, Ph.D. LL.D. Pres.

As for the entertainment craze which held Americans of that era in thrall, the *Purple and White* ran regular notices of performances by the Millsaps Players theater group, the singing Millsaps Collegians, various quartets, and the Men's and Girl's Glee Clubs. The *P & W* and *Collegian* also ran ads for the movies on tap at two of Jackson's cinemas, the Majestic and the Istrione. Popular movies shown during that era included *Four Feathers* with William Powell and Fay Ray, *The Lady Lies* starring Walter Huston and Claudette Colbert, and *Tom Sawyer* with Mitzi Green and Jackie Coogan.

But the booming '20s were doomed to give way to the hard times of the Depression Era '30s. And although Millsaps's and Mississippi College's football fortunes would soon suffer a fate similar to that of the nation's faltering economy, the football series they had established in the '20s was destined to grow into an unprecedented, emotionally-charged rivalry in the 1930s and '40s.

CHAPTER FIVE

THE RIVALRY
1930-1949

The Millsaps/Mississippi College rivalry took on an unusual dimension in 1930. The Majors' best hopes of victory over their Choctaw archrivals rested squarely upon the shoulders of their greatest coach, "Goat" Hale, who also happened to be the Braves' all-time greatest player! But Coach Hale's loyalties were not divided when his Majors met his former Choctaws; he was far too competitive to ever accept losing to anyone, even when the opponent was his alma mater, Mississippi College.

Beloved by everyone at both MC and Millsaps, Hale was also quite a character, as Millsaps legacy and Jackson consultant Floy Holloman remembers:

> My uncle was Bascom "Bo" Hollamon, who quarterbacked the '29 Millsaps team, and my father was Garland "Bo" Holloman, who played quarterback for the '33 Majors. My father told me a ton of stories about Coach Hale, who they both loved very much. Daddy once told me about how Coach Hale couldn't get the Alumni Field lights to come on for an important late afternoon practice, so he got everybody to aim their car lights onto the field, and he painted the field white, so the team could go ahead and practice. Daddy loved to tell the story about what happened in 1930, when he was a small, 165-pound freshman quarterback. That year, Coach Hale used him as quarterback for the scrub team which practiced every day against the varsity. One day, Daddy and halfback Dase Davis figured out a flaw in the first string's defense and decided they would take advantage of it in practice. Daddy said he broke free on the play he and Dase had cooked up to beat the defensive flaw, and was running full speed down field for a

touchdown. Suddenly, he heard footsteps behind him and then, out of nowhere, somebody hit him real hard and knocked him down. When he gathered himself together enough to look up, he saw Coach Hale standing over him. "Ain't no freshman going to score on my varsity!" said Goat, and my daddy could see that he meant it!

Both Millsaps and Mississippi College began the 1930s on high notes, posting records of 6-3 and 6-2, respectively. Sparked by all-conference halfback Punch McDaniels, Coach "Goat" Hale's 1930 "Militant" Majors swamped Memphis State (40-0) and Southern Mississippi (26-0) before preparing to face the mighty Mississippi A & M Maroons, a team they had never before bested. And even though McDaniels suffered a broken leg against Southern and was not available for the A & M game, Coach Hale had devised a game plan that he nevertheless believed would get the job done in Starkville.

Although the Maroons took a 13-6 lead into the game's second half, "Little" Jakie Miller heaved a fifty-yard scoring bomb to Claude Passeau to ignite a ferocious Millsaps comeback. The Majors' halfback, "Little Goat" Hale, Jr., kept the Maroon offense on the bench with his nifty down field running for most of the fourth quarter. By the time the smoke cleared, Millsaps had earned its first victory over the Maroons by a score of 19-13.

Although they added a shutout of Louisiana Tech (19-0) to their list of wins over big time southern teams, the Militants didn't fare so well against small college opposition, suffering crushing defeats to S.I.A.A. opponents Stetson and Birmingham Southern.

Mississippi College also hit the ground running in 1930, adding to Mississippi A & M's misery by sandwiching a 13-12 win over the Maroons between lopsided victories over Louisiana College (33-14) and Louisiana Tech (39-0). Stanley Robinson's "Indians" won the A & M game thanks to two scoring line-bucks by halfback McRee, and because A & M was incapable of converting either of their extra point attempts. The Choctaws also made Magnolia State history by being the first squad to play a foreign team on Mississippi soil, defeating the University of Mexico,

40-0, at Jackson's Municipal Stadium. Although they edged powerful Birmingham Southern by a score of 6-0, losses to Coach
Robinson's alma mater, Colgate (23-0), and Chattanooga (24-7),
took some luster off their winning record. Once again, their hopes
for a truly memorable season rested on the outcome of the big
Thanksgiving Day grudge match with Millsaps.

The *Mississippi Collegian* got right into the contentious spirit
by running a pre-game poem entitled, "Millsaps Beware," which
predicted "a great massacre day," and suggested that the Majors
"kneel and pray" at the sound of the "Redskin Braves'" war
whoop. Although the "massacre" never materialized, 7000 fans at
Municipal Stadium watched Mississippi College prevail by a close
margin of 8-7, thanks to a two-point safety that resulted from a
blocked punt deep in Millsaps territory. Neither team attempted
more than three passes in the game, although Millsaps's lone score
came by virtue of their sole completion. After the game, the *Collegian* fired another editorial volley, declaring that "Millsaps will
never again threaten the power of the Choctaw warriors, their day
is over, [and the] Choctaws will reign forever in glory over all
rivals to come." The Majors had to wonder if the prediction might
not be correct as they bid a sad farewell to Coach Hale, who had
become their most successful skipper to date with a 17-9-2 record.

But Millsaps soon became the first Mississippi college to install
lights on their campus stadium after the athletic department con-
tracted with the Stuart Irby Co. to erect lights on Alumni Field for
Millsaps's 1931 home opener. They also sold $10 season tickets
in anticipation of presenting their fans another winning season.
Even though 4000 fans turned out to see them play their first
game under the lights, new Head Coach Tranny Lee Gaddy, himself an A & M graduate, lost his inaugural contest to Mississippi
A & M by a score of 10-7. Except for lopsided wins over Southern
Mississippi and Delta State College, the rest of the 1931 season
proved a Major disaster. To make matters worse, their most
impressive win, a 19-7 victory over Stetson, was marred by the
death of junior tackle Connie M. Smith, who suffered a broken
neck in the game's first quarter. In deference to Smith, whom
the *Purple and White* described as standing "high in the esteem

of his fellow students," Millsaps canceled the next scheduled game with Rollins.

The Choctaws also suffered their share of misfortune in 1931, though their problems were strictly limited to poor play. An early season win over A & M was soon forgotten in the wake of consecutive losses to Birmingham Southern, Loyola, Colgate, and Louisiana Tech. Consequently, a 4-4 MC squad and a 3-4 Millsaps team rested their hopes for a decent season on the outcome of their traditional rivalry game. And much like the season before, a student newspaper couldn't resist the urge to throw kerosene on the fire.

This time the culprit was the *Purple and White*, whose November 21, pre-game editorial entitled, "Wallop Those Choctaws," declared that, "We want to win this game above all others, and we ARE going to win this game. . . and bring to the Choctaws one bitter defeat." This article obviously struck a nerve with one Mississippi College student who, under the cover of darkness, painted insulting signs all over the Millsaps campus. MC Student Body President James Sullivan promptly ended the bad blood occasioned by his fellow student's malicious mischief by offering an apology to Millsaps students at their next chapel service. Sullivan also promised to remove the offending signs and seek out the perpetrator for punishment.

With favorable relations between the two schools restored, their Thanksgiving Day tilt went off without a hitch, except for the embarrassment suffered by the "Fighting" Majors on an ill-fated trick play that Millsaps fans later dubbed the "High School Play." Down by a field goal at the half, Major quarterback Perimeter made a long lateral pass to Davis, who dodged a heavy rush and lateraled back to Perimeter, but his wayward toss was picked off by Choctaw end Taylor, who ran unchallenged to the goal line to close out the scoring at 9-0 in favor of Mississippi College.

The Majors gained a small taste of revenge a week later when their combined varsity/alumni team defeated "Goat" Hale and the Mississippi College varsity/alumni team, 6-0, in a fairgrounds charity game sponsored by the Jackson Chamber of Commerce. The Chocs had originally planned to play Ole Miss that weekend, but the Rebels canceled the match after being offered a post-season Orange Bowl bid.

Both programs lost ground in 1932, with Millsaps winning three of eight games and Mississippi College finishing with a 4-4 mark. The Majors' season highlight was a 19-0 Homecoming upset of Howard at Alumni Field, which came after they had dedicated the game to the memory of Connie Smith, "Majors' Football Martyr." Spurred on by the memory of their fallen comrade, the Millsaps starters fared so well against Howard that Coach Gaddy didn't make a single substitution the whole day. He had no reason to replace halfback Jesse "Taters" Magee, who thrilled the 5000 spectators with a seventy-yard punt return for a TD. In its description of the game, the *Purple and White* commented on a recent innovation in football attire by describing the only player wearing a chin strap as looking like a "visitor from Mars."

The Choctaws' 1932 high point came in their season-ending match with Millsaps, in which they eked out a narrow 7-6 victory. Dick Hitt, one of four talented Hitt brothers who terrorized Millsaps during the thirties, scored a rushing touchdown and an extra point for the Indians. The Majors failed to convert their extra point try following Frank Davis's TD reception, and a fourth quarter goal-line stand by the considerably heavier MC defensive line preserved the Choctaw victory.

As far as the MC faithful were concerned, the Chocs' grudge match victory was a satisfying tonic to the *Purple and White*'s brassy pre-game prediction of a Millsaps victory, and to a *P & W* editorial which had said that Millsaps students should enroll their dogs in Mississippi College. The *Bobashela*'s sour grapes comment, that Millsaps lost to "those *lucky* Choctaws" after gaining ten first downs to the Braves' one, must have further delighted the MC partisans.

The Chocs won their first three games in 1933, then failed to score a point in their remaining five contests. The Majors fared little better, taking a 3-4-2 record into the annual Thanksgiving Day rivalry game with Mississippi College. But this time the Majors backed up the *P & W*'s annual pre-game victory prediction when two of their defensive linemen, Bob "Bad Boy" Womack and Jimmy Morrison, blocked Choctaw punter Bruce Hitt's kick in his own end zone, and scored the game's only two points on a safety when they fell on Hitt after he recovered the oval in his own end zone.

Jackson Daily News sportswriter Craddock Goins wrote, "A blocked punt in the fourth period turned a traditional turkey-day classic into a Tribal tragedy yesterday as Bruce Hitt's Mississippi College Choctaws yielded to Major Jimmy Morrison's Millsaps stalwarts, 2 to 0, after a breath-taking battle in keeping with the legends of the ancient feud."

Goins's description of another play which almost yielded a Millsaps score is typical of the era's sportswriting prose: "One of the highlights of the contest came during the Majors' late drive when Bob Womack, finding the path beseiged by a determined Redskin ambuscade, undertook a placement kick from the 30 yard line. Although the ball had to travel 50 yards to reach the posts, it failed only because of being a few feet wide and short."

The victorious Majors' quarterback in 1933 was a gritty, 135-pounder named Garland "Baby Bo" Holloman, the third and last Holloman brother to don the purple and white. He saved the day for Millsaps on three separate occasions by making touchdown-saving tackles of rampaging Choctaw halfback Bruce Hitt.

As it turned out, all three Holloman brothers played quarterback, all were nicknamed "Bo," and all played key roles in Millsaps's first three wins against Mississippi College. The heroic Hollomans seemed anything but Little Bo Peeps to the Choctaws, although one Choctaw proved the exception. "I hope," he was heard to moan in the grandstands after the '33 game, "that the Holloman family just sticks to [raising] cotton and goes out of the sheep business and quits raising 'Bo Peeps'. "

That year, Millsaps students showed their Choctaw-defeating Majors how grateful they were for a victory over the "Raiding Redskins" by electing quarterback Garland "Baby Bo" Holloman as President of the Student Body, choosing Joe Stone as editor of the *Bobashela*, and naming halfback Dase Davis as the President of the "M" Club.

After the '33 season, the *Jackson Daily News* also sang the praises of two contestants in that year's titanic Millsaps/MC struggle. To the mythical All-Mississippi Football Team, which included seven Ole Miss Rebels and two Mississippi A & M Maroons, the Jackson paper added the names of Millsaps guard Jimmy Morrison and Mississippi College halfback, Bruce Hitt.

While Mississippi College struggled to a 5-4 season in 1934, Millsaps enjoyed its best season ever at a robust 7-2-1. The Majors' early season highlight came at Mississippi A & M's expense, as the Militants deflated the Maroons' "We're Orange Bowl bound" predictions by beating them in Starkville, 7-6. Under the headline, "Militant Majors Maul Cocky Cow College Cohorts—7 to 6," the *Purple and White* reported that Millsaps's faculty and students celebrated Gabe Felder's touchdown run, "Big" Bob Womack's conversion kick, and A & M's faulty extra point kicking by canceling Saturday classes and throwing a noontime "demonstration" of affection for the returning Majors at the campus's North State Street entrance. The *P & W* also threw in a little trash-talk for good measure, asking whether "anything other than horticulture" was taught at A&M, and joking that no one could tell Maroon players apart because they "all wear a number ten shoe and size six hat."

But the Majors' 1934 season highlight had to be a Thursday afternoon, 13-0, whitewashing of Mississippi College at the Jackson fairgrounds. Halfback Gabe Felder provided all the Majors' scoring with two rushing touchdowns, while the Millsaps defense snuffed the Choctaw ground game with five impressive goal-line stands, including one in which the Baptists had the ball on the Methodists' one-yard line with two downs to go.

The game's statistics reveal the relative unimportance of the passing game in 1930s college football: Major QB Fred Ezell completed one of two passes, while the Tribe's relatively prolific tosser, Billy Priester, connected on ten of twenty-four aerials, four of which were intercepted. The *Purple and White* took the heady occasion of Millsaps's second consecutive win over Mississippi College to declare that the newly competitive, annual grudge match had come to be regarded by both schools' fans as a "football classic."

The parity continued in 1935 as the two teams battled to a 0-0 tie at the fairgrounds. Millsaps, which had joined the Dixie Conference earlier that year, finished a respectable 4-4-2, including their first ever win against Birmingham Southern. Mississippi College stumbled through a dismal 2-6-1 season in which they were shut out by six of their nine opponents.

The two programs swapped places in 1936, with the Choctaws rising to a 5-3-1 record on newly-lighted Provine Field, and the Majors dropping down a few notches at 2-5-2. But even though both teams struggled through mediocre seasons during the early to mid-30s, something occurred that decade which changed the Millsaps/MC rivalry from a "classic series" to a "heated rivalry"—they began playing each other *two times each season from 1936 to 1938*!

The teams "played two" in order to solve a controversy that had raged for several years, i.e., whether to play an October game at the fairgrounds, as they had done during the early years of the series, or play a Thanksgiving Day tilt, as had become the custom in recent years. The ultimate solution—to play both games each season—made everybody happy. Nowhere was this joy more evident than in the streets of downtown Jackson on the day of the first 1936 game, where MC students put on a memorable pre-game parade.

Preceded by a large wigwam float and several blue and gold-decorated automobiles, accompanied by feminine backers from Hillman College and Mississippi Women's College in Hattiesburg, and followed by their barefoot freshman classmates dressed only in pajamas, a host of male Mississippi College students marched down Capitol Street from the viaduct to the State Street fairgrounds entrance. The procession was led by head cheerleader "Blue" Anding, George Neal, Jr., and future Mississippi Supreme Court Justice Roy Noble Lee.

Although the Choctaws were prohibitive favorites over a lighter, graduation-depleted Millsaps squad, Major head coach Gaddy had instituted a pre-season program of rigorous exercise which he hoped would whip his young men into top physical form for the '36 campaign. In addition to offering his players a new whirlpool machine and a state of the art training room, Gaddy enforced nine no-nonsense rules—(1) No smoking, drinking, or gambling; (2) No dating; (3) No boxes from home; (4) No eating between meals; (5) All meals eaten in the dorm; (6) No leaving the dorm after meals; (7) Radios off at ten; (8) Lights out at ten; and (9) No trips home without special permission. These restrictions apparently had little positive effect on the "Gaddymen"; they were shut out by five opponents. But when they met the Choctaws at the fairgrounds on October 23rd, the win-hungry Majors proved up to the task.

The winless Militants "upset the dope bucket" (i.e., fooled the pre-game prognosticators) by intercepting five of the Choctaws' fourteen passes and breaking up five more en route to a 7-0 upset win. The Majors pulled off the upset despite making only one first down to their opponents' nine, and being out gained by a margin of 218 yards to 47. The Methodists scored on a 57-yard interception return by Ross Shelton, and defensive back Fred "Pee-Wee" Ezelle intercepted three passes and batted down another in the end zone to preserve the Millsaps victory, despite being hampered with a severe shoulder injury.

The Choctaws took their revenge on Thanksgiving Day, walloping the Majors by a score of 19 to 7 in the second '36 match. It was a case of too many "Hitts" to the Millsaps gut as brothers Jimmie and Joel Hitt ran over, around and through the Majors. An interception return by safety Mervin "Red" Dunaway and an end zone fumble recovery by tackle Frank Blackwell also notched scores for the victorious Baptists. Jimmie Hitt went on to garner numerous post-season awards for his football prowess, including selections as halfback on the All-Dixie Conference and Merit All-American teams.

It came as no surprise that as soon as the Choctaws and Majors began playing each other twice a year, the fans brought a new level of intensity to the series. Shortly after the second 1936 game, the *Purple and White* ran a column entitled, "The Rudiments of Choctawism," which voiced numerous complaints about the recent conduct of the Mississippi College faithful. According to the article, the Choctaw band interrupted the Millsaps band's half-time performance when it "blared forth with sour notes and ear-splitting screeches" before the Millsaps contingent had finished its show. Apologizing for "contaminating the editorial page with the Choctaw name," the article then accused MC students of splashing a "bucket of dull grey paint over sidewalks, roads and walls on the Millsaps campus," and of painting a "reminder" of the second game's 19-7 score on a campus driveway in four-foot high letters. Millsaps students would have responded in kind, the editorial added, but "Choctaw driveways are not of concrete, but of dirt or gravel or something. Such a cultural appreciation of music and art seems to be typical of the Mississippi College student. We also remember," the story concluded, "that they like to blow car horns—especially on the Millsaps campus during classes."

In the spirit of journalistic fairness, a *Purple and White* editor also condemned several "ungentlemanly" pranks played by Millsaps freshmen during the "Choctaw victory pow-wow on Capitol Street." Although the "Chocs deserved a counter-insult for their rudeness during the game," an editorialist quipped, "unsportsmanlike" pranks did not constitute proper "Millsapsian" behavior, and an apology was "in order" to the Choctaws, "who [had] tallied a well-earned victory." The article ended with the author's sardonically-expressed wish that freshmen rise above being freshmen and "be something more worthwhile for a change."

These reported conflicts may have been the impetus for *Purple and White* editor Victor Roby's 1936 newspaper campaign to boot intercollegiate athletics off the Millsaps campus. When he ran the results of a straw poll which indicated that a majority of students polled wanted to discontinue the administration's practice of diverting nine of fifteen student activity fee dollars to the athletic department, 400 *P & W* issues mysteriously disappeared from the on-campus distribution centers. Under fire from the athletic department, Roby published the results of a second straw vote in which intercollegiate athletics received the polled students' approval by a two to one margin. Thus ended an attempt, however half-hearted, to end Millsaps football.

The 1937 season saddled the Choctaws and Majors with identical 3-6-1 worksheets. Although the Chocs suffered a humiliating, 84-0 loss to Tulane, they still got the better of their traditional rivals. They tied the Majors 0-0 at Alumni Field in a fumble-marred scrap, and won the Fairgrounds game by a 12-0 margin thanks to two rushing touchdowns by Choc halfback Otho Winstead.

Both '37 games were accompanied by the usual pre-game controversy. The *Mississippi Collegian* published an article prior to the State Fair contest quoting several Choc players' predictions on the Millsaps game, ranging from the confident—Co-captain Lamar Smith: "We're going to beat them but we are going to have to fight all the way"; to the overconfident—E. Hederman: "We're going to beat the stuffing out of them." Senior MC Class President Gene Cross predicted a hard-fought victory, but Freshman Class President Cleo Harris sounded a more impudent note, declaring that, "We are gonna beat the socks off of 'em."

The *Collegian* also ran two editorials before the Thanksgiving Day match which added to the rivalry's intensity. The first made sport of a *Clarion-Ledger* headline penned by a Millsaps graduate which stated that the Majors lost the first game because of "overconfidence" and then sardonically wondered what had convinced the Millsaps fans that they had anything to be overconfident about.

The second article attempted to rebut Millsaps students' public complaints about MC fans booing the Minors during a recent junior varsity ballgame in Clinton. While admitting that Choctaw supporters went too far by removing the ladder which allowed Millsaps sportswriters to climb down from the MC press stands, the *Collegian* editorialist argued that both the Minors and Majors *should* always be booed "except when the game might be interrupted by what is going on in the stands, or when a player is injured." Although it admonished Choctaw fans to maintain a "clean rivalry" with Millsaps, the article ended by saying, "If you want to boo, then go ahead and boo. But don't forget to do your best in cheering for our team. . . "

During the 1937 season, stalwart team captain "Pee-Wee" Ezelle proved the Majors' most effective player, while the fleet-footed, rifle-armed Joel Hitt staked his claim as one of Mississippi College's all-time greatest and most versatile players, starring as halfback, punter, defensive back, quarterback, and end.

Attired in new gold uniforms with blue numerals bordered by red stitching and blue arm stripes bordered by two red bands, the 1938 Mississippi College football team posted an impressive 7-2 mark, soundly whipping Millsaps by scores of 21-0 at the State Fair and 32-0 on Thanksgiving Day. Joel Hitt's 60-yard punts and key touchdown reception sparked the Redskins in the initial '38 contest, while they rode deft signal-caller's Bob Majure's rifle arm to victory in the Thanksgiving clash.

By sharp contrast, the 1938 Millsaps Majors not only lost all seven of their games, they also failed to score a single point all year. At season's end, Coach Gaddy resigned with an overall 28-34-10 record, and was replaced by a Millsaps graduate, the highly successful Copiah-Lincoln Junior College head coach, Henry "Hook" Stone. Stone immediately dropped Millsaps's outdated single-wing offense and replaced it with the more difficult to anticipate Notre Dame box offense.

The single-wing offense was a simple, run-oriented offense that succeeded on hard-nosed blocking for powerful or slippery backs.

The Single-Wing Offense

o o o o o o o
End Linemen End
o
Wingback
o
Quarterback (Blocking back)
o o
Halfbacks

In the Notre Dame Box offense, the backs stood in a line behind the center, then, after the signal was given, all moved in unison into the single-wing formation. Of course, the defense never knew in which direction the backs would move until the signal was given, and then the ball was snapped before necessary defensive adjustments could be made.

Choctaw coach Stanley Robinson ran the double-wing offense, which was slightly more complicated than the single wing:

The Double-Wing Offense

o o o o o o o
End End
o o
Wingback Wingback
o
Quarterback
o
Tailback

This offense relied on precise execution of various reverses, straight runs and passing plays.

(Years later in the 1950s, Robinson would eventually go to the Full-T formation which was the forerunner of modern offensive formations. This scheme featured backs behind the quarterback, who was now more a passer than a blocker, and a tight end on the line, rather than wingbacks just off it:

The Full-T Formation

o o o o o o o
o
Quarterback
o o o
Running backs

The modern Split-T formation with a quarterback, tight end, and two running backs evolved from this formation in the late '50s. But that eventuality was still decades away.)

In 1939, Coach Stone's new Box system helped new Millsaps

quarterback "Chunkin" Charley Ward complete 10 of 23 passes for 117 yards in a season-opening 14-0 win over Delta State. The Majors went on to a respectable 4-3-2 record that season, due in part to their decision to play only one game against their old rival, Mississippi College. The wisdom of that decision became readily apparent when the Choctaws invaded the Millsaps campus in October and dismantled the Majors by a score of 29-0

The '39 Millsaps win gave the Choctaws an 8-3-2 decade record against Millsaps, and their shutout victory was the Choctaws' fifth consecutive whitewashing of the Majors. With only S.I.A.A. "small" college opponents on their schedule, the Chocs fared even better against most of their opponents than they had with Millsaps. Indeed, the Braves closed out the decade with one of their best years ever, winning their last five games en route to a sterling 6-1-1 finish for the 1939 season.

The 1940s began as the '30s had ended, with Mississippi College continuing to dominate Millsaps in the annual grudge match. "Hook" Stone's 1940 Majors produced a decent 4-4-1 worksheet behind the able running of star halfbacks Henry Steinride and Ed Matulich, who led them to victory over in-state rivals Delta State (14-0) and the Southern Mississippi Confederates (14-7), and kept them in the game during the first half of a match with Orange Bowl-bound Mississippi A & M, although they eventually lost 46-13. Even so, as they prepared to invade Provine Field in early November, the Majors appeared to be no match for Stanley Robinson's 5-1-1 Chocs, who had easily steamrolled their way through all their S.I.A.A. foes with bruising wins over Spring Hill, Mercer and Louisiana College.

That the Choctaws were prohibitive favorites meant little to the *Purple and White* editors, who declared, "We're not going out on a limb when we say that the Majors will beat the Chocs, for Millsaps this year has a far better team, and the Majors are in better condition than they have ever been." The *Mississippi Collegian* also did its part to foster pre-game controversy by noting that the 4-1-1 Majors had racked up "unimpressive" wins over "mediocre" opponents, while the Choctaws had played a "tough" schedule to gain their 2-1-1 mid-season mark.

All pre-game bluster aside, the game turned out as predicted with Mississippi College winning, 27-0, on Robinson Field before 4000 ecstatic Choctaw fans. Brave halfback Charley Armstrong began the rout with a one-yard plunge after tackle Archie Mathews and center Hartwell McPhail cleared a gaping hole in the Millsaps line. Halfback Lonnie Tadlock buried the Majors with a long touchdown reception and a 34-yard interception return for six more points.

The *Purple and White* refused to admit that the Majors had suffered an embarrassing defeat. "The two teams battled on even terms throughout most of the fray," the paper related, and the Choctaws won only because they "got all the breaks."

The newspaper's "never-say-die" attitude was typical of the mentality shared by athletes at both schools in the 1940s. Charley Armstrong, a star Choctaw running back during this era and later head football coach at Meridian High School for twenty years, remembers the Millsaps/MC rivalry as the "get after 'em type" on the field and a wild one in the streets.

Charley Armstrong:

> If you played for Stanley Robinson or Hook Stone you hit hard. The Millsaps players hit hard and so did we. But there was never any ugliness on the field. No fights and nothing but hard-nosed football. In 1940, Coach Stone had brought some strong Co-Lin Junior College players with him to Millsaps and hoped to rub our noses in it that year, but. . . . (laughs) We beat their butts anyhow.

Even though the athletes honored the rivalry with clean hitting, hard-nosed play on the gridiron, both players and students engaged in considerably more vicious behavior off the field during the 1940s. The main source of this trouble was an ongoing beanie-snatching war. Beanies, of course, were the purple and white or blue and gold caps that newly-shaved freshmen wore as dubious badges of male freshmandom.

Hartwell McPhail, an MC player in the '40s and head coach of his alma mater from 1959-1973: "The freshmen fought over those beanies and hung them up as trophies in their rooms. But there was no fighting on the field. Both sides played it straight during the game."

Wendell Webb, MC's star quarterback during the '40s and later head coach of the Crystal Springs High School football team:

> Our upperclassmen drove a nail in our dorm room walls and told us they wanted to see a Millsaps beanie hanging on that nail right away. Raiding parties down Capitol Street were a common occurrence in those days. The MC men hung out at the Heidelburg Hotel and Barton Restaurant on the west end of East Capitol Street, while the Millsaps players were at Primo's Restaurant to the east on Capitol, closer to State Street. They met up a lot where beanies were at stake.

Choctaw halfback Charley Armstrong:

> If you went to a movie in Jackson wearing your beanie you'd lose it before the movie was over. There was also a lot of trouble on the streets. Once, I waited at the bus stop in front of the old Heidelburg Hotel, and when the bus stopped there, I spotted a Millsaps freshman sitting by the window, and snatched his beanie right as the bus took off. He raised a lot of Cain, but the driver wouldn't stop and I got away clean. Told everybody back in the dorm that I whipped him good for it!

Despite all the beanie-snatching conflicts, at this point in time, the rivalry was still largely good natured and free of any serious risk of bodily harm to anyone. Dr. Albert Gore, who, with brothers Granville, John, Jr., Bill and Dan, played ball for Mississippi College in the '40s and '50s, later recalled that the rivalry was based upon mutual respect and affection.

Albert Gore, of Clinton, former Choctaw halfback, now a retired Jackson physician:

> The main reason I went to Mississippi College was because I grew up hearing my father talk about that rivalry with Millsaps, and I wanted to be a part of that. Sure, there were many times when our boys came back to the dorm with a black eye and a Millsaps beanie in their hands, and we fought

real hard against Millsaps every game, but I never felt a moment's hate for any Millsaps player or coach. We all loved them because they were such competitors and never quit even when we were ahead of them thirty to nothing. Coach Stone was a true gentleman and David McIntosh was one of the greatest players I ever saw. We had nothing but respect for Millsaps.

David McIntosh, of Laurel, a Millsaps Little All-American half-back during the '40s, who later served as a Methodist minister for 40 years: "It was a good, clean rivalry and we at Millsaps had the utmost respect for Coach Robinson and his players. It was something special to be a part of."

World War II instituted a new American way of life in the early '40s, and eventually took many fine ballplayers away from Millsaps and Mississippi College. But that tragic conflict did little to interfere with the Mississippi College jinx against Millsaps, as the Choctaws again shut out the Majors for the seventh consecutive time in 1941, 21-0, thanks to the multiple-touchdown-producing aerial tandem of "Rip" Priester to Wilson "Lefty" Fulton.

And while MC finished their '41 season with a sporty 5-3 record against its S.I.A.A. foes, Millsaps persisted in scheduling major college opponents such as Mississippi State, Memphis State, and Mississippi Southern and suffered shutouts to all three teams en route to a 4-5 season record. Major coach Hook Stone promptly resigned with a disappointing 11-12-3 overall record, leading many Choctaw fans to wonder aloud how many more Millsaps coaches their beloved Coach Stanley Robinson would retire.

As for the Choctaw players, they had the utmost respect for their long-time head coach. "Stanley Robinson was a gentleman from the word go," recalls star running back James Coleman, who would later coach high school football and eventually retire as Dean of Men at Mississippi College. "He made a lasting impression on all of us as a caring, sincere man. He inspired me into coaching and taught me how to be demanding and well prepared without forgetting the needs of my players."

MC halfback Wendell Webb:

> Coach Robinson had learned his profession at Mississippi
> State and Mercer, and came to us a very knowledgeable leader,
> and he worked us hard, over and over so we were sure to prop-
> erly execute that double-wing. He let everybody play and was
> always available for anyone who needed to discuss their prob-
> lems of any kind with him.

Hartwell McPhail: "We had no scholarship money. We played
hard and were loyal to our school because we loved the institution we played for and the man who coached us."

Hartwell McPhail also remembers what happened in December of 1941, and how that shocking event affected his freshly
launched coaching career:

> I was on my first coaching stint at Greenwood High School
> in 1941, and hadn't listened to the radio all day long on
> December 7th. One of my players came up to me in my back
> yard and said, "Say coach, are you looking forward to going
> overseas?" I asked him what he was talking about, and assured
> him that I had no plans to go overseas. Then he told me that
> the Japanese had bombed Pearl Harbor. A little later I heard
> President Roosevelt declare war on the radio, and since I was
> unmarried and had no children, I knew right then where I was
> going—overseas!

Neither Millsaps nor Mississippi College fielded a regular team
from 1942 to 1945, although the Major Navy V-12 team went 3-6
in 1944, losing badly to Mississippi State (0-56) and Alabama
(0-55). Remembering that season, retired Vice President of Millsaps Enrollment and Student Services, John Christmas, who
played center and linebacker on the V-12 team, said, "Millsaps had
originally planned to bring in some great players on naval service,
but that never materialized. So we had 25 players when we traveled to Tuscaloosa to take on Alabama's squad of fifty men, which
included three All-Americans."

Retired Jackson attorney Rubel Phillips remembered the Alabama game in even greater detail:

> Walter Stokes and I rotated at defensive end. We weighed in at around 165 pounds, and our job was to block 200 pound, All-American tackle Vaughn Mancha. Mancha lifted me up and slammed me into the ground whenever he wanted to. Ole Walter was a tough guy and he could hang in there with Manch, but I didn't want anymore of him. (Laughs) I hunkered down on the bench and hoped the coach wouldn't put me back in!

But Phillips also recalled the special camaraderie that existed between players of the wartime era: "After the game, Mancha came by our hotel in Tuscaloosa and took me to an on-campus dance. He showed me the town in fine fashion as if to say, 'no hard feelings.' And there never were. Even at 55-0."

By the time regular play resumed in 1946, Millsaps had made three important decisions regarding its football future. Henceforth, the Majors would play home games against Mississippi College in Central High School's Tiger Stadium, which would later be known as Murrah High's Newell Field. Secondly, they would no longer schedule "big time" college opponents such as Mississippi State, Alabama and Ole Miss. And lastly, they hired a new head coach, McNeil "Doby" Bartling, an Itta Bena native and Ole Miss graduate who had played for the Rebels in their 1936 Orange Bowl appearance and had previously served as head coach at Meridian High School and Vanderbilt University.

Bartling had been visiting Mississippi to recruit McComb High superstar David McIntosh for Vandy's Commodores, then one of the South's strongest football teams. But McIntosh had turned Bartling down, saying that he was flattered by the offer, but was determined to go to Millsaps to become a Methodist minister. Several months later, while visiting the Millsaps campus and speaking with the school's Vice President, Bartling received an offer to take a job as the Majors' head football coach. He initially turned it down, but reconsidered the matter while driving out of town. Desirous of getting out of the big college grind and savoring the prospect of coaching McIntosh, the most graceful athlete he had ever seen, Bartling drove back into Jackson and accepted the offer to become Millsaps's ninth head football coach.

A new head coach and a more favorable football schedule paid big dividends for the Purple and White eleven in 1946, as they shutout Delta State twice while cruising to a 5-1 record. Unfortunately, they still had to play a 7-2 Choctaw squad, which gave them a tenth straight whitewashing in the series, 35-0. Mississippi College's yearbook, *The Tribesman*, summed up the game as succinctly as possible:

> Not for ten years have the Majors even had so much as a smell of the sacred soil behind the Choctaw goal line. The Majors showed very little offensive strength and did not even make a first down for the entire first half; their defensive strength can be gauged by the final score.

Statistically speaking, Albert Gore's hard-nosed running and Wendell Webb's precision passing shifted Coach Robinson's double wing offense into high gear, and a swarming Choctaw defense proved way too much for the hapless Majors, who went 0 for 7 via the air, and managed only two first downs and 43 yards rushing the entire game.

Choc halfback Wendell Webb: "We didn't expect to win the game, because David McIntosh was a great back and John Jabour was a heckuva lineman, but we pulled it off somehow."

Despite the crushing loss to MC in 1946, the "Bartling Era" had begun at Millsaps, and the Majors sensed that good things were about to happen on "Methodist Hill." Sure enough, in 1947, the greatest moment in Millsaps football history occurred.—when Doby Bartling's Majors broke the Choctaws' twelve-year-long winning streak in the series. The 4-2 Majors scored a 7-0 upset win over an allegedly superior 5-2-1 Mississippi College squad before 5000 screaming, Tiger Stadium fans. The *Mississippi Collegian* expressed shock at Millsaps's first win over the Chocs in twelve years, declaring that the Choctaws "were the victims of the greatest setback of all times. . . " Ten miles up the road, the *Purple and White* headline simply read: "MILLSAPS—7, M.C.—0."

The winning Millsaps drive was sparked by Little All-American halfback David McIntosh's 45-yard dash off a fake punt from the Majors' 17-yard line. McIntosh remembers the play: "We hadn't run a fake punt all year, but I noticed that their end was crashing in full speed, and decided that if he did it again, I'd pull the ball in and take off."

Millsaps QB Jay Jackson followed up on McIntosh's long gainer by hurling a fifty-yard bomb to McIntosh, who then fought his way to the Choctaw 11 before finally being brought down. After a few short gains, Little All-American center John Christmas, who called most of the plays in Bartling's single wing offense, cornered Jackson in the huddle and said, "Put your nose in my backside and follow me on the quarterback sneak!"

Jackson approved Christmas's plan, and caught the Chocs by surprise with a perfectly executed quarterback sneak. In so doing, Jackson scored Millsaps's first points against Mississippi College in twelve long years. He then successfully kicked the extra point to give his team a 7 point margin. It was a lead that Millsaps would never surrender, thanks to linebacker Christmas's second quarter interception in the Millsaps end zone, and a third quarter deflection of a sure touchdown pass by 'Saps defensive back R. C. Green.

However, the real stars of the '47 game may have been Millsaps's rugged offensive linemen, towering, 6' 4", 205 pound end, Mike Engle, 6'2", 230 pound center John Christmas, guards Van Stewart and Bill Winans, and monstrous tackle John Jabour, who opened big holes for McIntosh all day. While on defense, these behemoths dominated the line of scrimmage and completely snuffed the Choctaw attack. In any event, Millsaps's victory celebration lasted all weekend long, and the school canceled all Monday classes in honor of the eagerly-awaited triumph.

The *Purple and White* gave a lion's share of the credit to Coach Doby Bartling's inspirational pre-game pep talk, which it likened to Knute Rockne's immortal "win one for the Gipper" speech. Players from the '47 team also credit their success to Bartling.

Millsaps lineman John Christmas:

I had played ball with L.S.U. before the war, but came to Millsaps because of Coach Bartling. He was one of the finest men I've ever known. He took a bunch of war veterans and former SEC athletes and made human beings of us. At big schools like L.S.U., it was clear from the beginning that we were there as football players and everything else was incidental. But under Coach Bartling at Millsaps, we could thoroughly enjoy playing the game we loved and then be a serious student the rest of the year. Coach Bartling was a man's man, but also a very caring human being who was interested in us as people and not just as players. We'd go to the wall for him.

Millsaps halfback David McIntosh: "Doby Bartling was a real gentleman and a devout Christian, and even though I had passed up a scholarship to play football at Ole Miss or Vanderbilt and hadn't even planned to play at Millsaps, I couldn't turn Bartling down, and ended up playing for him for three years. I enjoyed every minute of it, win, lose or draw."

A week after the 1947 MC/Millsaps game, the *Purple and White* took the occasion of the victory to lambast MC students for allegedly defacing buildings and destroying property on the Millsaps campus, and for riding past the campus and "screaming obscene oaths," illegally detaining visiting Millsaps students on the Clinton campus, and dragging a Millsaps ministerial student named Harry Cannon onto a side street in downtown Jackson and assaulting him with a black-jack. "So long as some of your number persist in marring our buildings, such as our observatory, with your scrawlings," declared the sarcasm-drenched editorial, "it wouldn't be so bad [if you were] literate enough to learn to spell 'Millsaps.'"

But despite the renewed competitiveness of the series, and the few isolated incidents of bad behavior it spawned, the MC/Millsaps rivalry never got out of control in the late '40s as it eventually did a decade later. As retired Gypsum Company executive and former Millsaps football and basketball player Walter Stokes explained, "We had just come back from WWII, and we didn't take football or the rivalry as serious as we had before going into the service. After experiencing life and death struggles overseas, a lot of the boys never took athletics so seriously again."

David McIntosh: "The GI's came back as older freshmen in their mid-twenties. In years past, upperclassmen shaved every freshmen head, and many of the fights got started when the other folks tried to take our freshmen beanies, and vice versa. After the war, nobody wanted to shave the head of a twenty-five year-old ex-soldier. That stopped a lot of the trouble."

But even though the rivalry was many years away from getting out of control, no one doubted how important it was on either campus.

Buddy Bartling, son of Coach Doby Bartling, and later a star kicker at Millsaps in the 1960s:

> In the spring of 1948, my father Doby, who was also Millsaps's head baseball coach, was pacing back and forth in his office, sweating an upcoming baseball game with Mississippi College. A janitor named Lee Gibson took a break from his chores, propped an arm on his broom handle, and asked my dad what was bothering him so badly.
>
> "Oh," Dad said, "we've got a game against Mississippi College today, and we don't have any pitching and they've got a real good team."
>
> "That ain't no problem," said Gibson matter-of-factly, "Just get yourself some good umpires." Everyone from the head coach to the janitor knew how important any MC series was.

In the decade's final two years both teams struggled with mediocrity. The Majors finished a paltry 2-3-1 and 2-5, respectively, with Southwestern (later Rhodes College) their only certain victim, although they did establish the beginnings of a good rivalry with the University of the South at Sewanee. Mississippi College suffered through back-to-back 4-5 seasons, made endurable only by two consecutive wins over Millsaps and two "moral victory" losses to the Florida State Seminoles.

In '48 the Chocs beat the Majors, 20-14, behind the 103 yard, two touchdown rushing performances of halfback Sugar Green.

And on a rainy, muddy night in 1949, they smashed their arch-rivals, 42-6, on the strength of the bruising running of halfbacks David Lee and James Coleman, perfect place kicking by Hollis Rutter and Bill Causey, three touchdowns by quarterback Jimmy Pittman, and the disrupting defensive play of Rooster Case.

"Our blocking in the '49 game was great," remembered half-back James Coleman, who later became head football coach for Senatobia. "I ran to the right from my left halfback position all day. The holes were there and I just ran through 'em."

But the best description of the '49 game may have come from the Mississippi College yearbook, *The Tribesman*, which related that,

> the high point of the 1949 football season, so far as the Choctaws were concerned, was reached on the night of November 1, in Tiger Stadium, in Jackson, where they stomped the daylights out of their traditional rivals, Millsaps Majors, beating them by 36 points. . .

Choctaw halfback David Lee, now a doctor in Forest, Missis-sippi, recalls the '49 contest:

> Coach Robby, who was a great coach, but a little set in his ways, still ran that old double wing offense, in which the quar-terback was solely a blocking back but still called the signals. Even so, by 1949 I was telling him what to call in the huddle on most of the plays. In the double wing formation, the ball was usually snapped to the halfback, usually me, and I either handed it off, ran with it, or threw it. Since the quarterbacks called the signals in the double wing, Coach had a quarterback meeting every week, which I, a halfback, was not invited to. A few minutes before the '49 Millsaps game, Robby called us all together, and said, "Lee will be calling signals." Of course, I didn't know all the signals since I hadn't been at the quarter-back meetings. Even worse, the game had been postponed from Saturday to Monday because of rain, and again from Monday to Tuesday for the same reason. We didn't know if we could

keep up our intensity for another week. And we didn't know if we could execute our offense on that muddy field. But we were ready when game time came, and beat Millsaps, 42-6.

As the new decade approached, the Choctaws sported an intimidating 19-6-4 series lead over the Majors. But as the two church-supported schools waged all-out war for football supremacy into the 1950s, many of their students and fans approached the rivalry with what might best be described as a dangerous religious fervor.

Millsaps Head Coach Doby Bartling may have put the rivalry in the best possible context when, in 1949, he compared it to two other famous rivalries.

T. W. Lewis, who played halfback and kicker for Bartling's Majors in 1949 and 1950, and retired after 37 years as a Millsaps religious studies teacher and 40 years as a Methodist minister:

> Coach Bartling recognized how intense the rivalry was becoming in the late forties and early fifties. He had been a quarterback at Ole Miss in the early thirties, and had thought the Ole Miss/Mississippi A & M rivalry was intense until he coached at Vanderbilt during their glory days and discovered that the Vanderbilt/Tennessee rivalry was worse. Then he came to Millsaps and soon realized that our rivalry with Mississippi College was even more intense than Vandy/UT. He supposed that the Millsaps/MC rivalry was more intense because it was a "Holy War," to use Coach Bartling's expression.

The "Holy War" waged by Bartling's Majors and Stanley Robinson's Choctaws would lead to unprecedented success for both teams in the early 1950s. But by that decade's end, the off-the-field violence associated with the rivalry would rise to an alarming level and threaten the very existence of the series.

CHAPTER SIX

HOLY WARS
1950-1958

A prosperous United States of America was moving ahead full speed as the 1950s arrived, and so were Millsaps and Mississippi College. Academically speaking, both schools were well on their way to acquiring exemplary reputations. The National Research Council's 1951 Trytten Report ranked MC's chemistry department as one of the best in the South, while the American Council on Education ranked Millsaps's freshmen among the nation's academic elite. In an effort to promote an atmosphere commensurate with a top-flight academic reputation, the Millsaps administration adopted an unlimited class-cuts policy for its students, which mirrored a popular approach at Ivy League institutions.

The two schools' debate teams continued to clash every year, examining diverse topics ranging from whether a chicken could roost more comfortably on a round limb or square stick, to significantly more serious political, social and religious issues. A new teacher named Lance Goss arrived at Millsaps in 1950 and quickly fashioned the Millsaps Players into one of the nation's most admired collegiate drama groups, while Mississippi College's Classical Club gained renown by promoting the value of classical studies to those who wished to be "truly educated." Mississippi College's women's intramural sports received a substantial boost from one Mrs. Cleveland, who fought for and obtained an impressive women's intramural program that included soccer, tennis, volleyball, basketball, track, swimming and speedball. Men's speedball (touch football with nine-man teams) was the intramural rage at Millsaps, where in 1950, a team called the Ministers, led by future United Methodist Bishop Lavelle Woodrick, fought for league supremacy against a Pi Kappa Alpha squad headed by future Bar Association President Jack Dunbar.

As was the case on many American campuses in the '50s, social activism ran high at both institutions. In 1950, the *Purple and White* ran a column supporting the position taken by the editor of Ole Miss's school newspaper, *The Daily Mississippian*, wherein the latter had argued that blacks should be allowed to attend the Ole Miss Law School. That same year, the *Mississippi Collegian* ran a bold, ahead-of-its-time cartoon which effectively criticized corruption in sports, especially basketball fixes and college football commercialism. Students at both colleges wondered how far their institutions should go to avoid religious dogmatism without becoming typical secular institutions. A 1950 *Purple and White* editorial on that very subject offered a solution to the problem based on the words of Christ: "Be in the world but not of the world."

Millsaps coeds lauded the arrival of television in Jackson during the 1952 Christmas holidays, with one young woman telling the *P & W* that it "was about time" TV had finally arrived, and another opining that television "would do good if it was educational and entertaining." In October of 1950, Choctaw head coach Stanley Robinson suggested a healthier way for male students to spend their spare time; he published an open letter to MC students in the *Collegian*, urging all "interested" men to try out for his Choctaw football team.

The right men must have answered Robinson's call, because his team finished a robust 6-2 in 1950. The Choctaws' two losses came in mismatches with Arkansas A & M (27-0) and Florida State (33-0), while their most memorable win came at the expense of the Millsaps Majors by a score of 19-7 at Robinson Field. All-Conference back "Dixie" David Lee, the "Forest Flash," led the Choctaws to victory by running for 97 yards and one score and passing for another 89 yards and two more touchdowns. The Choctaws' gargantuan line, which sported a twenty pound-per-man weight advantage over the Majors, kept Millsaps star running back Johnny Miller bottled up all day except for a 54 yard touchdown gallop. Choc brothers Bill and James "Foots" Wilson were especially effective in the trenches, as was guard Mike Mullins, who made three tackles in a row on one Major offensive series.

Defensive back Gene Allen also played a good game, stopping a Millsaps drive on the Choctaw 14-yard line with a clutch interception.

Major lineman Tom Prewitt, now a retired realtor, remembers the 1950 game: "I was having a hard time passing my Spanish class that year. I was also having problems with getting knocked out in practice. Then we played Mississippi College, and I had to try to tackle David Lee, who was a great, great athlete. During the game, Lee ran right over me and knocked me out cold. When they finally woke me up, I still didn't know where I was, and the first words out of my mouth were, 'I can't remember my Spanish!'"

Choctaw halfback David Lee: "The 1950 game was an especially big rivalry game because we both had good teams. It was a tough, tough game, but we never had any fights or any dirty hits by either side. Both teams played well and we finally managed to win, 19-7."

The week after the 1950 game, the *Purple and White* ran a tongue-in-cheek article which posed the question, "Who dirtied our bell?" The historic Millsaps bell, a smaller version of Philadelphia's Liberty Bell, had reigned as a campus landmark since 1916, the article related, but had recently been mistreated by "renegades from an unmentionable southern institution." The Choctaw "renegades" had turned the bell on its side on a previous occasion, the article noted, and shortly after the 1950 MC/Millsaps game, had splashed it with red paint. The story included a photograph captioned, "For Whom The Bell Tolls," that showed Harvey "Sherlock" Nall investigating the "crime" attired in the famous detective's distinctive hat and pipe. Nall was facetiously quoted as saying, "Gadzooks, men, I believe it's blood." The caption ended in the spirit with which it began, declaring that, ". . . the pipe made [Nall] sick, and the investigation was postponed."

Although the bell article was penned in the spirit of good collegiate humor, it foreshadowed darker events to come in the 1950s, incidents which would run the gamut from humorous pranks to violent, occasionally sadistic acts. In the early '50s, the rivalry usually took the form of nothing worse than rough-and-tumble beanie snatching and drive-by insult. But as the seriousness of World War II gave way to the light-hearted prosperity of the 1950s, and as the football series grew more competitive and intense, these acts began taking on a progressively darker tone.

T. W. Lewis:

> Stealing beanies was a big challenge for us throughout the 1950s. There were frequent scraps over beanies on Capitol Street as the rivalry got more and more intense. And although the players were the best of friends on the field, because of the hype before the games, some of the students resorted to vandalism and theft of property. For example, in 1951 some of our Millsaps students stole an MC fan's noisemaker at a baseball game. Then shortly before that year's football game, Mississippi College students stole some trophies out of a glass case at the Millsaps Kappa Alpha fraternity house. On one occasion, five or six MC fans came to our campus and challenged five or six of our students to a fistfight. Needless to say, the challenge was accepted. But no one was ever seriously injured during the early '50s.

Although Coach Doby Bartling's Majors enjoyed a successful 4-2 season in 1950, Bartling resigned his role as athletic director, intramural coordinator and head baseball, basketball and football coach to take a position with Mississippi School Supply Co., in Jackson, in order to better support his expanding family. He was sorely missed at Millsaps, and a recollection by his son, McNeil "Buddy" Bartling III, himself a salesperson with Mississippi School Supply, may best represent the great impact Doby had upon his players. Buddy Bartling:

> I remember my father's funeral at Itta Bena in 1992. An incredible number of his former players from Millsaps, Vanderbilt, and his high school teams came from all over the country to pay their respects. I simply couldn't believe it. Every last one of them made a point of coming by and telling my seventeen year old son Neil how much his grandfather had meant to their lives. After that experience, Neil was determined to exert the same kind of impact on others as his grand-

father had. He decided on the spot that he wanted to go into coaching. In 2000, he finally made it, as head baseball and assistant football coach at Simpson Academy. I was headed that way myself when a job came along selling sports equipment to schools for the same company my father had worked for. I'm very proud that my son and I can both follow in my father's footsteps.

Doby Bartling was succeeded by his younger brother Sammy, also an Ole Miss alum, who vacated his post as head coach at McComb High School to take over the head coaching reign at Millsaps. Sammy Bartling's McComb teams had played championship-caliber ball in the Big Eight Conference, and he brought several of his senior stars with him to Jackson. With these talented football newcomers, several highly touted prospects from Jackson's powerful Central High School, two Ole Miss transferees, and the arrival of several battle-hardened Korean War veterans in the Major camp, Bartling fielded a strong nucleus with which to make an assault on the Majors' archrival, the Mississippi College Choctaws.

The new coach also brought a fresh style to Millsaps. According to 1950 Major halfback T. W. Lewis, the younger Bartling

was as brilliant a football mind as you'd ever want to encounter. He was a student of Ole Miss football coach Harry Mehere, from whom he'd learned valuable coaching strategies and the subtleties of 'T' formation. And unlike Doby, who never raised his voice on or off the field, Sammy was as feisty as he could be. He'd banter with the players, get very sarcastic with us, and kid us about our mistakes. He was a greatly loved and respected coach just like his brother Doby.

With a new coach on board, Millsaps enjoyed an unusual season in 1951, moving into position to capture their first Dixie Conference flag despite posting an overall 2-3 record. This was occasioned by the exit of Stetson and Florida State from the league, leaving only three football-playing teams, Mississippi College, Millsaps, and Howard, to compete for the conference title.

Mississippi College, which eventually went 1-6 in the year, lost a mid-season game to Howard, so the 1951 MC/Millsaps contest took on championship dimensions for the Majors. If they won the rivalry game, they had only to beat Howard the next week to win the conference crown. But the Choctaws hadn't been entirely eliminated by their loss to the Howard Bulldogs. If they could beat Millsaps, they could root for the Majors to whip Howard and create a three-way tie for the conference championship.

The bitterly contested 1951 MC/Millsaps game was played on October 29 at Jackson's Tiger Stadium. Prior to the game, the *Purple and White* did everything it could to stir up controversy by labeling the MC double-wing formation "antiquated," and derogatorily referring to the Choctaws themselves as "the South Pasture lads." This was risky talk, indeed, since Mississippi College was led by two former Mississippi State scholarship players, fullback Buddy Lee and tackle Wade Bass, who had transferred to MC earlier in the season. Such former SEC players always posed a serious threat in Dixie Conference play.

In an even more surprising move, the *Mississippi Collegian* laid off the pre-game editorial tradition of verbal volleyball, choosing instead to laud their own players for recent successes. In a statement that perfectly summed up the beauty of playing football at schools such as Mississippi College and Millsaps, the *Collegian* opined that the reason the Choctaws had fared so well over the years was that "they play because they love the game, because they are inspired by their coach, and because they are playing for the honor of their institution, and not because they are hired to play."

However, the old school spirit proved not nearly enough to save the Chocs as Millsaps rolled to a 12-7 win. Although MC had taken a 7-0 lead on a five yard scoring pass from Buddy Lee to Johnny Byrd, Major halfbacks Sammy Joe Glorioso and Buddy Kalil ran the ball down the Choctaws' throats, and Kalil ignited a rousing Millsaps comeback with a second quarter scoring gallop. Then, with only 3:40 remaining in the game, Major signal-caller Eddie Collins scored on a fourth-down quarterback sneak. Major defensive end Dave Powell and safety Glen Cain ended the Choctaws' final rally by sacking their quarterback on third down and batting away a fourth-down Hail Mary pass. The Majors, who completed only one of five passes for five yards, compared to MC's relatively successful 12 of 26 passing for 76 yards, got the job done on the ground by out-gaining the Chocs 212 rushing yards to 60.

With the victory over their archrival secured, the Majors only had to get by Howard the next weekend to claim their first Dixie Conference crown. But they would have to do it in Birmingham, and they would have to deal with a talented Bulldog quarterback named Bobby Bowden, who would later go on to glory as the national championship-winning Florida State head football coach.

With the score knotted at 7-7 in the third quarter, Major halfback Tommy Parker fielded a Bowden punt, ran laterally and faked a handoff to Glenn Cain, then turned up field and cruised 45 yards for a Millsaps touchdown. Fellow halfback Cain scored the next touchdown by evading several tacklers, including one who ripped off Cain's helmet, and running twenty more yards for the Majors' third score. "Big" Ollie Scott wrapped up the Majors' win in the fourth quarter when he intercepted an errant Bowden pass and returned it 72 yards to pay-dirt. Not content merely to claim Millsaps's first-ever football title, the *Purple and White* concluded its coverage of the game by saying that, "The game was well-played, [and] the weather was beautiful, with only the officiating marring the setting."

The 1952 season found the Majors and Choctaws once again vying for the Dixie Conference title. Coming into the traditional rivalry game, the Chocs sported a 3-1 record, including a 7-0 defeat of Howard, courtesy of a five-yard touchdown pass from quarterback Buddy Lee to end Bobby Hannah. The Blue and Gold desperately wanted to win the Millsaps game for several heretofore undreamed-of reasons: (1) to prevent Millsaps from winning two consecutive conference titles; (2) to avoid a second consecutive loss to the Majors, which would be the first in series history; (3) to win their first Dixie Conference title; and, (4) to properly celebrate Mississippi College's 125-year anniversary. In pursuit of these goals, Stanley Robinson eschewed his familiar double-wing formation in favor of the new Split-T formation, hoping to balance his capable running game with a more prolific passing attack.

Sporting a 1-2 record, Sammy Bartling's Majors focused their week-long practices on stopping the new Choctaw system and sharpening their running attack. Although the two teams were scheduled to meet on Robinson Field on October 27th, the game had to be rescheduled because the Mississippi State/Alabama contest in Starkville and comedian Bob Hope's appearance at Jackson's City Auditorium threatened to severely diminish the game's attendance. Consequently, the two teams met at 8:00 p.m. on October 25th, and played what many consider to be the most exciting game in twenty-two years. But before they did, they would become involved in one of the greatest pranks ever played in the history of the series.

The night before the big game, several Millsaps students snuck onto the MC campus with a can of gasoline and burned a giant "M" on the fifty yard line of Robinson Field. Although many Millsaps players and school officials publicly decried the students' vandalizing act, the Choctaws could do little about the "M" and it remained on the field throughout the entire game!

In the annual grudge match, Millsaps added injury to insult in the second quarter when Major defensive back Benny Kirkland intercepted a Buddy Lee pass and raced unmolested into the end zone. T. W. Lewis then successfully converted his first extra point attempt. As the first half drew to a close, the Major defense stuffed a Choctaw drive just five yards shy of the Millsaps end zone.

Choctaw halfback Joe Murphy got things started in the third quarter with a one-yard, fourth-down plunge for six points, but Jake Thompson missed his extra point try. Millsaps then followed the Choc touchdown with what was by far the game's most exciting play. Major quarterback Cain faked a hand-off to T. W. Lewis, then gave the ball to freshman fullback John Lowery, who broke off left tackle, ran over a linebacker, bowled over a defensive back, and flattened a safety, before racing thirty-five more yards to the Choctaw 15-yard line. There, another Choctaw leaped onto Lowery's back, and as he fell to the ground, Lowery lateraled back to an alert Cain, who scooted the remaining fifteen yards for a touchdown. Lewis's second extra point kick was perfect. Down, 14-6, the Braves came right back, capitalizing on a Major fumble when Larry Hill skirted left end for a Choctaw touchdown. This time Thompson succesfully converted the extra point attempt.

The fourth quarter began with Millsaps in the lead, 14-13, but the Choctaws went ahead for the first time when Lee completed a short pass to Charlie Ballard, who ran forty yards for paydirt. Thompson's successful extra point attempt put the Choctaws ahead, 20-14. But the Major defense soon launched a fierce comeback by forcing a Choctaw fumble at the Millsaps 46. On the next play, Cain hit Lowery with a fifteen-yard pass which the fleet back carried the remaining 35 yards for the go-ahead touchdown. All that was needed now, the Majors realized, was a successful extra point kick.

As the team huddled for the extra point play, Major lineman Tom Prewitt, Jr., approached kicker T. W. Lewis in the huddle and said, "Take your time, T. W."

"Get away, get away," shouted Lewis, who desperately wanted to be left alone with his thoughts before attempting the most important kick of his life.

The Majors' hearts soared as Lewis's kick sailed through the uprights and gave Millsaps a 21-20 lead with time running out. But the game was far from over.

To everyone's surprise, Major kickoff specialist Bill Irby tried an onside kick, which a jubilant Millsaps kick-off team recovered. But the Majors couldn't move the ball and had to punt it away. The Choctaws promptly fumbled the ball and the Majors again took over possession on their own 46 yard line. Cain fumbled the ball right back, but the Chocs were once again unable to mount a sustained drive and had to punt the ball away. After running out all but the last fifteen seconds, the Majors lined up to punt the ball one last time from deep in their own territory. To the delight of the home crowd, Brave end Bobby Hannah crashed through the Millsaps line and blocked John Little's punt, giving Mississippi College the ball on Millsaps's five yard line with ten seconds remaining.

After a pass completion gained but one yard, and with five seconds left on the clock, the Chocs called in their place kicker, Jack Thompson, to win the game with a short field goal from a difficult angle. As 5000 fans held their collective breaths, Thompson's kick fell short and to the left, and the Majors celebrated their most thrilling victory to date!

In a post-game column entitled, "The Statistics, Or How Did We Win That One?," the *Purple and White* reported that the Choctaws had "outrushed, outpassed and nearly outfought" the Majors. The published stats confirmed that Millsaps had rushed for 101 yards and completed two of five passes for 64 yards, while the "South pasture lads" had rushed for 309 yards and completed 10 of 18 passes for 152 yards. But two other statistics told the real tale of the 1952 game: Millsaps went three-for-three in the kicking department while the Chocs missed one extra point and a game-ending field goal attempt; and the Majors intercepted three MC aerials and recovered two of their opponents' fumbles, while losing the ball only twice on the ground.

Unfortunately, the Majors had little time to celebrate their hard-earned victory. The Howard Bulldogs were coming to Jackson the next weekend, and they were led by a 155-pound quarterback and Little All-American candidate named Bobby Bowden, who was planning to ruin both their Homecoming game and their conference title hopes.

But the Bowden mystique aside, everything went Millsaps's way in the very first game ever played in Jackson's new, 20,000-capacity Hinds County Memorial Stadium, appropriately located a city block north of the Millsaps campus. Major halfback Sammy Glorioso gained 125 rushing yards and scored three touchdowns en route to the Majors' 27-7 thrashing of Howard. Major defensive end Payton Weems put an exclamation point on the drubbing by blocking Bowden's end zone punt for a two point safety. Although a late, fourth-quarter touchdown dive by Bowden avoided a shutout, the Bulldogs had to watch in anguished silence as the Majors celebrated their second consecutive Dixie Conference Championship.

Although Millsaps quarterback Glenn Cain out-dueled Bowden

that day, and had better offensive statistics during the 1952 season, Bowden got the All-Star nod on offense while Cain was selected solely for his defensive skills. Years later, Cain, a teacher, coach and administrator, would tell the *Clarion-Ledger* that he wasn't offended by the All-Star oversight. "I'm just glad to see [Bowden] do well," Cain said. "He was the only famous one we [the Dixie Conference] had. It's kind of an inspiration to know you played against someone like that. It was a pretty competitive league."

Major lineman Tom Prewitt, who towered over Bowden at 6', 202 pounds, was somewhat less charitable remembering the Bulldog signal-caller. "I tackled Bowden several times," Prewitt recalls, "but didn't remember him particularly well, or whether he had much of a ballgame. But he couldn't have had too great of a game," Prewitt added with a grin, "when we beat him, 27 to 7."

As exciting as the 1952 season had been, 1953 brought even more thrills, as both the Choctaws and Majors whipped Howard before playing each other, setting up the annual grudge match as the battle for the Dixie Conference championship. Mississippi College started off slowly, losing to the University of Mexico for the first time ever, 34-20, and tying Austin College, 19-19. Millsaps also stumbled early, losing their first outing, 27-6, to Delta State. But both teams won their next three games, making the upcoming rivalry game as important a match as either team had ever played.

The 1953 game was especially significant for several reasons. To begin with, back in February, Millsaps President H. E. Finger had responded to rampant rumors that the Choctaws were paying their basketball players with a stern letter to MC President D. M. Nelson, threatening to end basketball competition between the two schools until the latter had given him written assurance that Mississippi College was complying with the N.I.A.A.'s no-scholarship rule. Upon receiving the asked-for written assurances, Finger promised to schedule future basketball games with the Choctaws, although he stated that it might not be possible to do so in 1953 since the schedules had already been completed for that season.

Despite a favorable resolution, the basketball incident stuck in the Choctaws' craw. They also wanted to win the Millsaps game because the conference title was on the line, and to stop the Majors from gaining a third-consecutive win in the series. Consequently, the Chocs planned to strive all the harder to "remove the Bartling hoodoo."

And of course, there were the usual rivalry shenanigans the week before the big game.

Choctaw tackle Jimmy Bradshaw, now a retired Baptist preacher:

In 1953, four or five upperclassmen put me in an old Pontiac, shaved head, beanie and all, and dropped me off on the corner of the Millsaps campus. They also called the Millsaps upperclassmen and told them where I was. Before long, some of their freshmen came to look me over and see what a real Choctaw smelled like. After looking at me for a while, and having a few things to say, they all went on about their business. They could see that I was like a rattlesnake and that they needed to give me my space. I wasn't but 5'8" tall, but I weighed 243 pounds after football practice and 255 pounds before (since Coach Robinson wouldn't let us have any water and made us run three or four miles every day). I had a 28" waist and a 54" chest and muscles you couldn't drive a nail through. My brother always said I looked like a fireplug sitting on a hydraulic spindle, movin' around so you couldn't get hold of me. But when I grabbed somebody they could get a'loose, but they'd have to leave what I was holdin' on to with me. (Laughs)

So I fended those Millsaps boys off pretty well. They left me alone out of fear of having their body parts removed or crushed. (Laughs again) Lots of folks are satisfied with the way they are, don't want their nose stuck in their ear. Anyhow, after a few hours of that my upperclassmen came and picked me up and we got off the campus before anything else happened.

Although the off-the-field rivalry fires still hadn't blazed out of control by 1953, that season's MC/Millsaps game was neverthe-

less predicted to be a hotly-contested affair. The pre-game prognosticators noted that the Choctaw line outweighed their Major
counterparts by eleven pounds-per-man, but also realized that
Millsaps had twenty-two returning lettermen compared to only
twelve for Mississippi College. Both teams ran the high-powered
Split-T offense, and both sported modern uniforms which differed
from today's uniforms only by the lack of plastic face guards. In a
sense, this game would not only have more on the line for both
teams than any previous MC/Millsaps meeting, it would also be
the first such tilt played in a purely modern context.

The teams kicked off the title match, which also served as
Homecoming for both schools, at 8:00 p.m. in Tiger Stadium. The
Majors took the field decked out in white, stripe-less jerseys with
purple numbers, and white helmets, while the Choctaws were
attired in blue jerseys with gold numerals and arm stripes, and
gold helmets.

After Millsaps fumbled a punt on the their own 23, the Chocs
took a 7-0 first quarter lead two plays later when fullback "Big"
Jack Bass ran through a gaping hole in the 'Saps line to score six
points. Glenn Cain brought the Majors back in the second period
by passing to John Lowery for a score. The Millsaps kick failed and
MC retained a 7-6 halftime lead.

Choctaw halfback Fred Morris skirted the left end for a third
quarter touchdown to give his team a 13-6 lead. A few minutes
later, Lowery bucked the line for a Millsaps touchdown, and Red
Powell's extra point tied the game at 13-all. Choc halfback Bill
Gore scored a go-ahead, rushing TD, and with a successful conversion, the Braves took a 20-13 lead into the final stanza.

Late in the fourth quarter, Powell completed a pass to Lowery who
outraced the Choctaw secondary to paydirt, bringing the Majors
to within one point of tying the game. But the Brave defense rose
to the occasion and blocked Millsaps's extra-point attempt to
clinch the game and claim their first-ever Dixie Conference title.

Ecstatic Mississippi College officials gave their student body a
one-day holiday to celebrate the Choctaw title game victory, and
a grateful *Mississippi Collegian* honored MC Head Coach and

Athletic Director Stanley Robinson with a column entitled, "Roses for Robby," which featured testimonials from several ex-players and students—

Future Mississippi Governor Ross Barnett:

> [Robinson] will go down in history as a truly great coach. He has instilled in the hearts and minds of thousands of young men every essential element of the highest type of sportsmanship and Christian ideals;

Future Mississippi publishing magnate R. M. Hederman:

> Football coaches are supposed to win—or to build character. [Robinson] has done both—for many reasons. His character on and off the field personifies better than anyone we know, the wholesome and courageous spirit of amateur intercollegiate athletics;

and, former All-American halfback "Goat" Hale:

> Coach Robinson instilled into my life true principles of character. He stressed team spirit, fair play, and courage. "Robby"has been an inspiration to the youth of Mississippi.

But perhaps no commendation speaks as loudly as the one given Robinson by an MC player who met "Robby" after the coach had stepped down and was serving the college as teacher and athletic director. John Smith, who played at Mississippi College in the late '50s and now serves as a Choctaw assistant football coach, credits Robinson for much:

> Meeting Coach Robby was one of the greatest things that ever happened to me. He was like a second father to me. When I came to MC, we only paid $6 per hour of instruction, but I only had $20 in my pocket and that wasn't enough for me to pre-register. Coach Robby counseled me to hang in there, and

loaned me $500 so I could register and stay in school. He told me that I should be responsible and pay him back, but that even if I couldn't, he would consider it a good investment if I'd stay in school. I worked my way through college, put away some "Robby" money in a sock whenever I could, and finally paid him back after my third year and offered to pay the interest as well. He wrote me a letter refusing to accept any interest on the loan, saying he was proud to help. I knew from being around him that I wanted to coach someday, and I credit him for helping to make that happen.

Stanley Robinson retired after the 1953 season as Mississippi College's greatest football coach to date with a 123-84-15 record, a .588 win percentage, a decisive edge over Millsaps, and the school's first Conference title trophy on display in the athletic department offices. He'd also earned well over 200 victories as head coach of the Choctaw baseball team. He was replaced by former MC star player Joe Murphy, who would become the eleventh "Choctaw Chief" in 47 years of MC football.

If Major and Choctaw fans thought the excitement of the 1953 season would never be topped, they were in for a pleasant surprise in 1954. Both teams won three out of their first five games, including close wins over Dixie Conference member Howard. Consequently, their October 23rd, joint-Homecoming Game would determine the conference championship for the second year in a row, and even more importantly, grant bragging rights to the winner for another 365 days. In addition, the schools introduced a new tradition to the feature-packed affair by putting up the Choctaws' Tomahawk and the Majors' Sword for the taking by the victor.

When the teams finally met before 6500 fans at Tiger Stadium, the Majors took an early 6-0 lead on halfback Walter Waldrop's two yard plunge, but Red Powell's conversion attempt failed. Moments later, Choctaw QB Ken Toler hit receiver Ken Halford for a 25-yard scoring strike, but the Majors blocked Dan Dubose's extra point try. Consequently, the teams went into the locker room with their big game knotted, 6-6.

In the third quarter, Millsaps quarterback Powell redeemed himself for missing a first half extra point boot by firing a thirty-five-yard pass to Waldrop, who sped the remaining twenty-five yards to paydirt. The Millsaps defense then shut down the Chocs for the rest of the game, and Major backs Waldrop and Hardy Nall (who would portray *Hamlet* on the Millsaps stage two weeks later) ran out the clock playing fumble-free ball control. The 13-6 win clinched the Majors' third Dixie Conference title in four years, and gave them an unprecedented three-out-of-four wins over their traditional rivals!

And by virtue of a more competitive series, to say nothing of the fact that a Dixie Conference title had hinged on the outcome of every recent Millsaps/MC contest, the rivalry between the two schools had intensified a thousand-fold over the past five years. As Major footballer Tom Prewitt remembered:

> The games were clean and never dirty, although they were very intense and focused. But they were never as important to us as they were to our student bodies. Oh, we wanted to win very much, make no mistake, but our practices for Mississippi College were not very different from those for our other games. There was never any dirty hitting on the field because we respected the Choctaws and I believe they felt the same way toward us. There just wasn't any bad blood on the field.
>
> But you know how it is with many college students, they've got to have something to do to get into trouble. They'd ride down the street ringing bells and waving blue and gold or purple and white streamers all week long before the Millsaps/MC game. The two campuses were so close to each other, and with all the hype before the big game, there was bound to be some trouble. The students couldn't resist raiding each other's campuses for beanies, and if one of them came back without one, he'd have to run a belt line gauntlet.

Jim Berry, '50s Millsaps player, now a retired Special Treasury Agent, remembers the shenanigans associated with the rivalry in the mid-'50s:

During my freshman "M" Club initiation, the upperclassmen stripped us down to our shorts and dropped us off on the
Mississippi College campus to steal the white rocks that the
MC students had used to spell out "Mississippi College" on a
hill facing Highway 80. Of course, one of our upperclassmen,
Ted Alexander, who recently retired as President of Pearl River
Community College, called over to Clinton and tipped them
off that we were coming. We had to try to escape through the
town. They didn't expect us to have any money, but I had been
a paratrooper overseas and knew how to tape money to my
foot. So I called my roommate James Hood, and he drove over
and picked me up. But while I was running for my life, I was
thinking, "I've been in a war and jumped out of an airplane,
and now I'm over here doing this fraternity stuff!"

Anyhow, to get us back, a big Mississippi College gang set
up some tom toms across the street from our Christian Center
and started beating them one night. My Kappa Sigma fraternity little brother, Jimmy Hayes, was one of the first ones there
to greet them. Jimmy was a 4.0 student and so poor he had to
sell his lunch ticket to stay in school, but he wasn't afraid of
anything, so he went right at 'em, and then the cops got him.
I tried to talk the cop into letting me take Jimmy out of there,
but he told me that if I didn't go home he'd arrest me too. So I
waited until they put Jimmy in the police car and then opened
the door on the other side and he went straight through and got
away. We were both in good shape and so we outran the police.

Whether they were involved in the action on the field or in
the streets, every Major or Choctaw agreed on one thing—they
were caught up in one of America's most intense collegiate rivalries!

The 1955 season found the Majors understandably optimistic
about their chances for gridiron success, led as they were by a
senior class which had garnered two previous conference titles
and whipped a championship-caliber Mississippi College squad
two out of the last three years. Mississippi College, guided by new
head coach Joe Murphy, abandoned the soon-to-be defunct Dixie

Conference in 1955 and joined the ranks of the small college independents. Unfortunately, neither Jackson-area team met with much success that season.

Millsaps struggled to a 4-5 record thanks to what lineman Tom Prewitt later described as "a bad case of senioritis. We thought we were good," Prewitt recalled, "but we didn't live up to our potential and didn't win the title in 1955."

Mississippi College fared better with a 5-4 winning season, but like Millsaps, lost badly to Delta State and Southwestern, and barely defeated old rivals Sewanee and Howard. Even so, the Millsaps/MC game remained the hottest ticket on both schools' schedules, and the '55 contest at Hinds Memorial Stadium was easily one of the best ever played in the series.

Since the game was Millsaps's Homecoming, the Majors put on a rousing parade in downtown Jackson the morning of the game. Floats representing the fraternities, sororities, independent organizations, honoraries, and the Christian Council kicked off the procession, with First Prize going to Kappa Alpha for their colorful whale with a "Whale the Chocs" theme. Chi Omega placed second with a garden-swing float entitled, "Get in the Swing," while Kappa Delta finished third with their pink, pearl-studded oyster shell, which denoted their members as "Priceless Pearls." The Millsaps Singers topped off the festivities with an on-campus concert, playing such songs as "Salvation is Created" and "Carol of the Drums."

The game was also Homecoming for Mississippi College, and during their afternoon parade, conflict erupted on the streets of downtown Jackson.

Jim Berry: "We weren't supposed to be in the streets during the MC parade. They were supposed to have them all to themselves. But some of us hopped into a convertible and watched their parade on Capitol Street. One of our players, Ted Alexander, mouthed off to the guys on one of their floats, and they all piled off and came right after us. We got into a fight right there on the front yard of the Governor's Mansion. The police came and we scattered. We weren't surprised that the police got there so fast, since we were fighting on the front steps of the Governor's Mansion."

The 1955 Homecoming game began as a hard-nosed, error-prone defensive struggle. On the first series, Millsaps tackle Tom Prewitt recovered Choctaw QB Ken Toler's fumble on the Millsaps 11 yard line, but the subsequent Millsaps drive ended with a fumble on the MC 37. The "Injuns" came storming back downfield only to lose the ball on downs when Major linemen Prewitt and James Hood sacked Toler on a thwarted pass play. Playing defense, Toler promptly ended the Majors' next drive by intercepting a pass, but another Choctaw miscue gave the ball back to the Majors deep in Mississippi College territory. Millsaps QB Crow Parnell, who played the whole game with a bleeding gash above his eye, capitalized on the Choctaw mistake by tossing a thirty-two yard touchdown pass to end Bennie Kirkland to break the scoring ice.

The Braves fought right back and Toler soon hit receiver Charles Bryan for a twenty-yard scoring strike, but their kicker, Bill Gore, later mockingly referred to by the *Purple and White* as "Golden-Toe Gore," missed the first of three failed extra point efforts. Two plays after the ensuing kickoff, Major quarterback Parnell connected with halfback Hardy Nall on a 75-yard scoring bomb, and the extra point staked Millsaps to a 14-6 halftime advantage.

After Toler intercepted another Millsaps pass to start the second half, the Choctaws drove for a second score which came on Sonny Emerson's eight yard stampede over right guard. With the Majors still leading by a score of 14-12, the Chocs dug in and held them for a chance to take the lead. The game's most exciting play soon came on a 41-yard sprint by Emerson behind a wall of Choctaw blockers, giving the Baptists an 18-14 lead.

But the favored Majors were not ready to surrender, and Militants return man Roy Wolfe ran the ensuing kickoff back to the Choctaw 46. After gaining a first and goal at the nine behind the blocking of Johnny Awad and Tom Boone, Millsaps gained just one yard on two more rushes. Parnell then heaved a jump pass to Kirkland, who was stopped at the three. On fourth down and with only seconds remaining, Parnell handed the ball to his best runner, "Big" John Lowery, who was swarmed over by a host of Choctaws, and the game belonged to Mississippi College.

Ken Toler, Choctaw quarterback, now a retired investment advisor: "We were down 14-12 and trying to put together a drive when our right tackle, Puddin Davis, got my attention in the huddle. Only the quarterback could talk in the huddle, but he caught my eye and pointed to his own chest. I knew that meant to run the ball his way. So I gave the ball to Sonny Emerson who ran off right tackle behind Davis for a forty-yard touchdown run. We had revenge in mind after losing to Millsaps in 1954. It was great to get that win over Millsaps!"

Sandra Toler, Millsaps alumnus: "After I transferred to Millsaps from M.S.C.W., I got engaged to Ken. One of my Millsaps friends was Roy Wolfe, who had played in the '55 game, which Ken had won, 18-14. Roy told me that he was about to catch the winning pass on their last drive when Ken's hand reached up at the last second and knocked the pass away. "You shouldn't marry that guy," he told me! (Laughs) He was really upset about it."

The Choctaws may have been the better team, declared a post-game *Purple and White* editorial, but their students were some of the most uncivilized people in America. In an October 28, 1955, article entitled, "Characteristics of the Majors," the *P & W* claimed that the "Mississippi College students were not satisfied with friendly rivalry, but resorted to property destruction." Although the article did not mention the alleged destruction, it did point out that Millsaps students had returned the MC Tomahawk they had stolen on the Friday before the game because Mississippi College students had cited a previous agreement banning student forays to their rival's campus the day before a game. But, the article continued, after Millsaps students honored the agreement, MC students promptly swiped the Millsaps dummy a few minutes later. "We can only wonder at the character of an institution," complained the *P & W*, "that uses a rule only when it works in their favor." The article also alleged that the majority of the fifteen-yard penalties went against the Choctaws during the Millsaps game, and chastised the MC student body for engaging in primitive horseplay before the game "every year."

That same *P & W* issue also contained another, even more caustic article entitled, "Custer's Last Stand, or Something," which accused Mississippi College students of "sneaking from their reservation rat-holes, and proceeding to paint, wreck and burn any part of the campus they could find not under guard." The article alleged that the MC students' pre-game actions had "reached an all-time low for any group of supposedly civilized adults." Millsaps students repelled the "Chocs' Pearl Harbor-like sneak attack on Tuesday night," the article continued, but on Friday afternoon, "four more MC students, including some of the ugliest human (?) females ever seen in Murrah Hall," came to get their "iddy-biddy tom-tom back." Several carloads of policemen were required, noted the editorial, "to disperse the ignorant mass."

Along with this very general yet highly incendiary language, the column tossed in several specific allegations, claiming that the Choctaw "savages" had splashed paint on the Millsaps-Wilson Library, "carted off some vases from the front of the library, wrecked the cannon between Murrah and Founder's, painted the bell and the M bench, smashed the glass bulb on the entrance gate," and committed several other "misdemeanors." The article further noted that the Mississippi College administration condemned the lawless acts of its students and requested that an itemized expense list of damages incurred be sent to its Dean of Men for payment. Not surprisingly, the *Custer* editorial was published anonymously.

In 1956, Millsaps and Mississippi College followed up mediocre 1955 worksheets with substantially worse records; the Majors fell to 2-2-3 and the Choctaws dropped off to 2-4-2. To no one's surprise, disappointing seasons failed to have any lessening effect upon the traditional rivalry's intensity.

Byrd Hillman, Millsaps alumnus, now a Jackson insurance broker:

> My father, Rev. Byrd Hillman, Sr., is now a Methodist preacher in Brandon, but when he was at Millsaps, he knew all about the rivalry. He told me that lots of fights took place at the Krystal in downtown Jackson. He also told me about the time that he went to the MC campus to get the Choctaw tom

tom. The MC freshmen had to beat tom toms all night long
every night the week of the Millsaps game. One night in '56 he
went onto the MC campus with several buddies, all of them
posing as MC students. One of their group had actually transferred from MC and knew all about the tom tom "program."
According to my dad, this transfer student told the girl beating
the tom tom that he would relieve her long enough for her to
go get herself some ice cream. After she left, he took off with
the tom tom! Dad also told me about the time he and some of
his buddies took some rye grass seed and planted it in front of
a dorm late one night so that when it grew up a week later, it
would spell "Millsaps." I think those guys had a good time
with that rivalry.

Rev. Byrd Hillman, Sr.: "After we got the tom tom that evening,
the Mississippi College student body representative, Talmadge
Littlejohn, and a group of MC students came to our campus the
next day and demanded its return. Our school officials ordered
us to return it and we did so immediately. It wasn't the sort of
thing that you wanted to act ugly about forever. (Laughs) We had
a fun, wholesome rivalry with Mississippi College back then,
before it got out of control."

And as had frequently happened in years past, the rivalry
shenanigans did get out of control the Thursday evening before
the Millsaps/MC football game.

According to an October 26 *Purple and White* editorial, around
midnight, "a large group of Choctaws began setting up drums,
sirens, and megaphones for a pep rally" across North West Street
from Millsaps's Christian Center. As the Choctaws began their
rally, a cry went up among the Millsaps faithful to "get that
drum," and about 200 "eager [Millsaps] *defenders* swarmed over"
across West Street and broke off a siren, "liberated" a megaphone,
ripped off one side of the big drum, and otherwise repulsed the
Choctaw "*invaders.*"

Major ballplayer Tom Prewitt remembers the event: "About
thirty or forty MC students began challenging us to a fight right
in front of the Christian Center, of all places. I stood there and

watched the whole thing happen. There were a few football players involved in the scrap, especially the ones who had been good
Gold Glove boxers. But mostly it was the regular students who
participated in that fight."

According to the *P & W* article, the police were finally sum-
moned and "bade the Tribe to return to their tepees." But on Friday night, the article continued, "the largest body of Choctaws
ever to visit our campus" returned for another engagement, and
"100 Millsaps men stood ready to defend our home." Amazingly,
the evening ended without any violence, and at noon the next day,
the Millsaps students and a large number of alumni threw "the
finest pep rally ever seen on [the Millsaps] campus."

That annual grudge match at Jackson's Municipal Stadium
proved to be yet another in a six-year succession of nail-biters and
heart-stoppers. The '56 match quickly shaped up as a defensive
struggle; the Choctaws gained only 119 yards on the ground and
completed but four of 14 passes for 47 yards, while the Majors
picked up 121 yards on the ground and were 0 for 1 through the
air. Fullback Rusty Smith led the Militant Methodists with 52
rushing yards while Baptist Brave Linus Bridges ground out 45
yards on the ground.

The Chocs drove to the Millsaps one yard line in the second
quarter, and faced a fourth and goal decision. While the Indians
huddled, Major lineman James Hood grabbed his roommate and
fellow lineman Jim Berry by the face mask and said, "We have got
to gut this one out!"

"Let's be in the *Clarion-Ledger* tomorrow," agreed Berry. And
when the inevitable Choctaw dive materialized on the next play,
Hood and Berry stuffed the runner at the goal line. The heavily
favored Choctaws failed to score, and ventured deep into Millsaps
territory only once more.

The Major offense fared even poorer, never driving farther than
the Choctaw 31-yard line. Memphis State transfer Rusty Smith
provided the Majors with their only offensive thrill by faking a
fourth down punt and dashing to the Millsaps 35-yard line from
the shadow of his own end zone. The Choctaws gained a final
chance to win the game by driving to the Millsaps nine-yard line

with time running out, but a Choc receiver dropped a pass in the end zone to finish the drive. The 0-0 score was the fifth tie in the history of the 36-game series.

Major lineman Jim Berry recalls an incident that occurred shortly after the '56 game:

> James Hood, was a big man, a 6'3", 245-pound lineman, but he was as nice as he could be. A real Mr. Clean, everybody's friend and always the peacemaker when there was trouble between us and the MC boys. But one Choctaw player had been riding him all game long, during that 0-0 tie. We had been favored, and so the guy was really laying it on James. When our teams were leaving the field under the bleachers after the game, the guy started giving it to Hood again. Hood finally lost his temper and hit the guy so hard on the top of his helmet that his helmet ended up crammed down onto his shoulders. When the MC guy finally recovered enough to know where he was, he got out of there as fast as he could.

In 1957, Millsaps floundered in mediocrity with a 2-5 mark, but the Choctaws dumped their doldrums with a 5-2-1 winning season. And for the first time since 1950, the annual October blood-letting, which again served as Homecoming for both teams, turned out to be less than exciting fare.

Writing for the *Mississippi Collegian*, future Ole Miss Law School professor John Robin Bradley declared that, "It wasn't in spectacular fashion that the Mississippi College football men thrashed the Millsaps Majors, but the 19-0 victory was decisive and left the Choctaw Homecoming fans quite contented." Terming the MC/Millsaps match "one of the nation's classic grudge tilts," Bradley noted that his Chocs were held to a minus 18 yards in the first quarter, but remembered "their mission" in the second period and overcame "the seemingly impotent Majors."

Don "Crick" Reynolds gave the yellow-helmeted, blue-jerseyed Braves the only score they needed in the first half by ramming into the Millsaps end zone from five yards out. Choc right halfback

Billy Reford scored another TD on a 61-yard run from scrimmage in the second half, and fullback Lynn Naylor concluded the scoring with a fourth-quarter, nine yard dash to paydirt. The gold-helmeted, white-shirted Majors, who failed to score all day, had to settle for "a large measure of commendation for a fine game and enthusiasm" from the supportive editorial staff of the *Purple and White* newspaper.

Collegian sports editorialist Albert Gooch memorialized the Choctaw victory with a poem, which, with apologies to "Casey At The Bat" poet Earnest Thayer, ended as follows:

> *They [Millsaps] won a Tomahawk all right, one buried*
> * plumb out of sight.*
> *Oh, somewhere in this favored land, the sun is shining*
> * bright.*
> *Somewhere, namely in Clinton, sports fans' hearts are*
> * bright.*
> *But there's no joy in Jackson, the mighty Majors goofed*
> * out*

One of Millsaps's star players in the '57 game, lineman Steve "Smiley" Ratcliff, who is now a Jackson real estate appraiser, remembers that time as the year his Majors began seeing the handwriting on the wall as far as Choctaw athletic superiority was concerned. "We simply couldn't compete with those boys," recalls Smiley, a star player for Jackson Central in 1955 before he arrived at Millsaps. "It was like a small high school playing against a large one; they had more students and their players seemed twice as big as ours. What's more, the two schools' academic standards weren't the same, allowing them to get players we couldn't take. Millsaps didn't even offer P.E. classes, and we had to go to our labs every day while they [the Choctaws] were outside practicing. Mississippi College just approached things differently and not so academically," Ratcliff said. "I wish we had had more of a balance of academics and athletics. But that's the way it was, so we really couldn't compete with them."

Millsaps running back Fred Belk, a former state senator, local prosecutor, and chancery judge, put it more succinctly—"We did poorly against Mississippi College, and they beat the hell out of us with a bunch of big, tough guys."

But although the 1957 game wasn't a close one, the rivalry kept heating up like a star going nova. After the game, *Collegian* columnist C. Earl Edmonson ran a story headlined, "Much To Crow About—Millsaps On Tail End," which denounced some Millsaps fans for raining on the Choctaws' pre-game Homecoming Parade. After noting that the Chocs paraded (with their Frosh boys and girls in full Indian regalia, no less) down Capitol Street at 10:30 a.m., four hours before the Millsaps Homecoming Parade was scheduled to roll, Edmonson wrote that a "black Ford full of Saps who had the audacity to rather loudly proclaim from whence they came," trailed closely behind the MC parade. According to Edmonson, a policeman walking in front of the Millsaps boys turned to them and said, in prophetic fashion, "That's exactly where you'll be tonight, at the tail end of things!"

On a less humorous note, Edmonson also reported that two Mississippi College freshmen, James Dubose and Bob Jenkins, were attacked from behind by "four of the rather barbaric Saps," who assaulted them in a Jackson parking lot. The Millsaps assailants were taking revenge for a Wednesday evening, Choctaw "raid to Sapland," Edmonson declared, and "through rather degrading violence, not cunning, stole the [Choctaw pep rally] tom-tom. . . "

Other late '50s-era students remember the frequent violence occasioned by attempts to steal their archrival's possessions.

Ex-Major running back/linebacker Cliff Rushing, who eventually retired as a Marine Corps officer, remembers beanie-stealing slugfests in front of the Millsaps Christian Center between Millsaps defenders and MC raiders, as well as several attempts by Millsaps students to steal the Mississippi College bell, which led to fisticuffs on the Clinton campus.

Choctaw track star Earl Walker, now a Jackson insurance salesman, remembers when he helped instigate a fight between over 250 of his fellow MC students and a large group of Millsaps defenders on Millsaps Street—"Some of our boys were swinging chairs, sticks and chains in a big fight over freshmen beanies. A few of the Millsaps boys had chains, too. I was right in the middle of the fistfighting, but when I saw Ted Alexander, one of Millsaps's football players and a former Gold Glove boxer, coming my way, I told my buddies that I was going to fight in another direction!"

Walker also recalls how MC upperclassmen motivated him to seek out Millsaps beanies—"They forced me to run through a Millsaps dormitory collecting beanies on the threat of having my ass whipped if I didn't go or if I came back empty handed. It was the same for the Millsaps freshmen; in one Millsaps dorm room, I saw over a hundred Mississippi College beanies stuck on the wall with tape. Most of the beanie scraps were all in good fun, but I could never understand how good Christian boys could use dangerous chains and sticks which could seriously injure somebody."

Millsaps alumnus Thelton Bryant, now a Laurel loan officer:

> I was a freshman at Millsaps in the fall of 1958, walking around campus with shaved head and beanie. And if you were ever walking downtown on Capitol Street wearing your beanie, you could be sure that somebody from Mississippi College would grab it for a trophy, jump in his car and go. I'm not saying we didn't do the same thing to them. But sometimes, they even came on our campus to get beanies. Once, during the week before the MC game, some of us freshmen baseball players were standing around talking near the Chapel on campus, wearing our beanies, when four Mississippi College guys grabbed our beanies and took off in their car. We got our cars, and some upperclassmen came with us, and we went looking for the MC gang.
>
> We found them parked at the gas station near the Farmer's Market at the corner of West Street and Woodrow Wilson Drive, and followed them into the station parking lot. One of their guys, obviously their toughest guy, got out of their car, and challenged one of ours, an upperclassman named Ray Wesson, to scrap it out. Wesson was a Gold Gloves boxer, and

he beat the coon dog "you-know-what" out of their guy. I grabbed a tire tool for protection and stayed out of everybody's way and waited for any of the MC guys to come after me if they wanted me bad enough. But Ray scared 'em all off, and that was the end of that business. I couldn't tell you if we ever got our beanies back.

Martha Fraiser Bryant, an Ole Miss alumnus, now a Laurel paralegal: "My husband Thelton loves to tell those stories about his Millsaps/Mississippi College beanie wars. I thought the Ole Miss/Mississippi State rivalry was something, but it's nothing compared to what he went through!"

Major athlete Fred Belk also remembers the riotous times during the middle-to-late 1950s: "For our Freshman 'M' Club initiation, the upperclass guys took us to Mississippi College, blindfolded and dressed only in t-shirts and shorts, and left us there with instructions to steal the white rocks which spelled out 'Mississippi College' on their campus. We got caught with the rocks on our shoulders, and I said to my group, 'I don't know about y'all, but I'm gone!' Two of our guys stayed behind to take on the MC students, and they got beaten up pretty bad."

MC footballer John Smith recalls the beanie-snatching climate of the late 1950s:

After we won the 1957 game, a big, strong Millsaps athlete named Ted Alexander, who would later become president of Pearl River Community College, had challenged some of our athletes to a wrestling match to prove that the Saps were really tougher than us even though we'd beaten them 19-0 the week before. It was to be a winner-take-all-the-beanies match. About fifteen of us showed up on their campus near the flag pole, where we met up fifteen or so of them. Alexander was talking over the rules with some of our guys when one of our players, Barry Landrum, hit him square in the mouth with no warning or provocation. We had us a sure enough fist fight then, and they soon outnumbered us pretty good. It wasn't very pretty.

As for the regular beanie-snatching episodes, we would ring our bell when Millsaps people came on our campus to steal beanies, and then we'd go run 'em off. So they came up with the idea to steal our bell. In the spring of 1958, two Millsaps guys got caught trying to do it. Some of our folks forced them to go over to the girls' dorm and serenade them for several hours. They were pretty upset about being forced to do that. Then, when they got in their car and left, another of our guys ran them and their car off the road. They got through it okay, but their car was wrecked pretty bad.

Mississippi College linebacker Barry Landrum, who later became a Baptist minister in Greenville, Mississippi, and Houston, Texas:

I came to Mississippi College to play football and to become an Ace. An Ace was someone who had snatched five Millsaps beanies and fastened their top buttons onto the bill of his own cap. Sort of a trophy you could wear on your head. This relieved you of going through any more Freshman initiation. So my goal was to become an Ace. So, one Friday night in 1957, my freshman year, the night before the Millsaps football game, I went with Ronnie Goddard, Freddie Hatten and Crick Reynolds to see a junior college game in Memorial Stadium, and from there we went to see the end of the Central/Murrah game at Tiger Stadium to see some of Ronnie's old high school buddies. Up in the stands, we saw two Millsaps beanies ready for the taking. I already had four beanies myself, so I needed one more to be an Ace. I said to Goddard, "Let's go up there, get behind 'em, count to three, grab 'em and run." We got ready to do it, and Goddard got cold feet. So I grabbed both beanies, stuffed 'em in my front shirt pocket, and took off down the steps. Everybody got up to chase me, and as I was heading down the bleacher steps, I saw a man coming up with a cup of coffee in each hand. With the crowd closing in on me, I didn't have time for any fancy side-stepping so I ran right over him. When I got to the ground, they surrounded me and finally chased me down with the help of a policeman. Of course, I had my fifth and sixth beanie and was going to be an Ace, so I didn't care if they put me in the penitentiary. One of the Millsaps guys told the cop I had taken his beanie. The cop asked me if I had it, and I refused to answer, pleading the Fifth Amendment. He saw the bulge in my pocket and made me give one of the beanies back. He then showed me where several guys were holding the man back that I had run over. This man was enraged and ready to kill me. The cop let me go, and told me that they would hold onto the man for ten minutes, and after that, I was on my own. I was happy to go. I had my beanie and was an Ace, at last!

As these stories make abundantly clear, the one-sided turn the series was taking as the decade drew to a close had no diminishing effect on the rivalry's intensity level. Without a doubt,the MC/Millsaps rivalry remained one of the most bitterly contested feuds in America.

The 1958 season brought a new man to the Majors' helm. Marvin G. "Erm" Smith, an Ole Miss alum who was serving as a Millsaps assistant football coach as well as head basketball and baseball coach, became Millsaps's tenth head football coach in almost forty years of Major football. Smith replaced retiring mentor Sammy Bartling, who had led the Majors to a 28-19-2 football record, an impressive .592 winning percentage, a 3-3-1 mark against the archrival Choctaws, and three Dixie Conference titles. Bartling stayed on as athletic director for another year.

MC head coach Joe Murphy would retire after the '58 campaign with a 16-21-4 record and a 2-1-2 edge over the Majors. But before he left, he would have one last shot at the Majors.

Erm Smith's Methodists did poorly his first year, finishing 1-6-1 and suffering shutouts in five of their eight contests. Their sole victory came at the expense of lowly Samford by a score of 14-9. Murphy's winless Baptists did even worse, losing seven games and tying one in a season that saw them whitewashed by five of their eight opponents. Despite their ineptitude, the

Choctaws took some measure of satisfaction in placing two players, end Hershel Hawthorn and fullback Tommy Alexander, on
the Little All-America team.

The Chocs also claimed a 0-0 moral victory with "Ole Mill,"
although the Majors probably noted with satisfaction that, of the
six ties in the longstanding series, the 1958 deadlock was the first
one which the *Choctaws* claimed as a moral victory. In any event,
the bitter rivals played a hard-nosed, low-scoring match which the
Majors led in first downs, 10 to 5, and in total yardage, 205 yards
to 108.

The Brave defense had to stop the Militants deep in Choctaw
territory on five separate occasions, and did so thanks in part to
several Millsaps fumbles and costly Major penalties. After Major
tackle John Woods recovered a Choc fumble on the MC 20-yard
line, "Injun" defensive back Tom Alexander intercepted a pass
in his own end zone to stop Millsaps's first threat, and linebacker
Jerry Napier recovered a fumble to end a second quarter Millsaps
drive. Then, after the Majors drove the ball to the MC three-yard
line on their next possession, a personal foul penalty disrupted
their momentum and they soon turned the ball over on downs.
Millsaps also attempted a field goal toward the end of the first
half, but the kick fell way short.

The Choctaws ventured into Millsaps territory only once when
John Flynt carried the pigskin from his own 47 to the Major 40-
yard line. But the Blue and Gold lost eight yards on the next play
and eventually turned the ball over on downs back at the midfield
stripe. Although both teams played exceedingly hard, their inabil-
ity to score left both schools' fans sorely disappointed.

"We were a selfish team in 1958," recalls Choctaw linebacker
Barry Landrum. He continued:

> All the talent in the world but too much bickering over who
> was going to score, call the plays, etc. . . . . After the first three
> losses, our morale plummeted. Then Coach Murphy tried to
> shock us back to reality for the Millsaps game by benching the
> starters on Monday and then putting them back in the lineups
> on Friday. The strategy obviously didn't work, and we played

as bad a game as I ever remember us playing. The Millsaps guys played poorly, too, and I could say that they were just as disappointed in themselves as we were in our effort.

Although the alumni, students and players at both schools were disappointed with the results of the '58 contest, that feeling was nothing in comparison to the discouragement they would experience a year and a half later when the violence associated with the football rivalry came to a riotous head at a downtown Jackson basketball game. Though none of them knew it at the time, the storied Millsaps/MC rivalry, which had flourished for almost forty years since its 1920 inception, was headed down a short road to extinction.

CHAPTER SEVEN

THE RIFT
1959-1960

Heading into the 1959 season, Millsaps and Mississippi College aficionados had little reason to expect that their beloved series was headed for disaster. True enough, officials at both schools were growing more and more alarmed at the recurring violence on both campuses. A 1958 incident in which two Millsaps students had been injured in an automobile crash had prompted some to consider establishing stricter rules of conduct in order to curtail the unwholesome aspects of the rivalry. But discontinuing athletic competition between the schools was not high on anybody's agenda.

For one thing, the two schools' basketball teams had just resumed competition in February of 1958, meeting on the court for the first time since Millsaps had refused to play a return game in 1954, and there had been no reports of inappropriate conduct at those games. For another, the spring of 1958 had ushered in a more serious controversy which gave both schools' officials something far more serious to worry about. This political football was the issue of the integration of Mississippi's colleges and universities.

Although the boards of trustees at all "white" Mississippi colleges, including those at Millsaps and Mississippi College, had voted to exclude all black students as late as 1958, Millsaps caused a significant uproar in March of that year when its faculty allowed Dr. Ernst Borinski, a white professor at the all-black Tougaloo College in Jackson, to give a pro-integration lecture at a race-relations forum on the Millsaps campus. It was also discovered that Millsaps was quietly running an educational exchange program with Tougaloo.

The thunderstorm got upgraded to a tornado when thirty Millsaps students attended a bi-racial meeting at Tougaloo College to promote racial harmony. In short order, the institution came

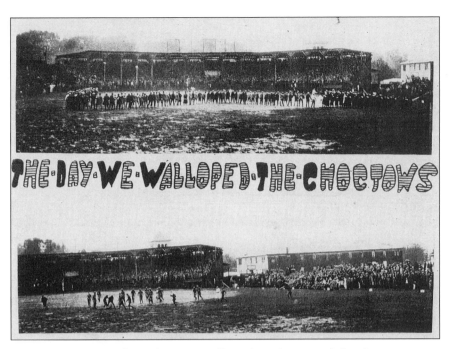

THE·DAY·WE·WALLOPED·THE·CHOCTAWS

Scenes from the 1925 Millsaps/MC fairgrounds battle
Photo courtesy of the Bobashela, Millsaps Archives

First Mississippi College football squad, c. 1906
Photo courtesy of the Bobashela, Millsaps Archives

Choctaws score against Majors in 1927 contest.
Photo courtesy of the Tribesman, Mississippi College Archives

1927 Choctaws versus Majors in Clinton, Mississippi
Photo courtesy of the Tribesman, Mississippi College Archives

Majors score against Choctaws in 1928 at the fairgrounds.
Photo courtesy of the Bobashela, Millsaps Archives

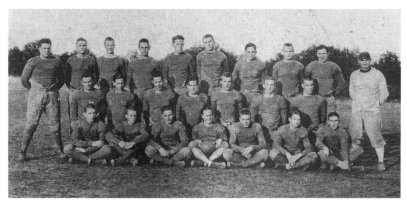

1928 Millsaps Majors, with Carson "Little Bo" Holloman,
second from left on front row
Photo courtesy of Millsaps Archives

Late 1920s Millsaps football team travel bus
Photo courtesy of Floy Holloman

1947 Mississippi College Choctaw team
with Coach Stanley Robinson, standing on far left
Photo courtesy of the Bobashela, Millsaps Archives

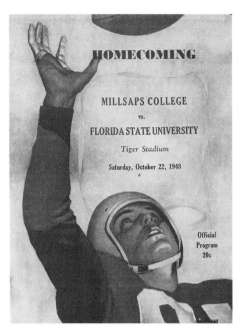

1948 Millsaps College football souvenir
program, Millsaps vs. Florida State

Photo courtesy of Millsaps Archives

1949 souvenir program for Millsaps/MC
Halloween contest

Photo courtesy of Millsaps Archives

1947 Mississippi College football souvenir program

Photo courtesy of Mississippi College Archives

Millsaps coach Sammy Bartling leads an early 1950s practice session.
Photo courtesy of the Bobashela, Millsaps Archives

1951 Millsaps Capitol Street victory parade in downtown Jackson
Photo courtesy of Millsaps Archives

In 1953 action, Majors (in white uniforms) gain ground against Choctaws.
Photo courtesy of the Bobashela, Millsaps Archives

1954 Millsaps linemen block for Homecoming Court belles
Photo courtesy of Millsaps Archives

1954 Game, Millsaps in white helmets

Photo courtesy of Millsaps Archives

Choctaws (in dark uniforms) vs. Majors, 1958 match

Photo courtesy of the Tribesman, Mississippi College Archives

1959 Mississippi College football team
Photo courtesy of the Tribesman, Mississippi College Archives

Majors (in white uniforms) vs. Choctaws, 1958 rivalry game
Photo courtesy of Millsaps Archives

Coin toss for home team. Pat Frascogna flips the coin for former MC athletic director Terry McMillan and Millsaps athletic director Ron Jurney.

Photo by Mark Hinkle

Florida State Coach Bobby Bowden (left) and retired MC Coach Hartwell McPhail at the 2000 National Championship Sugar Bowl game, won by Bowden's Seminoles

Photo courtesy of Hartwell McPhail

Former Millsaps players (from left), Mike Coker (seated),
David Russell, Wayne Ferrell, Paul Benton and Joe Whitwell
Photo by Jim Fraiser

Members of the 1959 Choctaws squad honored during halftime
of the 2000 MC/Millsaps contest. Hartwell McPhail displays the Backyard Brawl
Trophy. Rev. Barry Landrum is third from left.
Photo by Jim Fraiser

Joe Whitwell, MC Coach John Smith,
and Marguerite Whitwell at the downtown pep rally

Photo by Jim Fraiser

Millsaps Head Coach Bob Tyler, Mike Frascogna,
MC Athletic Director Mike Jones, and Pat Frascogna

Photo by Jim Fraiser

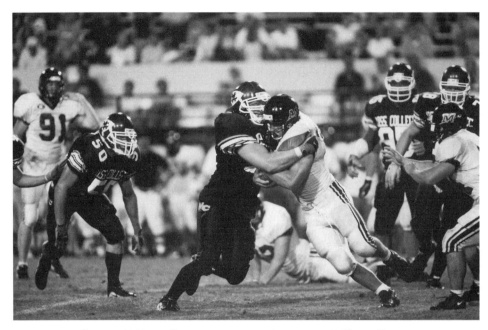

Holy War 2000, Millsaps Majors vs. Mississippi College Choctaws

Photo by Mark Hinkle

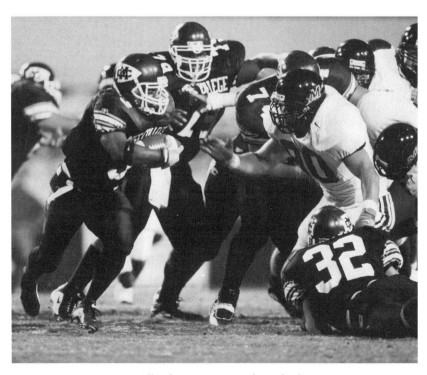

MC tailback Lamar Davis hits the line
as Millsaps lineman Jeff McIntyre gives chase.

Photo by Mark Hinkle

Millsaps QB Allen Cox dives for extra yardage
as MC LB Mike McKelvey moves in.
Photo by Mark Hinkle

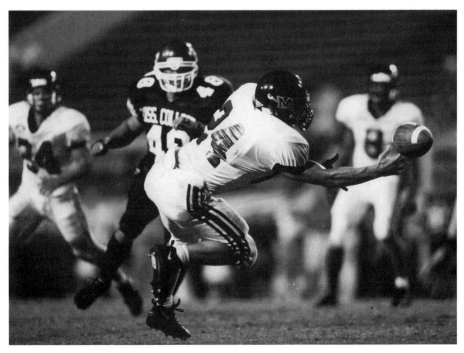

Major RB Chris Shiro dives for an Allen Cox
pass as Choctaw DE Scott Young defends.
Photo by Mark Hinkle

MC QB Payton Perrett prepares to throw
his second touchdown pass of the game.
Photo by Mark Hinkle

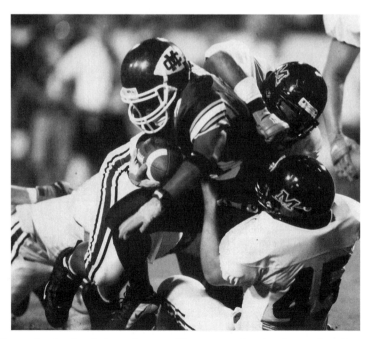

Millsaps linebacker brings down a Choctaw rusher in the Backyard Brawl.
Photo by Mark Hinkle

The Backyard Brawl line of scrimmage
Photo by Mark Hinkle

Millsaps's Marty Frascogna returns a punt to jump start the drive for
the winning field goal.
Photo by Mark Hinkle

MC linebacker Bryan Madden wraps up Millsaps runner Brent LeJeune.
Photo by Mark Hinkle

Millsaps kicker Derrick McNeal
boots the winning field goal out of Blake Huggard's hold.
Photo by Mark Hinkle

under fire from the staunchly segregationist Citizens Council, and Millsaps's Board of Trustees was forced to issue a statement that "segregation always has been, and is now, the policy of Millsaps College." But the board refused to give in to Citizens Council pressure and surrender the faculty's and administration's right to invite controversial speakers to the campus.

As reported by the *Jackson Daily News* and the *Memphis Commercial Appeal*, Millsaps's trustees, led by Bishop Marvin Franklin, also issued a statement supporting "the encouragement of academic freedom in the faculty and the spirit of inquiry in the students." President Finger further enraged the Jackson Citizens Council when he declared that, "College students have a right to hear various points of view. They are more mature in their judgment than they are sometimes credited with. . . Millsaps College has its weaknesses, but indoctrination is not one [of them]."

Of Millsaps's lonesome stand on behalf of academic freedom in the late '50s, *Delta Democrat Times* Pulitzer Prize-winning editor Hodding Carter said, "Millsaps College is perhaps the most courageous institution in the nation. . . it lets students and professors speak their minds. . . and has occasionally suffered for doing so. It has survived and attracted the best student body in Mississippi. They go there because Millsaps challenges their souls."

With the integration controversy continuously brewing in Mississippi for the next five years, Millsaps and MC officials had little time to worry about the possibility of terminating a financially lucrative, universally-adored football series. At least not in the fall of 1958.

In 1959, new Mississippi College head football coach Hartwell McPhail, himself a former Choctaw football star who had resigned as head coach at Greenville High School to take the MC job, unexpectedly guided his charges toward one of their best seasons in fourteen years. Teams such as Howard, Sewanee, Southwestern and Livingston University, which had been feasting on Choctaw incompetence in recent years, were ground under heel by McPhail's raging Braves.

As Barry Landrum recalls, there were several reasons for the turnaround in 1959:

First of all, Coach McPhail was a great, smart coach and we loved him. He and his assistant, Bernard Blackwell, called a fine game for us. Second, McPhail brought a talented group of guys with him from Greenville—Foshee, Pounds, Holland and Garrett. Third, he recruited some fine junior college players, especially Alton Greenlee from Brookhaven, who was a Little All-American and the greatest college quarterback I ever saw. If Alton had been a few inches taller he could have played for anybody in the nation. Finally, our great halfback Linus Bridges got back from the armed services that year. McPhail coached us well, and we played unselfishly and got the job done.

Choctaw Coach Hartwell McPhail: "Quarterback Alton Greenlee was a good passer and runner, but he was such a fine leader. He had more effect on his fellow players than any single individual I've ever coached. My players always told me they'd rather I got mad at them than for Alton to do it."

But things were not going as smoothly on Methodist Hill. Despite the return of fourteen lettermen and an exceptionally large turnout of thirty-six prospective players in September, second year Major boss "Erm" Smith found the going very rough in 1959. His hapless Militants failed to score in three of their first four games, and Sewanee, which had earlier fallen to Mississippi College 27-6, mercilessly routed the Majors by a score of 47-0.

After viewing the Millsaps/Sewanee debacle, and then scouting the Choctaws' impressive home win over the previously unbeaten Austin Kangaroos, *Purple and White* sports editor Ralph Sowell wrote, "At this point—if the Choctaws were to play the Majors, we would go down in defeat by several scores of points." In addition to provoking numerous angry letters from Millsaps students and faculty, Sowell's words also prompted the *Collegian*'s sports editors to run a gloating column, "*Purple and White* Editor Sees MC Victory," which declared that Sowell had left the Choctaw/Austin game "dreading the MC/Millsaps battle."

Further fanning the flames of pre-game controversy, *Collegian* "Ringside" columnist, Jack Curtis, Jr., wrote, in reference to the

Majors' lopsided loss to Sewanee, "It looks like the same old bunch of Saps over across town. I thought this year might be different and have them furnish a little competition. Oh well, you still have three weeks, Majors. If we keep your sword [which was at the time resting in an MC trophy case] much longer, you may as well give it to us."

Sowell fired right back, reporting Curtis's words in his next *P & W* column, and then boldly declaring that, "The Indians from the Choctaw Reservation will meet a band of Majors that would have still been standing when the smoke cleared from Sitting Bull's attack on General Custer at Little Big Horn."

Sowell then went even further, predicting that, "The Majors' sword will not be needed in action against the gang from across the pasture Saturday as a band of spirited, determined gridders bearing the colors of Purple and White, stomp the torn, mangled uniforms of Blue and Gold into the blood-soaked field of the Capital City." Sowell concluded by accusing the Choctaws of illegally and secretly handing out scholarships to their athletes, and scoffing at the Chocs for foolishly thinking they were ready to quit playing Millsaps and take on the likes of the Alabama Crimson Tide.

Another *Purple and White* editorial, signed only as "JDA," boldly declared that,

> The time is ripe for the season's biggest upset and Coach Smith's Purple and White are GOING TO BE THE ONE TO SLASH THE CHOCTAWS' THROATS WITH THE MAJORS' SWORD AND THEN SCALP THEM WITH THEIR OWN TOMAHAWK. . . . All the professors have been teaching this week is, "Spare the sword and spoil the Injun." All in all, Saturday, October 24, will be a day of rejoicing—MASTER MAJOR WILL AGAIN RIDE HIGH AND THE LITTLE INJUNS FROM ACROSS THE TOWN WILL BE GONE AND LOST IN THE SANDS OF TIME FOREVER.

In a more serious vein, the *Collegian* ran a pre-game editorial entitled, "Old Custom, New Spirit," which noted that MC's freshman football initiation had been canceled for 1959 because the "taunting and tormenting between the two schools had caused a serious and unfortunate accident [the year before] involving Millsaps students who were caught on the MC campus." The article declared with pride that, because of steps taken to avoid further conflict, "there was no mass invasion of the Millsaps campus this year [and] no reports of street fights in Jackson." Admitting that "this editorial is a little premature," and wondering, quite prophetically as it turned out, whether there would be "in the next four days another Millsaps incident," the article concluded by lauding the "strong," "good," "new spirit of Mississippi College."

Sure enough, the very evening of the day the *Collegian*'s "Custom" article ran, a gang of MC students invaded the Millsaps campus with an avowed purpose of "whipping some Millsaps butt." Congregating on a hill in front of the Christian Center Auditorium across Millsaps Street from the campus, the invaders were opposed by fearsome former boxer and current Major linebacker Ted Alexander, star receiver Joe Whitwell, and a small group of ready and willing Millsaps disputants.

Whitwell, now a Methodist minister specializing in pastoral counseling for marriage and family therapy, recalls the 1959 "Millsaps incident":

> The administration had put out the message to avoid fights, but what could we do when a group of MC guys, 75-100 strong, gathered right down from the Christian Center looking for a fight? We probably had no more than 20-25 Millsaps guys, so we were terribly outnumbered. I remember being in front of the pack, beside Ted Alexander, so I felt some comfort being with him.
>
> After some harsh words between the two groups, we charged into the crowd of MC folks—what a stupid move, huh? What happened after that is mostly a blur, but I recall being on the ground with several MC guys on top of me, and I was getting pummeled. The next thing I knew, I was headed back to my room in Burton Hall, dazed, in my underwear, with

one leg of my jeans in one hand and the other leg in the other hand. I was not really hurt in the scuffle, and in fact, thought it was quite funny. The torn jeans must have been a trophy of sorts representing my bravery since we had taken on the MC dragon.

Officials at both schools failed to share the participants' view that the usual week-of-the-game brawl was only harmless, college fun. But there was little they could do about it with the big game just a few days away. In fact, an event that probably occurred on the very same day as the "Millsaps incident" showed both administrations how totally involved everyone was in beanie snatching adventures.

The day before the annual bloodletting, the *Purple and White* ran a headline that every Millsaps man must have loved, entitled "Four Millsaps Co-Eds Swipe Choc Beanie." The article explained, in glowing detail, how Carol Malone, Barbara Griffin, Faith Craig, and Roberta Erwin relieved Choctaw student Lee Baxter of his MC beanie. An accompanying photograph showed the girls proudly displaying their prize, and the article hailed the "valiant four" as "martyrs to a dying cause" and "heroes forever."

But if the Millsaps coeds had won a minor skirmish with a Choctaw "ed," few prognosticators really expected the Majors to fare so well the next day. Almost everyone except the *P & W*'s Ralph Sowell, including Jackson *Daily News* sports editor Lee Baker, *Daily News* sports writer Albert Gooch, *Clarion-Ledger* sports writer Ned Wirth, ex-MC coach Stanley Robinson, and current MC coach Hartwell McPhail, predicted a Choctaw victory *in writing*. MC student body president Ken Lyle told "Ringside" columnist Jack Curtis, Jr., that he expected a 66-0 Choctaw rout, the *Collegian* sportswriter agreed only with the outcome, not with the score, writing that, "I predict a Choc victory by a safe margin, but not 66 points."

Confident of victory, Choctaw "warriors" held a Friday evening "funeral" for the "soon to be bruised and badly beaten Majors," burned the Major in effigy, and beat their tom-toms all through the night and into the early morning hours of game day. As the incessant tom-toms throbbed, the Choctaws led a 10:00 a.m., Saturday morning Homecoming Parade through the streets of downtown Jackson, and their alumni tabbed Governor-Elect Ross Barnett as Alumnus of the Year at a pre-game banquet. To everyone's delight, the 5-1-1, 1940 Choctaw team, which had defeated Millsaps, 27-0, twenty years ago, attended the game seated in a special cheering section. All thirty-six team members, except for five who were killed in the armed services, were in attendance. These included then-coach Stanley Robinson, and 1940s stars Wendell Webb, Charley Armstrong, Albert Gore, current MC head coach Hartwell McPhail, Bob Majure, Archie Mathews, and Lonnie Tadlock.

Across the "pasture," the Majors threw a Thursday night pep rally which was attended by 200 devotees behind Founders Hall. Their newly organized Booster Club, under the leadership of president Gail Garrison, offered new purple and white pom-poms for sale before and during the game, and *Purple and White* sports editor Sowell declared that Millsaps students' spirits were "blazing" at an all time high.

The two teams met for the 39th time at 8:00 p.m., on October 24, 1959, at Hinds Memorial Stadium. The Chocs crowned their Queen in a pre-game ceremony; the Majors were set to crown theirs during halftime. Each school's student body president stood eagerly by to receive either a Tomahawk or a Sword from his counterpart after the game's conclusion. Stirred up all week long by media hype, campus raids, parades, concerts, pep rallies, and the heightened emotions that always accompanied their most important game of the year, a crowd of 12,000 fans cheered at the top of their lungs as the Millsaps Majors, clad in gold helmets and white jerseys, and the Mississipi College Choctaws, sporting navy helmets and jerseys, prepared to go to war.

Unfortunately, the game turned out to be an anti-climactic, fumble-marred defensive struggle for the entire first period. The only thrill came when Choc return man Benson Holland fielded a John Wood punt at his own 35, and then followed guard Norvell Burkett sixty-five yards to the Millsaps end zone. But the Choctaws were penalized for being offsides and the Majors were whistled for illegal procedure, so Holland's electrifying run counted for nought. It was not until eleven minutes into the second quarter that things finally got interesting.

It was then that Millsaps end Joe Whitwell fumbled the ball and Curtis Nix recovered it for the Braves. Choctaw backs Holland and Linus Bridges began crashing through gaping holes created by precision trap blocking, and carried the ball to the Millsaps one-yard line in six consecutive rushing plays. Quarterback Lavon Nettles's attempted quarterback sneak was stuffed by a tenacious Major defensive line, but Bridges scored on the next play to give the Choctaws a 6-0 first half lead.

Midway through the third period, Choc rusher George Green blocked a Bob Lowery punt which his team recovered on the Millsaps 15. Two plays later, Holland ran the ball ten yards to the five, where a Major would-be tackler got a vise-lock grip on his foot. Determined to score, Holland lateraled back to an alert Linus Bridges who carried the ball the rest of the way for a touchdown. MC quarterback Milton Thomas faked an extra point kick and passed to Bridges for a successful two point conversion and a 14-0, third-quarter Choctaw lead.

As the third period wound down, MC quarterback Larry Therrell fired a twenty-yard aerial to receiver John Smith, who gathered it in at the Millsaps thirty-five and raced untouched for a score. Millsaps defender Roger Kinnard blocked the Choctaw conversion kick, so Mississippi College took a 20-0 lead into the fourth period. The Braves iced the game early in that final stanza as defensive end Hershel Hathorne blocked a Millsaps punt, Bridges scooped it up, broke several tackles, and scored the Choctaws' final six points. Kinnard again blocked the MC extra-point try, and the Chocs led 26-0.

Millsaps's Lowery received the ensuing kickoff on his own 13 and returned it to the 41. Major QB Larry Marett then scrambled across midfield for a thirteen yard gain. Marett quickly took charge of his huddle, turned to receiver Joe Whitwell, and simply said, "Get open, Joe." Whitwell expertly executed a down-out-and-down pattern, and the Choctaw defender bit on Marett's pump fake, lunging toward the sideline just as Whitwell turned to race up field. Whitwell gathered in Marett's perfectly thrown pass and raced the remaining thirty yards for paydirt, dragging a Choctaw cornerback the final five yards into the end zone. Marett's run for two points was stopped by a determined Choctaw line, and with neither team able to mount another scoring threat, the Choctaws settled for a solid 26-6 victory. They now held a substantial, 24-9-6 edge over their archrival in an amazing series which dated back to 1920.

After Millsaps student body president Gayle Erwin handed the ceremonial Major sword to Mississippi College SBA President Ken Lyle, the Choctaw fans began their week-long celebration. *Clarion-Ledger* sportswriter Ned Wirth wrote that "Coach Hartwell's rampaging Braves took the Majors' scalps," while the *Collegian's* Jack Curtis simply said, "It was a perfect day. . . and the win over the Majors put a delicious icing on the cake." In typical never-say-die fashion, *P & W* sports editor Ralph Sowell praised the Majors for "not letting up for one moment" and for offering "the Chocs their stiffest competition of the season." He concluded by declaring that the Majors only "lost because of bad breaks. . . "

With the win over Millsaps, the Choctaws brightened skipper McPhail's maiden voyage with a 7-2 worksheet, Mississippi College's best record since 1946. The Majors made their television debut in their final 1959 game on Jackson's WJTV, but lost, 25-6, to visiting Arkansas State. They finished with a disappointing 2-7 season record. But as the rivalry game had been played without any hint of violence or other bad behavior, everyone associated with both schools was looking forward to continuing the Millsaps/MC series for many years to come. But the new decade brought unexpected disaster to Jackson in the form of the worst incident that had ever occurred in the forty-year history of the rivalry.

On Monday, February 16, 1960, the Major hoopsters, led by sharpshooting Larry Marett, met the MC basketballers and their Little All-American candidate, Tommy Covington, at the now-defunct, 3000-capacity City Auditorium in downtown Jackson. At the time, the arena was located at the corner of Congress and Pearl

Streets, and the price of admission was $1 for adults and 50 cents for children. The basketball Chocs were leading the nation in scoring for small college teams, and were heavily favored to soundly whip a scrappy, but poorly-regarded Millsaps squad.

Knowing that they couldn't play the Choctaws' high-scoring, running game, the Majors decided to freeze the ball and keep all scoring to a minimum. The plan worked for a while, but after taking nine minutes to defrost, the Braves pulled ahead, 30-11. Seven minutes later, they held a commanding 30 point lead, 54-24. The Millsaps strategy led to a foul-marred contest; the Chocs would finish with 45 personal fouls and the Majors with 22. But there was something more ominous going on in the arena than a little shoving and elbowing on the court.

According to *Clarion-Ledger* sportswriter Albert Gooch, shortly before the first half ended, "The game was interrupted. . . when the Millsaps students stormed the Mississippi College stands after being provoked throughout the game. Police were required to break the battle up, but it erupted again in the concession room at halftime."

Choctaw guard Tom Lee, now a U.S. Federal District Judge in Jackson, was standing at the foul line preparing to shoot a free throw when the first melee erupted. "Some Millsaps boys were trying to retrieve something from our student section," Lee recalls, "something pilfered by MC people. Our students outnumbered them and whipped them pretty bad. The officials had to stop the game, but we were able to finish it after everybody calmed down." The Choctaws eventually won the penalty-marred contest, 131-72.

The brawl lasted for several minutes, and then began again during halftime. It made quite an impression on the participants and onlookers from both schools.

Hartwell McPhail:

> Our people were on the north side of the auditorium and the Millsaps people were on the south side. Some of our guys had a Millsaps flag of some kind up in our student section, and were parading it around. I thought that Wooky Gray used poor

judgment to come into our student section by himself to get it back. After the fight started Coach Robby tried to be a peace-maker, and Barry Landrum pushed him out of the way. Barry was a good ole boy from Laurel and he was quite a dude, believe me. But that really made Coach Robinson mad.

Millsaps basketball player Tom Royals, now a Jackson attor-ney:

Wooky Gray was a Kappa Sigma and a former football play-er who had been a manager for the 1959 football team. He died a few years ago, after coaching a Mississippi junior college football team to a national championship. After an argument broke out over some sign the MC fans were waving, Gray chased somebody into the MC stands. In the fight that ensued, they tried to throw him off the side of the bleachers onto the court.

Millsaps Kappa Sigma fraternity member Cliff Rushing, now a retired Marine officer:

I had already graduated Millsaps, but was living in Jackson when that 1960 basketball game was played. Wooky Gray, who later coached at Mississippi Delta Community College, called me at home and told me that some MC guys had stolen our Kappa Sigma sign and were waving it around at the basketball game. He asked me to come help him get it back. I was in the Marines at the time, and told him I couldn't go. He called me hours later, crying over the phone, saying they had beat him up pretty bad and thrown him over a rail fifteen feet above the hardwood floor.

MC linebacker John Smith, now an MC assistant football coach:

Sometime before the '60 basketball game, MC student Chuck Brandon had gone on the Millsaps campus and taken a Rebel flag with the words "Kappa Sigma" on it. At the basketball game, we were holding up the flag and waving it every time our basketball team scored. Finally, big Millsaps lineman John Wood, and 6'3", 220 pound lineman Wooky Gray, came up to our student section to get it back. They couldn't find it, and brought some reinforcements back with them a few minutes later. Gray said, "We don't want any problem, just our flag." Then, as he bent over to look for it, Barry Landrum, one of our linebackers who later became a preacher in Texas, hit him in the mouth and knocked him down the bleacher steps. Our students took Wooky and hung him over the railing, fifteen feet above the hardwood floor. If they had dropped him they would have killed him.

When the fight started, I was sitting two seats behind Landrum and had the flag under my chair, where he had put it. It was still laying there after the fight. Later on, after they got that one stopped, there was another big fight in the concession room under the stands. Before I knew it, I was fighting for my life again.

Barry Landrum:

A lot of the people who tell the "fight" story get it wrong. Wooky Gray jumped on me first! (Laughs) Wooky was sort of a Lone Ranger hero on their side, surrounded by about 300 or 400 of us. Chuck Brandon had a Millsaps Kappa Sigma flag or sign, I can't remember which, that he had swiped a year or so earlier on a raid of Kappa Sigma house. He was holding it up and waving it every time our basketball team scored, which was about once every minute. Gray came up by himself right before the half ended and ran up in the stands. He jumped on me when I was minding my own business, probably meditating on some scripture. (Laughs again) He came down the aisle he did just to come over me, because he and I had had some trouble before, which I had gotten the better of, and he just couldn't stand it.

Two weeks before the '59 Millsaps football game, Jerry Foshee, Paul Pounds, Charles Garrett and I had raided the

Millsaps campus for beanies. I had been waiting in the car for them to get back, and suddenly saw what looked like 400 mad Methodists running after them. I tried to close the car door after our guys got in, but John Wood wouldn't let me. Wooky Gray was also trying to get at me. Suddenly, one of the Millsaps guys asked Jerry Foshee if he was the Mid-South Gold Glove Boxing Champion named Foshee, and he said he was. They kind of backed off then, and told us to get the hell off their campus. Gray resented the heck out of that.

So Gray was mad at me, and he hit me first at the basketball game. Then we were fighting, the game was stopped, and the police showed up. They stopped the fight and the teams finished the first half of the game. During the break, with the teams in the dressing rooms, some more fights broke out in the concession area where 200 people were crammed in a room that could hold no more than fifty folks. It spread into the stands and there was more fighting everywhere.

Mississippi College official, Van "Doc" Quick, an MC football trainer in college, later an ordained Baptist minister and long-time Mississippi College administrator, and currently Vice President Emeritus of MC Student Services, who helped investigate the "brawl" for MC:

As I understand it, Chuck Brandon had the Millsaps Kappa Sigma flag in the stands. When some Millsaps folks, including Wooky Gray, came up to get it, Barry Landrum tried to stop them. Barry was a short, feisty linebacker who left Mississippi State to come to Mississippi College because he heard about the rivalry and wanted to participate in all the big campus fights. He swung the first blow, when Wooky Gray wasn't looking for it. And all-you-know-what broke out after that. Or so I gather from talking to people who were there.

Millsaps football player, Joe Whitwell:

I roomed with Wooky Gray, and he came back to the dorm early one morning after being released from the hospital following the 1960 basketball fight the night before. His clothes were torn and he was noticeably upset. He said some of the MC folks had been taunting the Millsaps folks and making negative comments to our team. Wooky got enraged and when he couldn't stand it anymore he got up and bolted into the group that was making all the comments, something he had done many times before. He was around 6'3", and weighed about 230 pounds, and was never one to back away from a fight. There was evidently a brief skirmish before others in the crowd helped to break it up. Wooky was a tough guy on the field, but most of the time he was one of the most tender-hearted guys I've ever known. Even though he was very sad about what had happened, I think Wooky wore his bruises proudly.

The "brawl" was by most accounts an all-encompassing melee, spreading as it did throughout the auditorium in the form of numerous individual scraps. Far worse was the highly concentrated fighting near the concession stand, where another Millsaps student, Gene Davenport, received injuries that required overnight hospitalization. The very occurrence of such a brawl, the fact the city police had to be called in to stop it, and the fact that two Millsaps students received serious injuries caused immediate concern for officials at both colleges. But when Millsaps Athletic Chairman, Dr. Milton C. White, was told that Wooky Gray's life had been imperiled by MC students' recklessness, he felt that he had no choice but to take immediate action.

Then Millsaps professor Dr. T. W. Lewis: "When Dr. White learned that Wooky Gray could have been killed, he knew we had to do something. There had recently been a similar situation in Birmingham, Alabama, where a Birmingham Southern student had been killed by a Howard student. Dr. White was convinced that, with all the past violence associated with athletic contests between our two schools, and with the schools in such close proximity, we just couldn't risk allowing it to go on."

According to a February 17 *Clarion-Ledger* article by sportswriter Jack Shearer, Dr. White immediately withdrew Millsaps's entry in the upcoming Mississippi College Invitational Basketball

Tournament to be played on the Clinton campus, because of "bad feelings between the two schools when their student bodies get together." White declined further comment, saying only that he had sent a letter to the MC athletic department and would not reveal its contents until they had been given ample opportunity to review it.

The newspaper article related that, in addition to the injurious fights involving Gray and Davenport, two Millsaps students had been "ganged" in the concessions room, but that the police had broken up the squabble before anyone had been seriously injured. The story also reported that Mississippi College students had made anonymous phone calls to Millsaps, threatening to "invade" the campus, but that no such raid had ever materialized.

Millsaps head football coach Erm Smith and his basketball counterpart James Montgomery both informed the *Clarion-Ledger* that the bad, unwholesome atmosphere between the schools had caused Millsaps's withdrawal from the MC tourney. Choctaw athletic director Stanley Robinson was quoted as saying that he had "heard nothing" about a possible decision by Millsaps officials to withdraw from *all athletic competition* with Mississippi College.

That decision came two days later in the form of a letter from Millsaps's Dr. White to Mississippi College's Faculty Chairman of Athletics, Dr. A. E. Wood, which was printed in full by the *Collegian* in its February 24, 1960, edition.

The letter read as follows:

Dear Dr. Wood:

Despite all efforts to the contrary, a very unwholesome atmosphere has developed in connection with our athletic contests, which seem increasingly to stimulate hostility and even some violence. We do not believe such an atmosphere should be tolerated in Christian institutions. In order to preclude further unfortunate incidents, which might possibly end in tragedy, our athletic committee has seen fit to call to an end all athletic relations with Mississippi College, and to cancel all existing contracts. It is regrettable that this action is considered necessary, but I believe that you, too, will see the wisdom of this course.

Sincerely yours,
Milton C. White

Although the *Collegian* reported that MC athletic director Stanley Robinson was "saddened" by the termination of athletic competition with Millsaps, the breach between the two schools was now far too wide for anyone to repair. For vastly different reasons, most Jackson-area sports scribes gave their approval to Millsaps's cancellation of athletic competition with Mississippi College. Carl Shavers, columnist for the *Clarion-Ledger:*

> The official action taken by. . . Millsaps College. . . is certainly to be regretted, but under the circumstances as now existing, probably a wise choice. . . Millsaps's action in terminating athletic relations between the two schools is appropriate. . . . No athletic event of any kind is worth a near-riot and mass fighting in which two [Millsaps] students were severely injured.

(Shavers went on to predict that Mississippi College, with a more ambitious athletic department and more coaches to pay, would suffer more financial hardship than Millsaps with its "low pressure," "play for fun program.")

Jimmie McDowell, *The State Times:*

> By ridiculing outclassed opponents, MC students certainly displayed none of that "Choctaw Spirit" which helped to make the college great. There was no move by a Mississippi College official to halt the brawl.

Anonymous *Purple and White* editorial:

> . . . a milestone in Purple and White history and the wisest decision made on the sports scene in many years. . . . The decision came after Mississippi College students exhibited some of the worst sportsmanship seen by local sports writers in many years

. . . . When a friendly attempt was made by Millsaps students to gain what was rightfully theirs ["a fraternity lawn sign"], a fight resulted with two of our students being seriously injured in a fight in which the Choctaws used "brass-knuks" to their advantage. . . . The [Millsaps] officials made a wise decision, appreciated by the Student Body and athletic participants.

Bill Turk, Sports Editor, *Mississippi Collegian*, in a column entitled, "A Slap in the Face. . . ":

Mississippi College lost several apparent annual athletic victories last week when Millsaps decided to cancel all future sports relations with our school. A football victory, and several baseball, basketball and tennis wins usually a certainty will be missed. However, this means that the Braves can schedule games with teams which can stay in the same competition on the field. And the many games with the Majors will never be missed. . . . Despite the efforts of local papers in Jackson, many of the fans. . . felt that the fight was a second rate incident which was completely overshadowed by the splendid Choctaw win of 131-72. Yes, indeed. If more had been said concerning the game instead of the fussing about minor details, MC and Millsaps might have been able to salvage something of their reputations. However, Jackson papers were totally unfair in several articles.

Tom Rawlins, *Mississippi Collegian* columnist, rebutting the three reasons why MC was supposed to be sorry the series was canceled—(1) traditional rivalry lost, (2) financial loss, and (3) damage to school spirit:

[Regarding the rivalry] To be traditional, a rivalry must continue for a number of years with both teams fairly evenly balanced and burning with a desire to win. With the exception of football. . . Millsaps has been markedly inferior and appears to have lost the desire to win as was evident in the last basketball game. [Regarding financial losses] There is a possibility that there will be a loss connected with the [Homecoming football] game. However, Homecoming is Homecoming and alumni will return to see a good football game and talk to old friends. Since very few adults and practically no Millsaps students attend the basketball games, MC students have been supporting not only their own athletic program but also that of Millsaps. [Regarding school spirit] I do not care what happens to the spirit at Millsaps. As for the spirit Millsaps instills in the Choctaw student body, it is practically null and void. Students no longer look forward to the MC vs. Millsaps game as a challenge and now feel that the game is just a means of improving the team record. . . . I think Millsaps took the best possible action under the circumstances and that Mississippi College should accept it and go search for another opponent that will compete on our level and will impart within us that spirit now lacking when we meet Millsaps.

Although Millsaps officials maintained that the series had been canceled for safety reasons, some Mississippi College officials saw another reason behind the cancellation.

MC coach Hartwell McPhail: "At that time our programs were beating theirs handily and they just took an excuse to get out. They may have thought we were scholarshipping players. Either way, I don't know but that I wouldn't have done the same thing if I had been in their situation."

The "Millsaps can't take it" attitude was perfectly expressed by Choctaw linebacker Barry Landrum: "We had beaten them in football, basketball, baseball, and tennis. Even our faculty had beaten theirs in faculty volleyball. They were just looking to get out of the series."

Writing for the *Clarion-Ledger*, Carl Walters argued that "sports enthusiasts" who alleged that Millsaps quit the competition with MC because the Majors "can't take it when they get their brains beat out," were mistaken. "They can and do [take it]," Walters wrote, "and have been taking it from just about every ath-

letic opponent they have met in recent years. And it is interesting to me that the only major trouble between Millsaps and any
other school has been between the Majors and Choctaws."

As for the football players themselves, most of them regretted
the loss of the long-standing series:

Choctaw football player John Smith (1959): "We were sad
because, as far as the guys were concerned, we had great friend-
ships with the Millsaps players in all three sports. It deprived both
schools of a big weekend and a great game to look forward to."

Major football player Joe Whitwell (1959): "To me, the BIG
GAME with MC was the highlight of the season. And even
though they usually beat us because they always had more players, we got 'psyched up' to play our best game. Therefore, when
the rivalry was terminated, it was like pulling the plug on a tradition and experience that added a lot of color to an otherwise
bland season. Most of us thought that canceling our games with
MC was an over-reaction. The students that I knew did not feel
like things were 'out of hand,' but obviously the administrators of
the respective institutions thought so."

But however the loss of the series was viewed by its participants, one thing could be said for the cancellation with absolute
certainty—American football fans in general, Mississippi gridiron
aficionados in particular, and Jackson-area pigskin-lovers especially, had lost one of the most colorful, intense, and beloved
cross-town rivalries in the history of American sports.

But as the Good Book says, "For everything there is a season
. . . ," and so it is with Mississippi football. Forty years and a new
millennium later, Millsaps and Mississippi College would once
again meet each other on the glory-laden gridiron of Jackson's Veterans Memorial Stadium. But before that would happen, both
schools' football programs would experience more modulations
and transfigurations than even far-sighted men such as Stanley
Robinson and Sammy Bartling could have ever imagined.

CHAPTER EIGHT

THE MODERN ERA
1961-1997

In the 1920s and '30s, Millsaps and Mississippi College had com-
peted directly with the University of Mississippi and Mississippi
A & M College in both academic and athletic endeavors. That
sportswriters commonly referred to Mississippi College as "Mississippi" (a moniker later reserved solely for Ole Miss), that MC
unsuccessfully challenged Ole Miss for the right to become Mississippi's flagship university, that Millsaps offered law school
courses, and the fact that both colleges played Ole Miss, A & M,
Tulane and Alabama in football, are all indicative of this competitive approach. With the advent of WWII, the two smaller colleges ceased competing directly with the larger universities, and
fashioned themselves as smaller versions of those institutions.
Millsaps scribes referring to the Majors as "Ole Mill," Mississippi
College's comprehensive, university-like curriculum in the 1950s,
and the two schools' annual battle for the Dixie Conference title
(which aped the Ole Miss/Mississippi State battle for Southeast-
ern Conference supremacy) were all reflective of this "smaller version" mentality.

However, by the 1960s, Millsaps and Mississippi College had
settled into their small college (later NCAA Divisions II & III)
roles and no longer attempted to mimic Mississippi's substantially larger state universities. Instead, both institutions strove for
well-deserved recognition as academically-oriented, liberal arts
colleges, and sought athletic success as small college independents. Once they accepted their liberal arts missions in the halls
of Mississippi academia and Division II or III status on the playing fields of Magnolia State sports, Millsaps and Mississippi College became nationally renowned for both academic achievement
and athletic prowess.

In February of 1965, Millsaps announced a historic Open Admissions Policy and achieved racial integration without violence or significant incident. In 1966, the Ford Foundation selected Millsaps as a "regional center of excellence," and awarded the school a $1.5 million challenge grant. Under President Edward M. Collins's leadership, the college overcame financial difficulties by beginning the commercial development of part of its campus, opening a Medical Center Holiday Inn on the north end of school property. The board added an undergraduate business program in 1974 to compliment Millsaps's celebrated liberal arts curriculum, and a School of Management with its Master of Business Administration opened its doors in 1981.

A 1983 poll of 1,600 college and university presidents by *U.S. News & World Reports* selected Millsaps as the top liberal arts college in the South, and by 1988, Millsaps had become the only Mississippi institution to be awarded a Phi Beta Kappa chapter. In the late 1990s, *Washington Times's Insight Magazine* ranked Millsaps in the Top 10 for adherence to academic rigor and traditional values, and *U.S. News & World Reports* ranked the college in the top 13% of American four-year liberal arts colleges and universities and also rated it the sixth Best Value among the nation's liberal arts colleges. With a 1999 enrollment of over 1300 students, a faculty/student ratio of 1:13, and an endowment of $93.1 million, Millsaps was also chosen by *Money Magazine, The Fiske Guide* and *Kiplinger's Personal Finance Magazine* as one of America's "Best Values" for prospective students.

The 1960-61 Mississippi College enrollment reached an all-time-high at 2,451 students, and in the mid 1960s, the institution's Board of Trustees followed Millsaps's lead and signed a historic "Assurance of Compliance" agreement which guaranteed a peaceful opening of the school's doors to African American students. Under the leadership of Dean Howard E. Spell, MC became Mississippi's first private school to be recognized by the National Council for Accreditation of Teacher Education, the nation's most prestigious education accrediting association. In 1970, the trustees expended $250,000 for aesthetic campus improvements, and in 1971, spent $600,000 to double the school's library space.

Mississippi College celebrated its 150th anniversary in 1976 by announcing an enrollment of 3,958 students, and by the late 1990s, Mississippi College had been selected by the esteemed Templeton Foundation as one of the country's top 100 character-building colleges for ten consecutive years. *U.S. News & World Report* listed MC in the top tier of regional universities in the South and named it "fifth best value among Southern universities." With a current enrollment of over 3,800 students, an endowment of almost $100 million, and a faculty/student ratio of 1:15, Mississippi College is ranked in the top 2.5% of the nation in education, top 3.5% in the non-sciences, and the top 17% in the sciences, according to a recent survey by Franklin & Marshall College.

And unlike many large universities which treated student-athletes differently from the rest of the student body, Millsaps and Mississippi College conferred the full benefit of an outstanding education upon their football players.

John Smith:

> Shortly after I arrived here as a player, I found that the faculty was very caring toward the students. Dr. Howard Spell, my academic Dean, and Dr. Wood, my chemistry professor, were, in addition to being excellent teachers, administrators who gave the impression that they cared a great deal for me individually. And they treated us football players with the same dignity they accorded the other students, and didn't look down on us. This certainly made recruiting a lot easier for MC through the years. When I came back here to coach and teach Biology, Mississippi College still had small classes, a caring faculty, and a President, Dr. Aubry McLemore, who was very involved with his students. My association with Mississippi College has been one of the greatest experiences of my life.

Joe Whitwell:

> I cannot say enough about the education I received at Millsaps. It was an education most football players only dream

about getting. Majoring in Philosophy and having a minor in Religion, I learned more than I ever hoped I could. Perhaps more important was that I was stimulated by Millsaps to have a curious and inquisitive mind. The academic work at Millsaps was always superb and I learned a lot in the classroom. But more than that, I learned "how to learn" and how to enjoy learning. Coming out of the small town of Senatobia, Mississippi, I had a very narrow perspective on life and religion. In many ways, life had been pretty simple for me. Millsaps helped me to see and appreciate the complexity of life and people. My education instilled in me that often quoted phrase from Plato—"the unexamined life isn't worth living." Dr. Bond Fleming, my philosophy professor, had a major influence on my education. I learned how to examine my life, and how to help others to examine theirs—and can truly say that I love my work!

In addition to receiving a first-class college education, athletes at both schools were also in for another treat in the mid-1960s—their schools made a complete about-face on the issue of granting athletic scholarships. As reported by the *Purple and White* in 1965, schools such as Millsaps had few options regarding football scholarships; they could either continue fielding losing football teams, drop football entirely, or fashion a winning program with the granting of athletic scholarships. And though the *P & W* had, for almost fifty years, opposed the granting of athletic scholarships, in early 1965, it too, did a 180-degree turn and wholeheartedly supported the payment of an estimated $28,000 to fund scholarships for football, basketball and baseball.

The reason for the change of heart was easy to discern—from 1960 to 1964, Millsaps had averaged one win per season in football and had no prospects for improvement as the decade rolled along. The only positive thing that happened to Millsaps football in the early sixties was when the Majors, who went 1-6-1 in 1960, were inexplicably invited to two post-season bowls, the Arkansas-based Rice Bowl, which they declined, and Huntsville, Alabama's Rocket Bowl, which they accepted. Unfortunately, the Majors were ambushed on the Rocket Bowl launching pad by Maryville (Tennessee) College and routed, 19-0.

Wayne Ferrell, who played football at Millsaps from 1964 to 1966, remembers the difficult pre-scholarship days:

> We had two coaches and a handful of players, and were playing teams with five coaches and up to a hundred players. Coach Harper Davis worked us hard—we couldn't take our helmets off or have any water during our two-hour-long practices—but we didn't have enough talent to win a single game in 1964. In our game with Sewanee, I was a 145-pound defensive end trying to stop a 6'2", 220 pound, running back, and they beat us 54-7. Austin College had an All-American quarterback and receiver, and they killed us, 34-0. Even lowly Quachita beat us when future Dallas Cowboys all-star, Cliff Harris, led them to a 21-15 win.

Many associated with the Millsaps football program believed that athletic scholarships would be the panacea for the school's sports ills. The seeds of non-scholarship change were sown on Methodist Hill when Harper Davis took over as head football coach for the 1964 season. Davis, a Clarksdale native and former All-SEC running back for Mississippi State in 1945, had played professional football for the Chicago Bears and Green Bay Packers. He was serving as West Point High School's football coach and athletic director when he accepted the Millsaps post. He immediately lobbied for the right to grant football scholarships.

Davis, who is now retired after twenty-five years as Millsaps's head coach, recalls the overwhelming need for athletic scholarships when he arrived in Jackson:

> Millsaps football was a disaster in 1964. They had been through five head coaches in five years [Sammy Bartling, Marvin Smith, Flavious Smith, Bill Dupes & Ray Thornton]. It was as low a point as a football program could reach. It wasn't the fault of the coaches or players—Millsaps was not in the NCAA and couldn't offer any financial aid to recruits. Football

was on its own. When I came in, my only paid assistant was coach Tommy Ranager, who had come with me from West Point.

We took over in June and started practice on July 1 with no time to spend on recruiting. We had forty players when the season began, and twenty-four left when it ended. We didn't win a single game. Fortunately, former Millsaps Little All-American, John Christmas, who later retired as Millsaps Dean of Admissions, was then serving as an assistant to President Ben Graves. John talked Dr. Graves into awarding forty-five full-tuition Diamond Anniversary Athletic Scholarships. Football got twenty-eight, baseball five, and basketball got twelve. I was also the head baseball coach, so I recruited five guys who could play both football and baseball. So we had thirty-three scholarships to work with to build us a football team. The fact is, John Christmas saved the football program at Millsaps. And from 1968, when those first scholarship players were seniors, to 1988, when I retired, we only had one losing season. Of course, we couldn't offer scholarships after 1971 when we went Division II, but we had built a program by then and still did all right. I was blessed with some fine football players, but never would have had them in the beginning without those badly needed scholarships.

As reported in the *Clarion-Ledger* in a January 8, 1966 article, Mississippi College also decided to award football scholarships. According to the article, Dr. D. Gray Miley, chairman of MC's Intercollegiate Athletic Committee, said that the scholarship awards would be made "on the basis of skills possessed, scholastic achievement, character and need." The school scholarship fund, Dr. Miley related, would be "supplemented by the Booster Club and friends of the college." Forty athletic scholarships would be awarded in the fall of 1966—twenty-seven and a half to football, eight and a half to basketball, and two each to baseball and track. The article also noted that the Choctaws' head football coach, Hartwell McPhail, would be succeeding the retiring Stanley Robinson as the school's new athletic director.

In the early sixties, Mississippi College had fared considerably better in football than had Millsaps, enjoying four straight winning seasons. However, by 1964, the Choctaws began experiencing a significant drop-off in wins, falling to 3-6 in 1965, and 3-7 in 1966. Scholarships were seen by many as the elixir for what ailed athletic endeavors at Mississippi College, and the Board of Trustees took the necessary steps to give the football team what it needed to return to its glory days of yore.

With the advent of scholarship football at Millsaps and Mississippi College in the mid-1960s, both programs had everything they needed except a traditional Homecoming Game rivalry. Millsaps had to settle for a lukewarm rivalry with Rhodes College in Memphis, while MC made the most of its annual match with fellow Baptist college, Howard. Both schools enjoyed some memorable battles with Sewanee, but neither found a comparable rivalry to that which they had once shared with each other.

The new rivalries they did find had little staying power. The Sewanee series didn't last very long at Mississippi College, according to Coach Hartwell McPhail:

> A lot of people we had been playing for years quit playing us after we started beating them pretty badly. Millsaps quit us in 1959, and Sewanee in 1962. Shirley Majors, Tennessee coach Bobby Majors's daddy, was coaching at Sewanee in 1961 when we beat them 42-6. I had been running a tailback named Billy Gore in the single wing formation on our scout team against the varsity to prepare for Sewanee, which still ran that old formation. We were way ahead of Sewanee in the fourth quarter, so I put Billy in to play some halfback, and he started running Sewanee's old single wing against them! I asked him what he was doing, and if he was trying to rub it in Sewanee's face by running their own formation. He said, "No coach. I've been running the single wing all week on the scout team, and I know their plays better than I know ours!" Anyhow Sewanee quit us a year later.

Billy Gore, Choctaw football legacy and son of Dr. Albert Gore, now a Mississippi Special Assistant Attorney General:

> I was a member of the infamous scout team that ran the sin-

‡

gle wing against the first and second teams to prepare for the '61 Sewanee game. After we ran up a big lead, Coach McPhail put the scout squad backfield in, and I said, "Fellas, we're going to run the single wing." In retrospect, it was not the thing to do, to embarrass a coach with the stature of a Shirley Majors. But it was all we knew how to do, and they couldn't stop us when we ran it. When, on a running play, I went out of bounds near Coach McPhail, he grabbed me and said, "Gore, get out of that danged single wing." We did, and we were stopped cold.

Hartwell McPhail: "After Sewanee quit us, we had a lot of close games with Howard in the early '60s, when their head coach was future Florida State coach Bobby Bowden. But I had Alton Greenlee at quarterback, and he was just too much for Bowden's boys, and we beat them every year. I see Bobby now and again, and he tells me I'm the only coach he never did beat."

One of the reasons that Mississippi College was unable to hold on to a rivalry opponent in the 1960s was because they had such an excellent head coach.

Dr. Van Dyke "Doc" Quick: "Hartwell McPhail was one of the finest football coaches around here. A great football mind. He was one of the few who ever beat Bobby Bowden at Howard. He would watch game films over and over until he learned what he needed to beat Bowden every time."

Hartwell McPhail:

Yeah, I learned about watching those game films the hard way. When I was head coach at Greenwood High School, my new quarterback was giving away our plays at the line of scrimmage by looking in the direction that a running play was going to go, and not looking either way if he was throwing a pass. After the Vicksburg coach beat us that year, he was good enough to tell me that all the coaches were picking up on my quarterback's movements when they saw our game films.

Well, years later at MC, I noticed on the films that Bowden's quarterback was dropping his right foot back if the play was going right, and his left foot if he was going to the left. We schooled our team on it and whipped Howard pretty bad. But they didn't drop us on their schedule because they started beating us after Bobby Bowden left.

"Doc" Quick: "Bobby Bowden didn't hold it against Hartwell McPhail for beating him every year. To the contrary, they became close friends. Earlier this year [2000], I received a letter from Bobby Bowden, which said with reference to their friendship, 'I love Hartwell McPhail.' I believe that if Hartwell was interested, Coach Bowden would find a place for him on the Florida State staff."

Like Mississippi College, Millsaps also had a difficult time maintaining a serious rivalry opponent. They developed a rivalry of sorts with Memphis's Rhodes College, recalls Harper Davis, because everybody in north Mississippi took the *Memphis Commercial Appeal*, rather than Jackson's *Clarion-Ledger*, so both teams got a good write-up in the *Commercial Appeal* whenever they met. The series was also an even one at first, with the teams going 5-5 against each other from 1959 to 1967.

But other factors prevented the Millsaps/Rhodes series from becoming a classic rivalry.

"Although we considered Rhodes to be our main rival," Davis recalls, "they didn't feel that way about us. They thought their main rival was Sewanee." In any event, by 1968, the Majors were making the most of their scholarship money by fielding some powerful football teams, and Rhodes took a four-year hiatus on the series.

Perhaps the best rivalry game played by either team in the mid-'60s occurred in the summer of 1965, when Millsaps and Mississippi College met on the Clinton campus for a hard-fought, pre-season scrimmage. "We scrimmaged them for about an hour and a half," recalls Harper Davis, "and did pretty good for the first thirty minutes. But they had about twice as many players as we did, and wore us down during the last hour."

But a one-shot, summertime scrimmage was a poor substitute for an annual rivalry like the one Millsaps and Mississippi College had formerly shared. And neither team ever found a rivalry that came close to achieving the same intensity level as had their annual pigskin tilt.

Coach McPhail's Choctaws continued to strive as independents in the late '60s, with no great rivalry series nor any conference championship titles to win. However, they did produce some fine athletes during that era. In 1967, All-American quarterback Larry Suchy ran for 919 yards and passed for 1047 more while leading the Chocs to a 6-3 mark. Billy Ray Dill helped out with ten TD receptions, while All-star defensive tackle Ed Trehern terrorized opposing backs who ran his way. Trehern, team MVP receiver Jamie Jones, and talented, all-star quarterback Andy Sumrall were the team's leaders in 1968.

Also playing as independents in the late '60s, the Majors had no conference titles to strive for, but nevertheless enjoyed several winning seasons. Their best year was 1968, when they went 6-3, beating Sewanee, 16-0, and destroying Rhodes, 61-8. Led that year by the dynamic running duo of fleet tailback Brett Adams and powerful fullback Robbie McCloud, the Majors featured an uncharacteristic, high-octane offense. Their quarterback, Mike Taylor, continued his success off the field, blazing a path to Hollywood stardom under the name of Michael Beck.

One of Millsaps's star players during that pre-Division III era, Buddy Bartling, was an heir to the Bartling football legacy. He learned a thing or two about good coaching from his father Doby and his uncle, Sammy, and credits his coach Harper Davis for much of Millsaps's late '60s success. "He was a demanding coach," Bartling recalled of Davis, "and made sure that we never beat ourselves on mistakes. Repetition was his thing. He taught us consistency and was always tough but fair with us. He pushed the fundamentals, because the other team was almost always bigger and better than we were. But we were usually more prepared and in better shape, so we always had winning seasons"

Bartling also thanks Davis for his own [Bartling's] personal football success: "I came to Millsaps in 1967 as a running back/defensive back, but got injured and couldn't play those positions.

Instead of running me off, Coach Davis turned me into a kicker, and gave me a chance, not only to keep playing, but to make a contribution to the team." Bartling repaid his coach with several game-wining kicks.

In 1969, he helped beat Maryville (Tennessee) College, 14-12, by successfully kicking two extra points. He also helped defeat Emory (Atlanta) College, 20-18, in 1970, by converting two field goals and two extra points. Later that season, Bartling contributed to a 24-21 Millsaps victory over previously undefeated Randolph Macon by kicking a clutch fourth quarter field goal.

Millsaps linebacker David Russell, now a Jackson oil company executive, remembers that Harper Davis occasionally used the steamy hot Mississippi weather to his advantage: "In 1970, we played an undefeated team called Missouri Southern State, that was way better than us. But when we played them it was a 90/90 day—90 degrees and 90 percent humidity. Their linemen were a lot bigger than ours, but we were faster than they were to begin with, and after they started dragging around in the heat, Coach Davis lined us up in the gaps and we ran right through them. I sacked their quarterback four times on the way to a 27-21 upset. It made them so angry that they beat us 41-0 the next year up in Missouri."

Coach Davis recalls how tenacious his players were in the late 1960s: "They had to try hard because they were always the underdog. I started off every game for four years with the 'Pro-Right, 26 Power' play, with the tailback running straight ahead, off tackle. Luther Ott, who is now a lawyer and an Episcopal priest in Jackson, played strong side tackle in our line. Before we ran the first play, he would say to the opposing team's defensive tackle, 'I know you know what play is coming, because you've seen our films. Well, you better get ready, because we're coming right at you!' Luther blocked for all he was worth and we gained yards on the play more often than not."

Just as head coaches Harper Davis and Hartwell McPhail crafted their players into hard-nosed, well-disciplined athletes, so to did they place their own indelible stamp on their players' uniforms.

Coach Harper Davis: "My teams wore white helmets, white pants, and either a white or purple jersey. But when I came to Millsaps, they had no emblem on their helmets. I said, 'What about a Majors' Oak Leaf, the symbol of a major in the army, in memory of Major Millsaps?' I came up with the design, took it to a company, and they printed 'em made to order."

Coach Hartwell McPhail: "My Choctaw teams wore white and later gold pants, and either gold jerseys with blue numbers, or blue jerseys with white numbers, and UCLA-style shoulder stripes. But I always liked white helmets because we felt that a quarterback could see his receivers faster when they were wearing white helmets."

Both coaches also took steps to ensure the health and welfare of their players.

John Smith, assistant MC football coach:

I believe that we had fewer severe knee and joint injuries in the fifties than players do today. In the old days, ballplayers had full or part-time jobs on farms or for construction companies, or doing some other kind of physical labor, where our joints got exercised all day long. Today, football players don't have jobs like that as a rule, and they come into high tech weight rooms and overwork their joints. We always tried to point this out to them whether they bought the theory or not.

Coach Harper Davis:

I served for a number of years on the NCAA's Rules Committee, and I tried to make as much input on injuries as I could. One thing I always tried to change, with no success, was the removal of the face mask. While the face mask saves many small cuts and bruises, I think it also leads to serious neck injuries. When players didn't have the masks, they didn't try to make tackles, nose-first. Now they do, and they suffer severe neck injuries for doing it.

The 1970s brought even greater success to the Millsaps and Mississippi College football programs. For one thing, both teams welcomed black players as soon as the decade began.

Coach Harper Davis:

Rowen Torry was our first black player, and he also became Millsaps's first Kodak All-American in 1972. He helped us win one of the greatest games in Millsaps history that year. Texas-Lutheran came to Newell Field undefeated for our last game of the season. We had a 3-4 record at the time. No one gave us any kind of chance to win. They marched up and down the field all day long but couldn't get into the end zone. They finally took a 7-0 lead toward the end of the game. We came back and scored, but went for two and missed it. We held 'em on third down the next series, and they went for it on fourth down at the fifty yard line and didn't make it. There were only three seconds left in the game when our quarterback, Dale Keys, threw a fifty yard bomb to Rowen Torry, who had two guys hanging off him at the ten yard line. Rowen tapped the ball up in the air at the ten, tipped it up again at the five, and with two guys literally hanging on his back, plucked it out of the air as he fell over the goal line with the gun sounding to end the game. We won, 13-7, and it was one of the greatest upset victories in Millsaps history. I told Texas-Lutheran's coach, Jim Wacca, who later coached at TCU and Minnesota, that I hated to take away his perfect season. He said, "Man, you earned it." But he waited on us the next year, and beat us 36-6 out in Texas.

As did Millsaps's Davis, new Mississippi College head coach John Williams also recruited the Choctaws' first African American players in 1972. Included in that group of six black recruits were talented running back Robert Felton and middle linebacker Larry Evans who, along with Kodak All-American receiver, Ricky Herzog, eased Williams's burdens during his first-year, 4-5-1, losing season.

Although the Choctaws didn't achieve immediate success in the early 1970s, MC fans knew they had a coach in John Williams who would take them where they wanted to go:

Dr. Van Dyke "Doc" Quick: "John M. Williams came to MC from Biloxi High School, where his teams had won two state championships. We soon found that he had a special talent for

turning mediocre players into good ones. They would come to us
scrawny boys and he would grow 'em into men. He instilled the
killer instinct into them and a strong desire to win. He made them
'killers' on the field and off the field, turned them into leaders in
their communities and churches."

Williams ushered in a new uniform design for the Choctaws—
solid black or white jerseys with matching pants and dark helmets
decorated with an MC/arrowhead logo. More significantly, he also
guided Mississippi College into conference play and full-scholar-
ship football in the NCAA's Division II in 1971. Once in the Gulf
South Conference, the Chocs could utilize full-tuition scholarship
grants; Coach McPhail had previously offered only half-tuition
scholarships.

Unlike Mississippi College, Millsaps remained in Division III,
where the granting of scholarships was not allowed. But even
though the two schools were now worlds apart, competition-wise,
players and students at both schools continued to feel the heat
generated by the still smoldering Millsaps/MC rivalry. In the
late '60s, the two schools participated in season-launching
"Denominational" basketball tournaments in the Jackson Coli-
seum, and in 1967, the Millsaps Dean of Men had to order his
cheerleaders to write an apology to Mississippi College for leading football players and students in an impromptu "Go To Hell,
Mississippi College" cheer. Although they hadn't played each
other in football for over a decade by the time the '70s rolled
around, players at both schools still considered themselves part
and parcel of an ongoing feud.

Jim Moore, early '70s MC defensive end, now a Jackson lawyer:
"We hadn't played Millsaps in football since the late '50s, so most
of our players didn't know anything about those old-time games.
But it didn't take any of us long to work up hard feelings against
the Millsaps players we saw around town. We'd run into them at
nightclubs like the Zodiac, and although we never had any big
fights, there were some harsh words and a little shoving on occasion. We really wanted to play them because we felt like we could
murder them, but they wouldn't play us. Once, when we heard
some of them had said something about us, a carload of us drove

over to the campus looking for trouble (laughs) but couldn't find anybody who wanted any!"

Brad Chism, late '70s Millsaps receiver & former Rhodes Scholar, now Executive Director of the Jackson Medical Mall: "We had some trouble with the Mississippi College guys in the late '70s and early '80s, especially at night clubs such as the old Zodiac disco. Nobody had forgotten about the rivalry, even though we hadn't played each other in twenty years."

In 1971, Millsaps chose to return to its former policy of competing only with true student athletes. Even so, the Majors continued to field winning football teams just as they had in the late '60s. They even did well enough in the early '70s to prompt *Sports Illustrated* to cover one of their games during the 1973 season. And with everyone on a more or less level playing field in Division III, the Majors were able to reach the NCAA Division III playoffs in 1975 by posting an all-time best 9-2 season record.

Coach Harper Davis:

> We had a great team in 1975. A smart team, with lots of future lawyers and doctors. Ricky Haygood was a Kodak All-American quarterback, with a great arm and smart as a whip. Haygood led the nation in passing and set an NCAA record with 241.8 yards of total offense per game. He had some fine receivers, including tight end Paul Benton and wide receiver Dees Hinton. I believe that Hinton led the nation in receiving. Ron Jurney was a great linebacker, Paul Walker was strong in the offensive line, and Ted Rumke was a fine, talented running back. Rumke had 130 rushing yards called back on penalties in a game against Georgetown, which was more total yards than Georgetown gained all day. We went 8-1 that year and made the Division III playoffs. We went out to Colorado and beat Colorado College, 28-21, when Rumke ran up over 230 total yards. We lost the next game to Wittenburg University, but I was sure proud of that '75 team.

Millsaps running back Ted Rumke, now a Gulf Coast attorney:

We won that Colorado game because our quarterback, Ricky Haygood, and our receivers, Dees Hinton, Sonny Aldee and Paul Benton were so talented that the Colorado defense keyed totally on them and ignored everybody else, and the rest of us had a fabulous game. Our receivers ran down-and-out patterns, and I just ran up the middle all day long. We had a third and twenty at our own 20-yard line, and Coach Davis called for me to run up the middle. Ricky Haygood sent all the receivers on sideline patterns and I practically walked 80 yards for a touchdown. It was really great playing for that team with Haygood and all those talented receivers to take the pressure off me.

Millsaps tight end Paul Benton, now a Gulf Coast lawyer, also recalls that the Majors enjoyed playing football in 1975, and not just because they made the NCAA playoffs:

Because of the school's approach, I really enjoyed playing football at Millsaps. Coach Davis worked us hard and made us all shave and cut our hair the first game of the season or else we wouldn't get to play. But that hard work paid off and we wound up being a good team. But playing at Millsaps was more than just good football. The coaches took the pressure off the athletes. The coaches were real characters and the guys played because they truly loved the game. This was no ride to the big leagues, this was an emphasis on getting an education. Some of our seniors even came back for their fifth year to play ball so they could get a double major. There were no late night football meetings; they expected us to be studying.

There was only one thing wrong with Millsaps football. We should have been playing Mississippi College. It was crazy not to play such a great cross-town rivalry game. Every morning we all looked in the paper to see how MC was doing against the same teams we played.

But although the Majors missed out on a great cross-town rivalry, they didn't lack for football success throughout the 1970s. They wound up the decade with a 7-3 mark in 1979, thanks in part to the key contributions of two-time Kodak All-American linebacker, David Culpepper.

David Culpepper, now a Millsaps professor of accounting: "The year before I came they went to the playoffs, and the year after I left they went undefeated. But in-between, we played winning ball because Coach Davis worked us hard and assistant coach Tommy Ranager was such a super competitor. He made no excuses and accepted no excuses for losing. Before every game Coach Ranager had the linebackers going head to head with each other, trying to get us mad and fired up for the game. We all liked him and called him 'Fat Daddy,' but we knew he was serious about winning. He had a speech that every one of us could testify to today, in which he would say, 'Personally, I'd rather eat shit than lose." And everybody knew he meant it!'

Although Millsaps never found a great rivalry series in the '60s and '70s, John Williams's Choctaws fell into a ready-made rivalry with fellow Mississippi Division II opponent, Delta State University. The Chocs had difficulty competing with the Statesmen early on, with DSU winning the first five contests, often by embarrassingly large margins. However, after dedicating a new football stadium to "Goat" Hale and Stanley Robinson in 1978, the Choctaws rose to the challenge by winning their first five games, including a 27-0 whitewashing of Delta State. The Chocs thrived on the strong running of backs Ezra Tate and Major Everette, and the fine defensive play of 6'1", 220 pound, nose guard Kent Adams. Unfortunately, they dropped their next five games to finish 5-5 for the year.

But despite the disappointing finish, Coach Williams declared the '78 season a success for reasons having nothing to do with wins. Touting his program's success at instilling character in young athletes, Williams told a *Clarion-Ledger* reporter that, "At MC we demand strong morals to survive. If we don't turn out outstanding young men, our program is a failure."

Speaking to the *Jackson Daily News* in a subsequent interview, Williams continued in the same vein. "At MC," he declared, "winning is important, but it's whether I can put some fine, responsible young men on the field that's very important. I feel very strongly about the idea [of recruiting] the kind of young man that has a chance to get a degree, the fine, young, outstanding Christian men. I agree that winning has got to be real, real important because it all kind of stems from that. But when it is the only thing, that kind of turns me off."

But by the very next year, the Chocs had also found success on the field, posting a 9-2 record for 1979, and whipping Delta State, 27-19, to win the newly established Heritage Bell Trophy, annually awarded to the winner of the annual MC/DSU game. The DSU win also gave the Chocs their first ever Gulf South Conference Title.

In the ensuing NCAA Division II playoffs, Mississippi College beat the University of North Dakota, 35-15, on the strength of tailback Major Everette's unstoppable rushing effort. They then moved on to a semi-final match with the University of Delaware, which they lost 60-10. But even though they lost their second round game by an embarrassingly large margin, the Choctaws had tasted NCAA playoff blood, and felt certain that their future in Division II was exceedingly bright.

In the 1980s, both Mississippi College and Millsaps would accomplish goals that players and coaches of former decades had only dreamed of achieving. The 1980 Millsaps squad posted an undefeated, 9-0 season, and although wrongfully shunned by the Division III playoffs, they took great satisfaction in having pulled off one of the greatest upsets in Millsaps football history.

Dan Roach, early '80s football player at Sewanee, now head football coach and history teacher at Jackson's St. Andrews High School:

> I played for Sewanee, and we had some great games against Millsaps in the late '70s and early '80s. But one team we both played, and had a rough time with, was Central Florida, which is now a Division I-A team, like Florida or Florida State. They hadn't had a football team in the '70s, so they ran articles in the Florida newspapers asking for guys to come try out for the

team in 1980. They had no limit on the number of players on their team, so they usually dressed out about a hundred players. They played their games in what was then known as the Tangerine Bowl in Orlando, which is now known as the Citrus Bowl.

Coach Harper Davis:

We had already beaten Fisk, 51-0, Rhodes, 26-10, and Sewanee, 33-7. But then we had to play undefeated Central Florida. They had so many players they tilted the field. (Laughs) We didn't even get to use one half of the field for our pre-game workouts, because their players took up space all the way across the fifty yard line to our forty.

Anyhow, in the first quarter, we ran a play called, "Sweep Left/Melvin Pass," in which our quarterback, Byrd Hillman, started a sweep to the left, handed off to wingback Melvin Smith, who threw a bomb to Jessie McRight, who went into the end zone untouched. Then we called a play we only ran two times during my years at Millsaps. It was called "Geronimo Left," and Mississippi football fans will remember it as the "Gobbler Play" used by Virginia Tech against Ole Miss in the '68 Liberty Bowl.

On the play, our holder and kicker lined up behind the center as they ordinarily did on extra point attempts. But our offensive line and backs all congregated ten yards to the left of our center. The Central Florida defensive team lined up on our center, as they ordinarily did. Our center then flipped the ball to Orman Knox, who walked into the end zone for a two point conversion. Those Florida boys weren't worried about our 8-0 lead, because they knew they were going to whip us by at least five touchdowns. They were so confident, that when they scored a touchdown on the next series, they kicked the extra point, not thinking they'd never score again. But they didn't, because we held them out of the end zone for the rest of the day.

We shut them down because we came up with a plan to contain their great, scrambling quarterback. Our two great defensive ends, Frank Lyle and Gus Morris, keyed on him all day, and sacked him over and over. Even though the press had started out making fun of us over the names we gave our plays, such as "Sweep Left, Melvin Pass," they ended up calling us "The Alabama of Division III."

Former Millsaps quarterback Byrd Hillman, now a Jackson health insurance broker, remembers Coach Davis's penchant for crafting successful game plans:

> We played an all-black school one year, and they were a very fast, talented team. We really shouldn't have had a chance against them. But Coach Davis knew our only advantage was that we were probably in better shape, just like we almost always were, so he used the whole field every time we were on offense, running end sweeps to the left or right on every single play. The other players were wheezing in the fourth quarter, saying, "Y'all run right at us!" We won the game because we wore them down.

Major receiver Brad Chism, a Millsaps Rhodes Scholar, now a Jackson health services executive, remembers how Davis whipped the Majors into shape during the mid-'80s:

> We couldn't have any water during practice, and we practiced hard the whole time. At the end of practice, we ran from five to eleven laps around the field depending upon how we'd done that day. We focused on the running game and the short pass, and we finished third in the nation in rushing in 1980. We won the Central Florida game that year because we were in better shape than they were. But after that game, on the bus ride back to Mississippi, everybody got drunk except Jessie McRight, the receiver who caught the game-winning touchdown pass, because he was sitting next to Coach Davis and couldn't drink a thing! Coach Davis was famous for his "Boozer and a Loser" speech, but we snuck it on the bus anyhow and celebrated that Central Florida victory.

Led by Kodak All-American tailback Edmond Donald's hard running and NCAA record-breaking punt return average (21.3 yards
per return), the Majors went 7-2 in 1983. They had an even better campaign in 1984, posting an 8-1 mark. But Coach Davis's
most vivid memory of the '84 season was not edging Sewanee, 28-
26, or suffering his sole loss, a 32-8 drubbing at the hands of
Rhodes College. It was, he says, the traumatic events suffered on
another memorable Major bus trip, this time to Western Tennessee.

Coach Harper Davis:

In 1984 we played four games on television, and one of
those was against Maryville College, in West Tennessee. We
stayed the night before at a hotel in Sweetwater, Tennessee,
about forty miles from Maryville. We had a 10:30 a.m. game to
accommodate their television broadcast, so we got up early to
go to breakfast at our hotel restaurant. But when the manager
realized we had black players on our team, he refused to serve
us breakfast! I almost fainted. I couldn't believe it! I thought all
that kind of stuff was behind us, like it was in Mississippi. But
apparently not in Sweetwater, Tennessee.

So we had to scramble around to find a place that would
serve us, and the only place we could find was Sweetwater's
Burger King. There was only one employee there early that
morning, so I had to help out with the cooking in the kitchen.
When we got on the bus, we had forty miles to go and an hour
to get there, so we taped their ankles and they got dressed on
the bus. We pulled into the stadium five minutes before the
game started, never had time to warm up, and still won the
game, 14-13.

Mississippi College began the 1980s with a 4-5 season, but by
decade's end had accomplished more than most schools ever do in
their entire football history. The first thing they accomplished in
the '80s was to take command of the Delta State rivalry game:

Choctaw Hall of Fame tailback Major Everette: "We beat Delta
State all four of my years, from '79 to '82. We beat 'em in 1979 to

win the conference championship, but my favorite DSU game was in 1981 when it went back and forth all game long. They were a passing team and we were a running team, and it was an exciting archrivalry. We had to get ready for DSU!"

Early '80s Choctaw assistant football coach Terry McMillan, who later became head coach and athletic director: "That '81 Delta State game was one of the greatest I ever saw, and Major Everette set the single game Choctaw rushing record with 307 yards that day. We had taken him out of the game until somebody told us he was close to getting the record, so we put Major back in. He got the record, and that was one of the best performances by a player I've ever witnessed."

Although back-to-back 8-3 seasons in '82 and '83 gave way to 6 and 7 win campaigns from '84 through '87, the 1988 season brought a 9-2 record and a Gulf South Championship to Clinton. The Chocs wrapped up their season with a satisfying, 7-3, win over Delta State, then began preparing for an NCAA Division II playoff game against Texas A & I University. Although they lost that game, 39-15, the Choctaws knew they had assembled the nucleus of a championship-caliber squad.

In 1989, John Williams's Braves enjoyed a respectable 7-3 season, but lost their final game to archrival Delta State, 17-7. After that loss, *Clarion-Ledger* sportswriter Rick Cleveland asked Coach Williams if his Choctaws would be going to the Division II playoffs that year. "Not a chance," replied a despondent Williams. "It's over for us this year. We're sending the players home."

But the Choctaws got an unexpected invitation to the big dance, and made the most of the gift by crushing Texas A & I in a Division II playoff rematch, 34-19. They followed that win with a second round, 55-24 upset over St. Cloud (Minnesota) University, then whipped Indiana University of Pennsylvania, 26-14 in a semi-final match. In the Championship Game, they edged the Jacksonville State University Gamecocks by a score of 3-0 to win the Division II National Title!

"Doc" Quick, who witnessed the Choctaws' extraordinary 1989 playoff run:

We had some great players in the late '80s and early '90s. One of the best was running back Fred McAffee, who went on to have a long pro football career. Another was receiver Nathanial Bolton, and still another was quarterback Wally Henry [Henry threw for 2253 yards in 1989] who was a great punter besides. And many of our players were great role models for kids, with some of them going to inner city schools and helping out with the poor, disadvantaged children there.

But we got some divine help to win that national championship in 1989. We were down from losing to Delta State and the Committee had just thrown us in the playoffs as an afterthought also-ran. No one expected us to win, including ourselves. But the Lord smiled on us during the playoffs. There had been a long drought in Texas, but it rained all day when we played Texas A & I. It snowed when we played St. Cloud up in Minnesota, and rainy or snowy weather usually helps the underdog. It was a warm, sunny day when we played Indiana up north, so our players didn't freeze. And the officials had to scrape snow off the field the day we upset Jacksonville (Alabama) State to win the championship game!

"The good Lord was with us during that playoff run," agrees then assistant coach Terry McMillan, who is now Choctaw head football coach and athletic director. "Texas A & I hadn't allowed 30 points all year, we upset them in the rain. Jacksonville had beaten us bad during the regular season, but it snowed when we played them in Alabama. They didn't even have any snow equipment, so they had to get it off the field by pulling bleacher stands behind tractors. That was just an incredible season!"

The Chocs won the semifinal game with St. Cloud thanks to Wally Henry's 358 passing yards and Milton McGee's dominating play on the defensive line. But to win the title game, they had to rely upon a forgotten second-stringer to overcome an undefeated, 13-0, Jacksonville State team that had whipped them earlier in the regular season by a score of 23-3.

The Chocs played the title game on a frigid, December day in north Alabama after the groundskeepers cleared two inches of snow off the field. Consequently, neither team was able to mount any consistent offense. This was especially true for the Game-cocks, who never crossed the Choctaw 34-yard line. After a hard-fought, defensive game, it all came down to a field goal attempt by bench-warming kicker, Shane Stewart, who had been demoted to second string oblivion earlier in the season. Although another kicker had been handling the field goal chores throughout the playoffs, and Jacksonville had blocked Stewart's first field goal try earlier in the game, Coach Williams called Stewart's number on MC's second drive of the third quarter.

The Choctaws had driven to the Jacksonville 2-yard line from their own 48 when Stewart trotted out onto the field. Despite the windy, frigid conditions, the snap was good, holder Stephen Crawford made a perfect placement on the nine-yard line, and Stewart kicked the ball straight through the uprights! "I expected to make it with my eyes closed," Stewart told the *Clarion-Ledger* after the game. "It was the most calm I've ever been on a kick."

For the rest of the game, the MC defense stuffed the highly-touted Jacksonville wishbone, allowing them a mere 166 total yards on the day. "This is just an emotional time for us," said Williams after the win. "The kids did fantastically well. This group had the ability to come back all year."

Mississippi Lt. Governor Brad Dye congratulated the victori-ous Choctaws on their outstanding championship run. "Missis-sippi College has always been noted as a fine academic institu-tion," Dye proclaimed, "and now it has risen to the pinnacle of athletic achievement. Winning the national championship is not only an honor for Mississippi College, but an achievement all Mis-sissippians can be proud of."

Even though the Majors and Choctaws did not compete in foot-ball in the 1980s, they did play each other in baseball and basket-ball. Although these contests never experienced the level of fan or player intensity of the past football games, some of the old-timers nevertheless kept the memory of the infamous rivalry alive.

Chuck Barlow, MC alumnus, now legal counsel for the Mis-sissippi Department of Economic Development:

In the early '80s, MC and Millsaps had just begun playing baseball and basketball against each other. But a generation had passed since the rivalry had been so intense, and Mississippi College was a much larger school and in Division II, besides, so the rivalry just wasn't as intense at it had been. The games weren't very well attended, especially since they didn't play football anymore. Of course, my father-in-law, Clarence Lentz, who had attended MC in the '50s, felt differently about it than I did. He once told my wife Deleslynn and I about his freshman year, when the upperclassmen forced him to sneak onto the Millsaps campus one night to make a one-man beanie raid. He told us that he hid in the bushes, knocked a Millsaps freshman down, took his beanie, and took off for Clinton on foot. Anyhow, he still felt strongly about the rivalry when Deleslynn went to college, because he told her that he would pay for her to go to school anywhere in the world except Millsaps College!

Mississippi College's and Millsaps's football programs had experienced extraordinary changes and unprecedented success from 1960 to 1990. They had abandoned their traditional rivalry game in 1960, and had opened their doors to black student-athletes in the early 1970s. Under Harper Davis's leadership, Millsaps had won a Division III playoff game in 1975 and had enjoyed a perfect 9-0 season in 1980. Under John Williams, Mississippi College had not only won two Gulf South Conference Championships in 1979 and 1988, they had also won Mississippi's first Division II National Championship in 1989. But the changes they had undergone during those three decades would pale by comparison to the transformations they would experience in the 1990s.

Harper Davis had retired as Millsaps's head football coach after another winning season in 1988. His 25-year, 138-79-4 record and .633 winning percentage had made him Millsaps's most successful football coach, although "Goat" Hale did achieve a higher win percentage (.679) during his three head coaching seasons at Millsaps. Davis's longtime assistant, Tommy Ranager, had succeeded his former boss, and brought formerly independent Millsaps into a Division III football conference, the Southern Collegiate Athletic Conference (SCAC), in 1989.

Ranager hit the ground running in the '90s with a 5-4 winning record, then led the Majors to a 7-2 season in 1991. More importantly, Millsaps won the1991 SCAC title with a 20-6 win over rival Sewanee, thanks to the strong play of three-time Kodak All-American tackle Sean Brewer, and All-American defensive back Murray Meadows. Meadows set an NCAA record in 1991 with 11 interceptions in a nine game season. Ranager also recruited Kodak All-American tailback Kelvin Gladney, who, in 1994, led the 4-6 Majors to back-to-back victories over rivals Sewanee (35-20) and Rhodes College (17-10).

But after a 2-7 mark in 1995, Ranager was replaced by former Millsaps player and West Georgia head football coach, Ron Jurney. Jurney gave the Majors' uniforms a new look when he designed a purple helmet decorated with an oak-leaf and a new "M." His new-look Majors responded to their school's sixteenth head coach by winning the 1996 SCAC Championship with an 8-2 record.

Coach Ron Jurney:

We called 1996 the "Miracle Season." Millsaps had gone 2-7 the year before, and we didn't have an especially talented team in '96. But our players had good chemistry and a never-say-die spirit. They were capable of coming back from almost anything. But considering our talent level, everybody picked us to finish last in the conference that year. Our key game was the first of two that we played against Rhodes. We played it on campus the second week of the season under the brand new overtime rules. Our game went into overtime, and we won, 28-22. Our tailback, Brad Madden, who was the Most Valuable Offensive Player for the conference that year, scored the winning touchdown in overtime. He had been injured in the second quarter, and I thought he was done for the game. But he came back to score the winning touchdown for us. We played Rhodes a second time that season and beat them14-7 on their campus.

The crowning glory of the '96 season came when we beat

Trinity in the last game of the year. They were undefeated at 9-0, and ranked second in the nation. We were unranked at 7-2. We played them on our campus before a packed house and upset them 13-10. That was a tremendous victory and the only time our fans ever tore down the Millsaps goal posts!

After just three seasons at the helm, Jurney, who continues to serve as Millsaps's Athletic Director, handed over the head coaching reigns to former Mississippi State head football coach Bob Tyler for the 2000 season. Tyler had ended years of frustration in Starkville by taking Mississippi State to the 1974 Sun Bowl, but had been out of coaching for nine years before he took the Millsaps job. "I was hoping for something like this," Tyler told the press. "I didn't want to leave Mississippi or the mid-South. I thought about coaching high school, but I was hoping for something like this. I wanted to coach Division III."

The Northside Sun reported that, although Tyler's arrival coincided with the completion of a new $17.3 million Physical Activities Complex, the new coach was more impressed with the team he had inherited. "The NCAA doesn't allow spring practice or the coaches to go on the field with the players," Tyler said, "but they've been working real hard on their own—out running and in the weight room."

Athletic Director Ron Jurney downplayed the NCAA rules sanctions that Mississippi State had suffered under Tyler's leadership. "We did our research on that," Jurney told the press, "and we found that he was not directly involved. We have no concern about that whatsoever. He's a proven winner. He completely dazzled our search committee with his plans for the program."

"So far, I think he's a good selection," star running back Marcus Dudley told the *Clarion-Ledger*. "I didn't know much about him, but I hope he brings the kind of winning attitude he showed in the press conference."

Tight end Roman Raybourne was even more optimistic about Tyler's arrival. "I think he's going to do a lot of good things for the program and hopefully will help win us a national championship." The changes Mississippi College went through in the 1990s were even more profound than those experienced by Millsaps College. The Choctaws carried their '80s success right over into the '90s, winning the 1990 Gulf South Conference Championship with a 10-1 worksheet. The Chocs succeeded thanks in part to All-Star tailback Fred McAffee's 1583 rushing yards and 19 touchdowns, and quarterback Dexter Roulhac's 1276 passing yards. The balanced Choctaw attack was ably complimented by a stingy Brave defense which held opponents to an average of 14 points a game. Lineman John Knox led the defensive charge with 127 tackles, while Terrence James sacked opposing quarterbacks eleven times.

Mississippi College beat Jacksonville State, 14-7, in the first round of the 1990 playoffs, after having already whipped them during the regular season, 17-7. But their National Championship defense ended a week later when they lost a playoff rematch to Indiana University of Pennsylvania, 27-8.

Personal troubles led to the departure of John Williams after the 1990 season. He had compiled a 124-78-4 record and .612 win percentage during his 19 seasons at the Choctaw helm, thereby becoming MC's winningest head coach, surpassing the legendary Stanley Robinson by just one victory. Williams was replaced by his assistant coach, Terry L. McMillan, for the 1991 season. McMillan had played quarterback for the University of Southern Mississippi, and was coaching at Biloxi High School when Coach Williams hired him as an assistant in 1972.

McMillan led the Choctaws back into the Division II playoffs in 1991 with a 6-3-1 record and a season-ending, 27-10, victory over archrival Delta State. The Chocs defeated Wofford College, 28-15, in the first round of the playoffs, but succumbed to longtime playoff antagonist, Jacksonville State, 35-7, in a second round match.

But cheers turned to chagrin in January of 1993, when the NCAA sanctioned Mississippi College for various NCAA rules violations committed during the John Williams regime. The NCAA stripped the Chocs of their 1989 National Championship Crown and their 1990 Conference Title, placed them on two-years' probation, and ruled them ineligible to compete for the conference title until the fall of 1995. Everyone associated with

Mississippi College, particularly the membership of the Mississippi Baptist Convention which supported the institution, was deeply troubled by the news.

This was, of course, not the sort of thing that was supposed to happen at academically-renowned institutions like Mississippi College or Millsaps, which prided themselves on both their religious heritage and their reputation for instilling character in student-athletes. It was one thing, many small college fans said, for Mississippi's Division I-A universities—Mississippi State, Southern Mississippi, and Ole Miss—to get slapped with probation for recruiting violations during the '70s, '80s and '90s; such things were a common occurrence in win-at-all-costs Division I-A schools. But it was something else entirely for a Division II program like Mississippi College to engage in such inappropriate behavior.

The reaction of Mississippi College's faculty was swift and to the point. They fired off a scorching memorandum to the president and board of trustees—

> The faculty. . . is disappointed and profoundly saddened by the recent revelations of dishonesty and mismanagement in the operation of our athletic program. By monetary standards, this college has never been wealthy, but it has always cherished its reputation for academic integrity and its commitment to high moral values. Most of us have committed our careers to Mississippi College primarily because of its fundamental mission to have the essence of the Christian faith permeate the entire process of education. Now, through mismanagement of an extracurricular program, the reputation of the entire institution has suffered. Our school motto, "Truth and Virtue," has become a point of ridicule, and every facet of the institution's integrity, even our own individual reputations, has come under scrutiny.

The faculty requested that the purpose of Mississippi College athletics be reexamined, especially the "level of participation that is justified in view of available resources." The faculty further asked that "adequate supervision" of the football program be maintained, and also requested that "additional fitness and intra-mural programs" be added to "benefit a greater number of Mississippi College students."

In a February 2, 1993, follow-up memorandum to the college president and board of trustees, the Athletic Department staff, headed by coach Terry McMillan, unanimously supported the faculty's requests, saying that, "No one is more ashamed and embarrassed about the recent events involving the NCAA than the Athletic Department."

In early 1995, newly appointed Mississippi College President, Dr. Howell Todd, announced to the press that Mississippi College would "move up" from NCAA Division II to the non-scholarship awarding Division III. "We need to be in focus with what we are all about," Todd told *Clarion-Ledger* reporter Robert Wilson on March 24, 1995. "We are making this move to help the school concentrate on the student experience. MC is known for its academic success, and that must be our priority. We want to move to Division III as quickly as possible. We will officially become a Division III program in 1997."

Although Athletic Director and head football coach Terry McMillan was disappointed by the move, he supported President Todd at the press conference. "I don't like it," McMillan said, "but I work for MC. If they told me to hook up a mule and plow the field, I'd do it. I'll play Division I, II, or III, whatever they tell me to do."

McMillan also told the *Clarion-Ledger* that, without their scholarships, the Choctaws would no longer be playing their 1990s archrival, Delta State University, or any other team that had thirty-six scholarships to use for football recruiting. "I guess our biggest rivalry *will be Millsaps*," he predicted.

After confessing their wrongs, offering sincere repentance, refocusing upon their moral and academic missions, and making amends by surrendering their scholarships and dropping down to Division III football, Mississippi College quickly found redemption in the American Southwest Conference (ASCC). In 1997, their first year in Division III, Coach McMillan's Choctaws won the ASCC Title with an impressive 8-2 record.

But even after ascending to college football's pinnacle, stumbling off the mountaintop, and then rising like a Phoenix from the ashes of probation to the jubilation of a conference championship won by non-scholarship student athletes, the Mississippi College faithful still sensed that something was missing insofar as their football program was concerned.

Van "Doc" Quick: "During the past few years MC hasn't established a good rivalry in the American Southwest Conference. We played Austin College back in the fifties, so maybe something will develop with Austin now that we're playing them again. But they're a Texas team in a mostly Texas conference, so I doubt that a big Austin/MC rivalry would ever develop. At least not anything like MC and Millsaps had. Besides, what everybody around here has wanted since we got into Division III is to start playing Millsaps again."

Several miles to the east, Millsaps true believers knew exactly how their Mississippi College neighbors felt.

Millsaps College football fan Luther Ott: "After we quit playing Mississippi College in 1960, we would read the newspapers every Sunday to see how MC did against teams we also played. If we beat the same team they did, but by a larger margin, we felt like we had earned a moral victory against MC. But what our players wanted then, and what Millsaps fans have wanted ever since MC dropped down to Division III, is for Millsaps to play Mississippi College again."

As the saying goes, sometimes dreams do come true. And to once again paraphrase the masterfully eloquent author of *Ecclesiastes*, there is indeed a season for everything under the sun. Or at least that's what MC Athletic Director/Head Football Coach Terry McMillan believed back in 1995 when he began pondering the prospect of life in Division III football.

What, McMillan wondered, would most appeal to Choctaw football fans who had grown accustomed to championship football in Division II, but were now being asked to accept non-scholarship Division III action? What would induce Choctaw fans to throw pep rallies, march in parades, and pack a football stadium to watch their Braves play? And what cross-town team had almost every Choctaw ballplayer wanted to play, but couldn't, for the past forty years?

These were the questions McMillan had begun asking back in the spring of 1995. And knowing full well that springtime was a season for renewal, the Choctaw Chief had taken the initiative in April of that year and contacted Ron Jurney, the athletic director of a cross-town, small college football program that favored Major purple and white over Choctaw blue and gold.

After forty years had come and gone, McMillan reckoned, it was time to resurrect the ghosts of autumns past. The time had finally come for the Choctaws and Majors to bury the hatchet, smoke the peace pipe, and renew the Deep South's most intense football rivalry. And if a new treaty could be signed, then an unschooled generation, living in a newly-dawned millennium, would finally have the opportunity to experience an extraordinary event that its forebears had appropriately called "Holy War!"

CHAPTER NINE

THE RENEWAL
1998-1999

Upon learning in 1995 that his team would soon be playing Division III football, Mississippi College Athletic Director Terry McMillan immediately contacted his Millsaps counterpart, Ron Jurney, about reopening athletic competition between their two schools. Jurney essentially replied that he would be willing to discuss the matter further when the Choctaws were official Division III members and all their current scholarship players had graduated. So when all of that came to pass in 1997, McMillan contacted Jurney once again.

MC Coach/A.D. Terry McMillan:

> The idea of the Millsaps series was a good one for us, especially after we lost our rivalry with Delta State. It was good all around, because it would give us both a cross-town rivalry, and would be a boost to Mississippi Division III football. So I had been pushing the MC/Millsaps series since 1995. Eventually, I and Ron Jurney, and both our Presidents, Dr. Howell Todd and Dr. George Harmon, all got together and worked it out in April of 1998. We had to work out our schedules to accommodate the first football game in 2000, but we got it done.

Millsaps A.D. Ron Jurney:

> Terry called me about a game in 1995. We waited for them to go down to Division III, and once they did, we became open to looking at it. We talked back and forth, and both of us felt it would be great for the community and would develop good school spirit on both campuses. And we knew it would be a financial boon for both of us, not only because of the atten-

dance at the game, but because we could save money by not having to travel across the country to play a game as we both do in our conferences, playing a lot of Texas teams.

Dr. Harmon asked me to research the positives versus the negatives, and we went through an in-depth review at the end of the 1997 season. I put together a package which clearly showed that the positives outweighed the negatives, and Dr. Harmon eventually approved the renewal in April of 1998.

Millsaps President Dr. George Harmon: "We were glad to start the rivalry back once they came down to Division III and everybody was on a level playing field. We're looking forward to a long series with Mississippi College."

Mississippi College President Dr. Howell Todd:

When we made the transition decision in 1995 I thought it would be a good rivalry and I was ready to play it. But Ron Jurney had no interest then. Fortunately, Mike Frascogna, the attorney for the Mississippi Sports Council, acted as an intermediary to help bring the two schools to an agreement to play. I look forward to the renewal of this rivalry. It's good for both institutions and for the community, as well. I know we had a little problem with behavior years ago, but I hope both schools can overcome that. As I told Dr. Harmon, a tank of gas and a bus is our travel budget, so this in-town game will work out perfectly for us. Both student bodies can be actively involved in this series and there will be a minimum of travel for our student athletes. We were proud to "go up" to Division III football where you play true student athletes, and we very much look forward to this game with Millsaps.

Choctaw head coach/A.D. Terry McMillan: "The Mississippi Sports Council helped a lot by settling any questions about where this first game would be played by proposing that it be played at a neutral site, at [62,500 capacity] Memorial Stadium. We now have a chance to set an all-time Division III attendance record when we renew the series."

Pat Frascogna, President, Mississippi Sports Council:

My brother, Mike, who is the attorney for the Mississippi Sports Council, had encouraged the Council for several years to consider sponsoring a college football doubleheader featuring all Mississippi teams. He eventually convinced the Council's Events Committee to try to arrange a doubleheader with Delta State University against either Mississippi Valley State University or Belhaven College, and a game between Millsaps College and Mississippi College. All members of the Events Committee were pretty much convinced the Millsaps-MC series would never happen because of the violent way the series ended in 1959. Nonetheless, Mike received the Committee approval to try to make the doubleheader a reality.

I remember Mike met several times with the Presidents of both schools. I teased him about his Henry Kissinger shuttle diplomacy going back and forth to the Presidents. But damn if he didn't get Presidents Todd and Harmon to agree to play the game after a forty-year hiatus.

The Council is thrilled about helping to bring this once-great rivalry back to life. Everyone wins. The two colleges, their students and fans, the Mississippi sports community, and most of all the young men on each team who will be given the opportunity to experience playing in one of America's most historic football rivalries. The renewal of the Millsaps-MC rivalry certainly enhances Mississippi intercollegiate football both on a local and national level. The Council anticipates the renewal game in 2000 to break the NCAA Division III single game attendance record.

The Council is proud to have played a small part in the history of this great series.

On April 16, 1998, the *Clarion-Ledger* reported that "Millsaps College and Mississippi College plan to resurrect their long-dormant football rivalry with a game at Mississippi Veterans Memorial Stadium. One game, to be announced at a news conference today, is scheduled for the year 2000. A 1999 game is possible. The schools, just a 20-minute drive apart, haven't played football since 1959. . . . The game is being promoted by the Mississippi Sports

Council, the private group that promoted NFL exhibition games at the stadium in 1995 and 1996."

In a follow-up article the next day, the *Clarion-Ledger* reported that the first MC/Millsaps football game would be played in September of 2000 as a season opener for both schools, and that basketball competition would also be renewed. [Tennis, basketball and baseball had already been renewed in the early 1980s, but the basketball series had been subsequently discontinued.]

The two April *Clarion-Ledger* articles quoted several players, fans and alumni who all welcomed the rivalry's rebirth.

Former MC footballer Charley Farmer: "It was always a good, intense rivalry. It would be a big game, and both schools need some big games."

Millsaps football player Wes Ingram: "It saves a ten-hour bus ride to somewhere else. It gives you an in-state rivalry, and we don't have an in-state rivalry now."

Former MC football star Puddin Davis: "It'll be like the Mayor's Cup baseball game for Ole Miss and State. It doesn't count in the standings, but it's a big game."

MC receiver Matt Murphy: "Right now we're playing everybody in Texas. It's hard to develop a rivalry. Our biggest rivals now are Howard Payne and Hardin-Simmons. [That] may be changing soon."

Millsaps linebacker: "You watch the news and see MC doing so well, and you wonder why you don't play them."

Millsaps Athletic Director Ron Jurney: "We fully intend to play MC in all sports."

MC Athletic Director Terry McMillan: (On whether the 2000 game could be the first in a series of season openers) "I'll just keep that date open. I want to play."

On April 20, 1998, *Purple and White* news editor Jason Stine weighed in with a "vintage Millsaps" perspective on the renewal of the MC/Millsaps football series: "As if awakened from a long slumber, the age-old rivalry between Millsaps and MC is reborn, and through this athletic epiphany, these two schools can perhaps put behind them the differences of the past and celebrate the dawning of a new golden age of intercollegiate sports"

The *P&W* article noted that the two schools had accepted an invitation given by the Mississippi Sports Council to compete in a football doubleheader, with their game following an afternoon meeting between Belhaven College and Delta State University. Once again, the key figures in the renewal gave their glowing approval to the deal.

Dr. Howell Todd: "This is one of the most exciting developments in Mississippi intercollegiate athletics in many years, and this is a wonderful opportunity for our students, our institutions, the greater Jackson sports area, and even the state of Mississippi."

Dr. George Harmon: "It is my hope that the renewed rivalry between our two institutions will increase and expand the awareness of the quality of NCAA Division III athletics throughout the state of Mississippi. On behalf of the faculty, staff, alumni, student athletes, and our entire student body, we eagerly await the renewal of this exciting rivalry."

Mississippi Sports Council President Pat Frascogna: "I'd like to see this game the most attended in Division III history."

That same day, the *Mississippi Collegian* also broke the renewal news to MC students, but utilized a decidedly more flamboyant approach. "What happened," asked assistant editor Mary Beth Evans, "to the intense rivalry Mississippi College had with Millsaps College which ended almost forty years ago? Well, it apparently got so vicious, with fistfights among athletes and students, and accusations of cheating at games, that in 1960 the two schools decided to end the football rivalry. . . "

As expected, the *Collegian* article contained the usual supportive quotes.

Terry McMillan: "We're looking forward to a long term association with Millsaps."

Dr. Van "Doc" Quick: "We had a lot of fun before and I believe we'll have a lot of fun again. This time we'll keep it under control."

But certain aspects of the *Collegian* article seemed to indicate that the old hotly-contested rivalry was well on its way back to the Jackson area. Choctaw basketball player David Horne was quoted as saying, "I understand that we're supposed to keep a friendly atmosphere, so I won't comment on how we're going to spank their tail. Every rivalry had to start with a little controversy."

And under the headline, "Millsaps begins its losing streak with coin toss," the *Collegian* article revealed that, at the press conference, "a sports official tossed a coin to see which college's president would speak first. Dr. Todd won the toss. Let's hope this winning trend continues," the article concluded.

As Julius Caesar declared after crossing the Rubicon, "The die is cast," and so it was with the renewal of the MC/Millsaps rivalry. As the great Roman general had metaphorically surmised, war had become inevitable as soon as he led his legions onto Roman soil; only its outcome, like the falling spotted cube, was still "up in the air." Similarly, the $64,000 question for Millsaps and Mississippi College players, coaches, alumni and fans was, "Who would win the first MC/Millsaps football war of the twenty-first century?"

The public's reaction to the series renewal was overwhelmingly positive, and as for the two schools' partisans, their perspectives could best be summed up by the words of two once and future MC/Millsaps rivalry fans.

Rose Crumby Downs, of Greenwood, retired teacher/homemaker, and MC alumnus: "I went out with some football players in 1950, and they talked about those Millsaps fellows pretty bad. Talked about stomping them and eating them up. I'm not a big sports person in general, but I'm glad they're playing again this year! I hope those Choctaws shoot those Majors down, and I and my husband will be there in Jackson to see them do it!"

Adelyn Gerald Stokes, Greenville, Millsaps alumnus: "I enjoyed the football games at Millsaps, and so did my husband, Walter, who played football and basketball for the Majors. Even we girls knew that the Mississippi College football game was the biggest game of the year. Unfortunately, they beat us in '46, and everybody was so disappointed. We are both looking forward to seeing Millsaps beat those bad ole Choctaws in Jackson. Go Millsaps Majors!"

The only ones not completely sold on the series renewal were a few of the administrators and faculty who had experienced the riots and brawls forty years before. For them, the more appropriate question concerning the renewal game was, "Is this game going to precipitate the most riotous disaster in Mississippi since the Great Flood of 1927?"

Dr. T. W. Lewis, retired Millsaps professor of religious studies: "There's always a potential problem with two teams from the same town playing each other. My fear is that the renewal will cause problems. I don't think they considered that when they decided to renew the series."

Dr. Van Quick, retired Vice President of MC Alumni Student Affairs: "I hope it's not the same rivalry it was before. I told my students that I better not catch them starting a fight! I said they better behave themselves and they knew I meant it. But. . . (laughs) I also told them that if somebody started a fight with them, they better not lose it!"

And that was how one of America's greatest football rivalries was reborn! The only thing everyone needed as the 1990s drew to a close was a Millsaps/Mississippi College football game, but that wouldn't happen until after Mississippians had celebrated the arrival of a new millennium. And though few were surprised that the dawning of Y2K did not lead to world-wide chaos, many began preparing themselves for another version of Armageddon 2000—the version that would come to be known by Millsaps Majors and Mississippi College Choctaws as "The Mississippi Backyard Brawl!"

CHAPTER TEN

ARMAGEDDON

2000

Millsaps vs. Mississippi College

When Jackson lawyer Reeves Jones strolled across the Millsaps campus on a crisp, early January afternoon in search of the newly relocated bookstore, he found that the new century had brought unexpected changes to his alma mater.

Reeves Jones:

> When I was here back in the late '60s and early '70s, sports in general, and varsity football in particular, weren't empha- sized as they had been in earlier years. The facilities were very humble, to say the least. So I couldn't believe it when I saw a new multimillion dollar Physical Activities Center, new bas- ketball courts, an outdoor pool, racquetball courts, and a light- ed football field. It was all very impressive. I was glad to see that, having insured its academic reputation, Millsaps was focusing on much-needed student and player athletic facilities.

A similar experience awaited Brandon homemaker Libby Hogue when, shortly after moving to the Jackson area from the Delta, she asked a friend to drive her across the Mississippi College campus.

Libby Hogue: "I couldn't believe how big the campus was! About twice the size as when I was here in 1948. There was a new Medical Health Complex where the old football field used to be, and the new stadium was tremendous. And there were so many beautiful new buildings. I was very impressed."

While the recent physical improvements to both campuses were extensive, the winds of change would bring even more aston- ishing surprises for the Millsaps and MC faithful in the year 2000.

On February 11, Millsaps President George Harmon announced his resignation as of June 30. He had provided Millsaps with twenty-two years of outstanding leadership which included the establishment of Mississippi's only Phi Beta Kappa chapter, the Else School of Management and a graduate MBA program.

Harmon informed the press that he would be succeeded by forty-three-year-old Francis Lucas-Taucher, formerly the Senior Vice President of Campus Life at Emory University and herself the daughter of a former university president in Mississippi. Dr. Lucas-Taucher became Millsaps's tenth President, and its first woman President in the 110 year history of the college.

Monumental as it was, the presidential change at Millsaps had little direct effect on the football program, but the same could not be said for the stunning transitions which followed at Mississippi College. On May 1, Terry McMillan resigned as athletic director and football coach, ending a twenty-eight year tenure with MC, the last nine of which he had served as A.D./Head Coach. "My wife and I have talked about it and prayed about it and come to this conclusion," McMillan told sportswriters. "Call it burnout, I guess. I just think it's unfair to the players and the school to keep a job just to have it and not have your heart and soul in it. That's just me."

In an interview with *Clarion-Ledger* sports columnist Rick Cleveland, McMillan denied that his resignation had anything to do with recent budget cuts occasioned by MC's two million dollar overall budget shortfall, or the Choctaws' move to Division III. "I've been playing or coaching football for forty-one years," he explained, "and I think it's just time for a change. I need a new challenge. I'm ready to try something else. And I'm going to spend more time with my three grandkids."

A few days later, Johnny Mills, a former Mississippi College player and defensive coordinator on McMillan's staff since 1996, became the new interim Choctaw head football coach. "This is the most exciting thing I've ever been around," Mills told the *Clarion-Ledger.* "The kids, my coaching staff and the alumni are excited. We're anxious to put a product on the field that will make people proud. There's not a place I'd rather be."

Mills lost no time predicting a wide-open Choctaw offense.

"We've got a great quarterback in Payton Perrett and some great receivers, so it's no secret we're going to throw the football." Regarding the upcoming Millsaps game, Mills opined, "This will be a big game for us. The best way to put it is every day it seems like somebody comes by who played in that game or remembers that game. They all tell me, 'Coach, we've got to beat 'em.' To those people, it's really a big deal."

Of the new head coach, Choctaw junior tight end Whit Lewis said, "Everybody is kind of excited with Coach Mills. We know his attitude and love for the game. He's a great Christian guy and a great friend, but he is also a guy who is going to work with you to do your best."

Then, on August 8, Mississippi College tabbed Mike Jones as the school's interim athletic director. A 1975 MC graduate, Jones had previously served as the Choctaws' head basketball coach during the past twelve years, guiding the Chocs to an impressive 241-86 roundball record. "I know I have a big challenge ahead of me," Jones told reporters, "but we have an excellent group of coaches and student athletes that are dedicated to Mississippi College, and the transition will be a smooth one because of them. I'm really excited about the position, because I've always wanted to do it."

Of the renewed rivalry with Millsaps, Jones agreed with his new head football coach that the game was a welcome event. "Of course we played them in basketball in the '70s," he said, "but I'm glad we renewed the football rivalry. It's a great thing for both schools."

With all the new chess pieces in place, the only thing remaining was to play the match. And to deal with the pre-game hullabaloo.

COUNTDOWN
TO GROUND ZERO
The Look of War

Devotees of Millsaps/MC sports contests had their appetites whetted on the third weekend of March, 2000, when the two longtime rivals met on the baseball diamond for a doubleheader in the Choctaw Classic in Clinton. The Majors took the first game, 4-2, on the strength of a two-run, seventh-inning homer by Brandon Page, while the Choctaws salvaged the second contest by a score of 3-2, thanks to a seventh-inning, game-ending home run by Luke McAlpin.

And then summer arrived and things really began to heat up. The hottest July in recorded Mississippi history gave way to an even more hellish August in which rain became a thing of the past and daily highs of 100 degrees were considered a break in the weather. By the time the two schools' football players reported for varsity practice in mid-August, temperatures of at least 105 degrees had become the rule rather than the exception.

The heat wave only intensified the fans' football fever, as did the promotional materials disseminated by both schools. A Mississippi College press packet reminded everyone that the Choctaws won the last meeting in 1959 by a score of 26-6, thanks in part to the play of now-defensive coach John Smith, and led the series by a 24-9-6 mark. The release also noted the Choctaws' favorable opening game record over the past eleven years, and that they were undefeated in games played at Mississippi Veterans Memorial Stadium.

The August edition of the Millsaps Football Alumni Newsletter announced that a book entitled *For Love of the Game: The Holy Wars of Millsaps College and Mississippi College Football,* covering the Millsaps/MC football rivalry from 1920 through the upcoming September 2 renewal contest, would be published by the Mississippi Sports Council in November. It also ran a picture of the Majors' new "Centennial Jersey" specially designed by Nike for the college's 100th year of football.

The new purple home jersey featured an "M & Saber" logo on each sleeve, a Centennial Patch on the right front shoulder, the Nike "batwing" logo on the back, and white numbers shadowed in black. A black helmet would also feature the "M & Saber" logo.

As the visitors in the renewal game, the Majors would wear a white jersey of the same design with white, purple-striped pants, which would contrast sharply with the dark blue uniforms of Mississippi College. As they had for the previous few years, the Choctaws would wear dark blue jerseys and pants highlighted by gold numbers, gold arm and leg stripes, and the letters "MC" in gold on the hip. Dark blue knee-length socks and a dark helmet with white "MC" arrowhead logo would complete the Choctaw uniform.

Without question, both the Majors and Choctaws would be dressed very smartly for the big September 2 dance. But with Ole Miss, Mississippi State and Southern Mississippi playing key opening games that same weekend, the archrivals needed to send Mississippi football fans the right kind of invitation to the party. Fortunately for them, as had been the case throughout the twentieth century, there would be no shortage of newspapers seeking to throw kerosene on the already blazing fire.

COUNTDOWN
TO GROUND ZERO
The War of Words

The *Clarion-Ledger*'s annual college football insert section, which ran on Sunday, August 20, not only included full page stories on head coaches Bob Tyler and Johnny Mills, it also gave what it considered to be the keys to both Millsaps' and Mississippi College's seasons. Predicted stars for the Choctaws, who had gone 6-4 in 1999, included 6'1", 200 lb., quarterback Payton Perrett, whose nearly 2000 passing yards and school record 19 touchdown passes had garnered him the 1999 ASC Rookie of the Year Award; fleet receiver Vance Andry; first team

All-ASC offensive lineman Craig Waddle; honorable mention All-ASC selections nose guard Tim Bivens and cornerback Jonathan McMillan; and preseason All-American punter Wilson Hillman.

The paper also tabbed several Millsaps players as potent weapons, including running backs Brent LeJeune and Marcus Dudley; sophomore linebacker William Jorden; cornerback and return specialist Marty Frascogna; and senior kicker Derrick McNeal. The *Clarion-Ledger* also reported that Millsaps football alumnus and Gulf Coast lawyer Paul Benton had made a one million dollar donation "for all the things that surround a football player," and opined that the contribution should go a long way toward helping to improve Millsaps's 2-8 record from 1999.

In a subsequent article, *Clarion-Ledger* sportswriter Mike Christensen kicked off the week-of-the-game publicity in fine style by running an August 30 article entitled, "Future preacher helped end Millsaps' scoreless futility at hands of MC." The story noted that after the Majors had failed to score on the Choctaws from 1937 to 1946, halfback David McIntosh, now a semi-retired Methodist preacher, helped break the ice and launched a touchdown-scoring, game-winning drive with a fake punt dash from his own end zone.

It wasn't long before the war of words broke out in earnest. When the Mississippi Sports Council's all-out media blitz treated the populace to daily newspaper ads and television commercials asking fans to come see the Millsaps/MC contest "for the love of the game," both coaches couldn't resist getting in on the act.

Major Coach Bob Tyler wasted no time praising his opponents in television interviews, saying that he had the utmost respect for "the Mississippi College powerhouses of past and present." MC mentor Johnny Mills responded by saying, "Coach Tyler, he'll blow some smoke, let me tell you. We'll be ready on Saturday night."

The Sunday before the game, the headlines of Rick Cleveland's column read, "Millsaps vs. Mississippi College? Let's just hope it doesn't get ugly." With the 1960 series-ending

riot as the focus of his story, Cleveland interviewed former MC
player, the outspoken Rev. Barry Landrum, who repeated his version of the cause of the brawl. After James "Wooky" Gray
charged into the MC student section at a downtown Jackson basketball game, Landrum related, he leveled Gray with a hard right
to the jaw. Then all hell broke loose.

"You know," Landrum said with a chuckle, "people who were
there say I attacked Wooky, but we all know a preacher wouldn't
do that." When asked if he knocked Gray out, as some witness-
es claimed, Landrum replied, "If he was out, he wasn't out long,
because he hit me back." Then the concession area fight broke
out, Landrum stated. "They started fighting like sardines in a
can. It was bedlam."

After Landrum declared that he would be in attendance at
next Sunday's game, Cleveland concluded his column with the
admonition—"Millsaps fans, be forewarned." The Thursday
before the game the *Planet Weekly* ran a column headed,
"Return of an Old Rivalry: College Football for the Love of the
Game," which declared that "Millsaps versus MC is the hottest
ticket this September," and that the two teams would resume a
series that was "second to none in terms of take-no-prisoners
warfare." The article concluded by declaring that, "If you think
November football in Mississippi is hot, wait until you see this
Brawl. And don't forget to bring your riot gear!"

Not to be left out of the picture, the always controversial
Purple and White ran an August 31 front page article which
trumpeted the return of the rivalry, but also noted that some students responded to "the so-called 'most heated rivalry in the
South' with glazed eyes and blank stares" because the rivalry
was such "a thing of the past." Nevertheless, the article continued, officials at the Mississippi Sports Council believed that the
renewal would make a significant contribution to school spirit at
both schools, albeit possibly "at the risk of jeopardizing an age of
peace between schools."

The *Purple and White* also ran another article in the same edition entitled, "Millsaps vs. MC. . . who cares?" Noting that the
pregame "propaganda displayed by Millsaps has far outshined

that of MC," the story quoted several Millsaps students as being excited about the upcoming football contest. "This is a totally different ballgame," allowed sophomore Akram Al-Turk. "It'll get more fans at the game because it's something different."

Most of the MC fans quoted in the article had a different view, however. Typical of their comments were those of Jim Young, an MC junior, who said the renewal match was "really just an average game. Not many people care."

But if the students had not yet gotten as fired up about the game as the coaches, players, alumni and sportswriters, it was only because they hadn't experienced the time-honored pre-game rituals that had whipped students of past seasons into a raging, seething fury. These rituals were pep rallies and parades, Millsaps/MC style.

COUNTDOWN TO GROUND ZERO

Prelude to War
The Mississippi College Pep Rally
Thursday, August 31, 2000, 8:00 P.M.
Mississippi College Campus

Mississippi College Athletic Director Mike Jones wiped the sweat from his brow as he watched the cheerleaders working the crowd before the newly-erected stage. Even an hour after darkness had descended upon his campus, temperatures continued to hover around the ninety degree mark. The past four days had brought triple digit temperatures to the Jackson area, and no change was expected through the weekend. But despite the oppressive heat, and his fears that his Choctaws might have to endure ninety-plus temperatures while they played one of the most important games of their lives, Jones was for all those concerns a very happy man.

He was, after all, finally living out a lifelong dream. His alma mater had honored him by choosing him as athletic director, albeit on an interim basis for now. His head football coach had also played for Mississippi College, and both of them had come to understand how special such a circumstance could be. What's more, their football team was a nine-point favorite over their once and future archrival from Millsaps College. And the game was going to be played in two days at Mississippi's largest stadium, and in the spotlight of more fan interest and press coverage than either school had garnered in any recent season, much less one game.

With those happy thoughts in mind, Jones stepped onto the podium nestled on the grounds of the B. C. Rogers building in the heart of the MC campus, and took control of both the microphone and the Choctaw Pep Rally. The tom tom which had been beating for the past ten minutes grew immediately silent.

"I hope we're excited about Saturday," Jones said, "we've been working hard, and we're ready to play that other school from across town." The crowd of four hundred students sent up a rousing cheer. "We're gonna kick their. . ." Jones shouted, paused, then added, "britches down!" The crowd went wild. The MC cheerleading squad, which had recently finished as runners up in the 2000 Division III National Championship on ESPN2, added their voices to that of the crowd.

Around twenty members of the Laguna Tribe girl's social club, many with faces painted half blue and half white, others sporting blue "MC" logos on their cheeks, offered a few well choreographed cheers of their own. They cheered loudest when head coach Johnny Mills took the stage holding a large trophy in his arms.

"This trophy," exclaimed Mills in reference to the gold football mounted atop a wide, square base, "will go to the winner of the Backyard Brawl every year. We have it now because we won the last game, and we don't ever want this trophy to leave our campus. The way we do this is to win now and every other year!"

When the crowd finally settled back down, Mills invited his players, all 108 of them, to ascend the podium and give their names, numbers, positions and hometowns. The first one complied, and then added, "Saturday is the first day of hunting season, and some people will want to shoot a bird or two. But I think it'll be more fun to come see us beat down Millsaps!" The Laguna girls yelled their approval, and the player responded by saying "Laguna rocks."

After sophomore quarterback Payton Perrett introduced himself to the crowd and stepped off the platform, a friend shouted, "Are you ready for the big game, Payton?"

"I'm ready, we're all ready," Perrett replied. "We've had two [practices] a day in this heat for two weeks and we're ready to play."

Two nearby coeds offered their opinion to anyone who would listen. "We're gonna cream 'em," said Spirit Chairman Kristen Bracken, a sophomore from Jackson.

Brittany Walker, a junior from Brandon, agreed with Bracken. "I'm very excited about this game," she said. "This is the first pep rally we've had with a rock band and which was not held in the football stadium. I love it."

As the cheerleaders broke into their "two bits" cheer, the Lagunas began executing the Florida State "tomahawk chop" en masse. Everyone was deep into the spirit now, but that was not why Mike Jones was grinning from ear to ear. All around him, he realized, stood a veritable city of beautiful new buildings, the result of sixty million dollars of endowments given by alumni since the 1970s. Below those edifices were several hundred students, every one of them clean-cut, smartly dressed young men and women, who were drinking, of all things, tea, which had been provided by a local delicatessen. This was, he noted with pride, a college to which he would gladly send his own children.

Jones paused for a moment and offered up a silent prayer of thanks for living long enough to see so many of his dreams come true. Then he turned to watch his football players introduce themselves, and allowed himself the luxury of wishing for just one more blessing—a victory over the Millsaps Majors.

COUNTDOWN
TO GROUND ZERO
Prelude to War
The Millsaps Pep Rally
Friday, September 1, 2000, 6:00 P.M.
Capitol Street, downtown Jackson

The police motorcycle escort veered eastward up Capitol Street toward the Old Capitol Museum Building as the purple Millsaps bus pulled in and parked beside the federal courthouse. Moments later, five coaches and seventy-five football players disembarked and gathered themselves atop the courthouse steps. Family members, friends and fans who had followed the bus from the campus to the courthouse mingled with the players, asking them how they felt about the big game, now only twenty-six hours away.

"This is unbelievable," said senior Millsaps cornerback Marty Frascogna as he surveyed the Capitol Street scene. Throngs of people lined the street a half block to the west, just in front of the majestic Walthall Hotel. A stage had been erected in front of the Deposit Guaranty Bank Plaza building at the far end of the block, and it was there that a band played, cheerleaders danced around the podium, and the head coach of Delta State University addressed the crowd. The Statesmen, Frascogna well knew, would be playing the Belhaven College Blazers the next day at 3:00 p.m. in the first game of the doubleheader now known as the Salvation Army College Football Classic. He and his fellow Majors would take on the Choctaws in the second game at 8:00 p.m. All four teams and their fans would participate in this pep rally, the first of its kind in Mississippi.

Frascogna glanced across the street at the Trustmark Bank sign which displayed the current temperature—a sweltering ninety-five degrees. He mopped his brow and smiled. This was what college football was supposed to be all about, never mind the heat. He and his teammates were in great shape and ready to meet the Choctaws.

"How do you feel about the game, Marty," asked a fan. "No predictions," he replied with a grin. "Talk to Payton Perrett about that." As the fan set off to do just that, Frascogna turned to join his teammates huddling around Coach Tyler, who was about to speak.

"All right now," Tyler shouted, "I want you guys to meet somebody. This is Paul Benton, the man who gave you a million dollars."

After the cheering subsided, Benton addressed the team.

You've been working hard all summer long, in this heat, getting ready for tomorrow," he said. "And because of all that hard work you're going to have a lot of fun tomorrow night. But even though they outnumber you, are bigger and faster, and are predicted to beat you badly, you know you're in better shape than they are, and you know you can win this game in the fourth quarter. And if you give your all in the fourth quarter, when those guys will be sucking air, then you'll really have some fun.

Moments later, as Tyler led the exuberant Majors down Capitol Street toward the rally, Benton's wife Merrill echoed her husband's optimism. "We're going to win it," she said. "I believe that."

"So do I," agreed Millsaps kicker Derrick McNeal as he hustled off to join the team. "And if it comes down to a last minute field goal, I'm going to be the one to win it."

Joe Whitwell stepped out of the lobby of the Walthall Hotel at 6:15 p.m., just in time to see Bob Tyler ascend the podium with his three game captains by his side and the rest of the Millsaps team surrounding the tiny stage. As Tyler introduced his captains, Whitwell turned to his wife, Marguerite, and smiled. "It was a long trip from Lawrenceville, Georgia," he said, "but it was worth it."

"If you say so," she replied patiently. With his white goatee and mustache, her husband looked for all the world like the quintessential southern gentleman. Except, she noted gleefully, for the purple Millsaps football jersey he had just donned.

A few yards away, two purple jersey-clad gents, former players Luther Ott and Wayne Ferrell, kidded a group of current Mississippi College players, themselves dressed in navy blue Choctaw jerseys. "You'd better be ready for our wishbone," Ott urged half-seriously.

"No way," said the disbelieving Choctaw players.

On the podium, Bob Tyler concluded his comments. "I speak for our seniors, the whole squad, and our fans, when I say thank you to the Salvation Army and Mississippi Sports Council for making this possible. This will be four great football teams playing on one day. And we have great respect for the Mississippi College powerhouse and wish them good luck for the rest of the season. Most of all, I want to say that I'm very proud of my players."

As the Millsaps pep band struck up a tune, Paul Benton turned to answer Joe Whitwell's question about their team's chances the next day. "It's going to be a close game," Benton predicted.

> If we win, it'll be in the fourth quarter. They've worked hard all summer, forty-four of them for nine months on their own. That may be the edge, because they'll sure need one. I don't think it'll be a blowout, but those MC guys have been eating well. They made the street shake when they were walking down here a while ago. But there's one thing I believe for sure, and that is that our guys believe they're going to win.

Moments later, after the Millsaps band grew silent, the MC pep band immediately picked up the slack, playing the FSU "Chop" song. The entire Choctaw team, assembled now to the right of the podium, responded with "tomahawk chops" in unison. MC head coach Johnny Mills then introduced his three captains and also thanked the Salvation Army and Sports Council for helping to create such a "great atmosphere for Division III football."

It was then that Whitwell spotted a familiar foe in the crowd and began pushing his way through the onlookers. Moments later, Whitwell and MC assistant coach John Smith shook hands and embraced. They had not seen each other since the fall of 1959, when the Choctaws had won the last football game in the series.

After catching up on old times, they discussed the subject of the 2000 game. "We've got a lot of injuries," Smith allowed, "including our best running back and some key linemen. But you've got to play with what you got, and I think they'll be ready. I sure hope they are."

As Coach Mills finished his speech on the stage, another unusual meeting took place in the middle of Capitol Street. "Hey, Marty," shouted Payton Perrett.

Marty Frascogna turned and took his friend and former Jackson Prep teammate's hand. "Hey, Payton," he said.

For a few moments, the star players of two teams which had once been the bitterest rivals in the history of Mississippi football exchanged pleasantries and wished each other good luck on the coming day. They even allowed Frascogna's mother to snap a few photographs of them standing side-by-side as if they were discussing girls or sports in the Frascognas' back yard.

Then it was time for old friends to part and ready themselves for the next day's battle. But what neither of them knew at the time, what no Choctaw or Major, friend or foe, fan or player had predicted, was that the Saturday contest was destined to be more than just another game which failed to live up to the hype. The 2000 Backyard Brawl between the Mississippi College Choctaws and the Millsaps Majors would prove to be the most exciting game ever played in the history of the series, and one about which everyone who either played in it or watched it could say was worth the forty-year wait.

GROUND ZERO
Millsaps vs. Mississippi College
September 2, 2000, 7:45 P.M.
Mississippi Veterans Memorial Stadium

As the Millsaps Majors slipped out of their locker room and prepared to charge onto the field of Mississippi Veterans Memorial Stadium, they were aware that few of the twelve thousand fans in attendance were expecting them to make a very impressive showing. In that morning's edition of the *Clarion-Ledger,* all seven sportswriters (and even the guest picker) had predicted a Choctaw victory, with scribe Rick Cleveland giving a final score of 21-10, Mississippi College. They also knew that MC was picked to finish in the middle of their conference while Millsaps was predicted to finish last in theirs. And they had just heard that favored Delta State had crushed Belhaven 55-18 in the 3:00 p.m. game, a turn of events that every Major hoped was not a foreshadowing of things to come.

Of course, they were well aware that their head coach Bob Tyler had been sandbagging when he had told the *Clarion-Ledger* reporter that the Majors were "obvious underdogs" and "just trying to establish ourselves and compete with [MC]." But the Majors hadn't failed to note that Choctaw head coach Johnny Mills hadn't appeared to take the bait, and had said that Coach Tyler "knows every trick in the book and he's had closed practices. Millsaps will come out fired up and ready to play," Mills had added. "We aren't taking them lightly."

What's more, all-star Choctaw quarterback Payton Perrett's quote in that morning's paper indicated that he fully appreciated the importance of this game. "It was a big deal way back then," Perrett had declared, "and it's a big deal now, too."

But despite all the negative prognostications, and the extreme unlikelihood of catching the heavily favored Choctaws by surprise, every Major agreed with senior cornerback Marty Frascogna's quote—"When you play in a rivalry, anything can happen."

As Coach Tyler led his team onto the field, he perfectly summed up his team's pre-game perspective. "We're eager to play," he said with a determined look in his eyes. "These guys are very focused."

A few yards away, Joe Whitwell voiced the feelings of the twenty or so ex-Millsaps footballers who were lined up on the sidelines in support of the Majors. "We got to win this game," he said excitedly. "We're the underdog but the Choctaws are going to have a fight tonight!"

As the Mississippi College Choctaws came rushing through the end zone and followed their cheerleaders to the home team's sideline, the tom tom began its familiar refrain and the blue and gold clad MC fans went wild. Head coach Johnny Mills gave his assessment of the situtation. "I've never seen us as focused as we are. They are all really focused. I feel great about it. These are the best young men in the world. Good students and good citizens. It's a different caliber of kids here in Division III. A notch above, for sure."

Assistant coach John Smith was also feeling confident. "It's our night from the word go," he said. "It's a great feeling being out here with these boys. And it sure brings back a lot of great memories, especially from 1959."

Behind Smith, hundreds of blue and gold pom poms danced to the steady rhythm of the tom tom as a banner with the words "Scalp 'em Choctaws" fluttered in the welcome breeze. Although the temperature was a toasty ninety-five degrees the breeze made the evening a perfect one for college football, and the frenzied Choctaw fans whooped it up in fine style.

On the visitors' side, Millsaps students and fans were also caught up in the spirit of rivalry. They had earlier paraded several city blocks from their campus to the stadium with floats, a marching band, and banners that read "Choke the Choctaws" and "The Only Good Choctaw is a Dead Choctaw." Without question, fans on both sides of the field were seizing the moment and giving a rowdy account of themselves that would have made the previous generations who supported the MC/Millsaps rivalry extremely proud.

The moment everyone had been waiting on for over forty years had finally arrived. For Choctaws and Majors, Baptists and Methodists, Millsaps and Mississippi College, it was time to go to war.

HOLY WAR
8:00 P.M. —The First Half

Shortly after Millsaps took the opening kickoff to their own 34 yard line, the players served notice on the fans that this game was more than just an ordinary Division III affair. On the first play from scrimmage, MC linebacker Bryan Madden slammed Major tailback Brent LeJeune to the turf for a three yard loss, and even the fans in the nosebleed seats could feel the shockwaves caused by the blow. Moments later, after a Millsaps punt and two fruitless Choctaw plays, Payton Perrett's third down pass to flanker Clint Harrison was broken up by Major defensive back Jahreese Jones, who hit Harrison so hard the lick was heard all the way up in the press box. The Mississippi Backyard Brawl was on with a vengeance.

The Majors gained the game's initial first down on their second drive when quarterback Allen Cox made a six yard dash to the Millsaps 49. But the signal caller fumbled the ball away two plays later and MC safety Deuce Harrison recovered for the Chocs at the MC 37.

The Indians achieved first down two plays later when Perrett completed a twenty yard pass to wide receiver Vance Andry, who was brought down by cornerback Marty Frascogna at the Millsaps 47. The drive stalled and the Chocs punted to Frascogna, who gave his mates a scare by fumbling the ball and kicking it towards his own goal line. But an MC player kicked it through the end zone and the Majors took possession at their own 20-yard line.

The Major ground game proved ineffective, however, and the MC band and fans began serenading the Millsaps faithful with the familiar Florida State "tomahawk chop." After the Chocs downed a punt for excellent field position on their own 49, Perrett went straight to work on their first scoring drive.

Three straight completions moved the Choctaws to the Millsaps 25, and after MC tailback Lamar Davis ran for two more yards, Perrett dropped back to pass. He hit Harrison on a down and out ten yards downfield and the flanker raced down the sideline, broke a tackle at the 10-yard line, and darted into the end zone for a touchdown. With Jeff King's successful conversion, the Choctaws led by a score of 7-0 with 3:54 remaining in the first quarter.

Frascogna returned the ensuing kickoff from his own 15 to the 28, but the Majors couldn't move the ball and had to punt. MC return man James Hobson returned the ball to his own 32, but the Chocs also found the going very tough. Major linebacker William Jorden ended the drive by breaking up a third down pass attempt.

As the first quarter expired, both schools' bands played the famous Southern Cal fight song—"We're gonna beat the hell out of you." But neither side looked poised to run away with the game. As had so often been the case in the past, Millsaps seemed tied to the running game, and the Choctaws had stopped it pretty convincingly. As for the Chocs, they were airing it out in the Mississippi College tradition, but were misfiring as often as not.

Neither team got anything going in the second quarter until Hobson made a good punt return for the Chocs, but his gain was nullified by a clipping penalty and MC took over at their own 4 yard line. A run up the middle lost three more yards and the Chocs found themselves with their backs against the wall. On second down the first big break of the day went Millsaps's way as Perrett fumbled during a quarterback sneak and the Majors recovered the ball on the MC 15 yard line.

Two Millsaps running plays produced negative yardage, but a Choctaw penalty pushed the Majors forward inside the MC 10. Allen Cox then completed a pass to receiver Josh Jeter who was stopped at the 6. Two more running plays gave Millsaps a first and goal at the 1. From there, fullback Matt Walker plunged through the middle of the line for paydirt. McNeal's successful PAT made the score 7-7 with 5:17 remaining in the first half.

The Choctaw offense immediately made up for its charity to the Majors by launching the most impressive touchdown drive of the game. Payton Perrett began by hitting Vance Andry for two straight first down completions to the Millsaps 49. Perrett notched a third straight first down by hitting tight end Whit Lewis for a fifteen yard gain before Frascogna tackled Lewis on the Millsaps 33. A red hot Perrett then hit wideout Joseph Ferritta for a nine yard gain to the 23 yard line. Tailback Lamar Davis then carried the ball around left end for another first down at the 18. On the very next play, Davis charged around right end for an 18-yard touchdown dash. King's PAT was blocked, making the score MC 13 Millsaps 7 with 2:39 left in the first half.

On their next possession, the Majors moved to midfield before running out of gas and punted to the Choctaw 28. Perrett quickly picked up where he had left off and completed two more passes to move his team out to their own 31 yard line, but the gun sounded to end the first half before Perrett could do any further damage to the shell shocked Major defense.

The first half of one of the greatest games ever played on Mississippi soil had ended. And the best was still to come.

HALFTIME

During the intermission, Mississippi College saluted ten members of the 1959 Choctaw team which defeated Millsaps 26-6 in the last meeting between the schools. Honored at midfield were head coach Hartwell McPhail, assistant coach Jim Parkman, Norvell Burkett, Charles Faulkner, James Garvin, Barry Landrum, Martin McMullen, Jim Parton, Larry Therell, Larry Tucker, and Gerald Welch.

After the ceremony, Landrum, whose knockout punch had started the riot that ended the football series in 1960, lauded the rivalry's renewal. "I just wish I could be out there on the field for one play," he said with a wry grin. "If they'd give me just a little daylight I might could get two or three yards."

MC athletic director Mike Jones was also in a jubilant mood. "Our team showed a lot of character answering their touchdown with a scoring drive," he beamed. "I'm proud of 'em, and glad we've got such a great crowd and this great atmosphere." Jones then spoke prophetically when asked about the game's ultimate outcome. "It will be decided," he answered, "by who makes the least turnovers and who has the best conditioning."

The Millsaps locker room was more subdued, but if the players were worried about trailing 13-7, it wasn't evident in their faces. The offensive players merely sat quietly and listened to Bob Tyler as he explained plays and formations on a black board, while the defensive squad listened attentively to assistant coach Ron Gray's strategic suggestions. The atmosphere seemed more like that of a Millsaps classroom than a football locker room; no motivational speeches or harangues, just a calm explanation of what the Majors needed to do strategy-wise to stage a second half comeback. And though Real Pure Beverage Group had donated free bottled water and sports drinks to all four teams playing in the Salvation Army Classic, the Majors seemed thirstier for information than for liquid refreshment.

After the lectures ended, Ron Gray made the coaching staff's only appeal to the players' emotions—"Hit 'em right in the mouth," he urged as his charges moved purposefully through the door onto the field.

The Mississippi College band and two high school bands. Hillcrest Christian Academy and Copiah Academy concluded their halftime performance just as a determined group of Choctaws resumed their place on the sidelines. The truce was over; it was time to return to the trenches.

THE SECOND HALF

Mississippi College couldn't move the ball in their opening drive of the third quarter. Major defenders Craig Bowman and Jeff

McIntyre killed the Choctaw drive with a quarterback sack, and Frascogna's punt return from the Millsaps 39 to the 50 gave the Majors excellent field position.

On second down, Chris Shiro exploded up the middle for a sixteen-yard gain to the MC 29. Consecutive rushes by Brent LeJeune moved the ball to the 15. Two more rushing plays and a Choctaw offsides penalty pushed the ball to the 3. From there, LeJeune skirted the right end for six points. With McNeal's accurate conversion boot, the score was now 14-13, Millsaps, with 9:30 remaining in the third quarter.

The Chocs were unable to answer the Majors' score this time and Hillman drove a tremendous punt to the Millsaps end zone. The MC defense proved up to the challenge and forced a fumble on the Majors' first play. Choctaw lineman Joe Bayone recovered the ball at the Millsaps 24, where Payton Perrett went right to work.

Perrett hit his favorite target Vance Andry on a down and out at the 10, and the fleet receiver raced down the sideline for a touchdown and a 19-14 Choctaw lead. Playing by the book, Coach Johnny Mills went for two, but linebacker William Jorden forced an incomplete pass by hurrying Perrett and causing him to throw off balance. With 6:07 to go in the third quarter, the Choctaws held a five point lead. The incessant pounding of the tom tom suddenly seemed much louder to the Millsaps students who were forced to endure a Choctaw loudspeaker carefully placed right in front of the Millsaps student section.

Frascogna again gave the Majors good field position with a return to the Major 29, but Allen Cox's first down pass was intercepted by the Choctaws. Fortunately for the Purple and White, the MC defensive back fumbled the ball right back to the Majors when tackled at the 31. Given new life, the Majors drove to their own 40 but could go no further. They punted the ball away to the Chocs, but return man James Hobson couldn't find the handle on the increasingly slippery pigskin and Tamond McKinsey recovered the ball for the Majors at their own 23 yard line.

Hard running by Cox and Walker brought the Majors to the MC 10-yard line where the third quarter expired with the Chocs still clinging to a five point lead. McNeal opened the final stanza with an 18-yard field goal to cut the MC lead to 19-17. The McComb High School band struck up the Notre Dame fight song as the Millsaps Delta Delta Deltas and SAEs cheered loud enough to drown out the infuriating tom tom.

Hobson returned the ensuing Millsaps kickoff to his own 25, but the Choctaws were again unable to mount a sustained drive. The Majors took the ball deep in their own territory after a driving Hillman punt, then drove to the midfield stripe where they faced a tough decision on fourth and one. Tyler decided to go for it, and Walker's half-yard dive gave the Majors' drive continued life. But the charge stalled moments later and the Majors were forced to punt on 4th and 16 at their own 44.

Hobson made another strong kick return from his own end zone to the MC 25, and Perrett quickly passed the Choctaws out to the 44-yard line. But two consecutive QB sacks by McIntyre and Jorden, and a pass break up by Jorden, ended the Choctaw threat.

Millsaps couldn't move the ball either, as Scott Young sacked Perrett on second down and McKelvey stuffed a Major third down running play. Mississippi College got the ball back on their own 23 with 4:12 to play and a chance to run out the clock with a time-consuming drive. But Perrett suffered an eye injury on a third down quarterback sneak and had to be taken out of the game. As the Choctaw fans chanted "warm up the bus," Hillman punted the ball back to Millsaps.

Marty Frascogna jump-started the Majors' last gasp drive by returning the ball to the Millsaps 45. With 2:06 remaining in the game, Millsaps fans started praying for a miracle.

Quarterback Allen Cox, who had suffered a leg injury in the second quarter and had gamely played through a discerniable limp throughout the second half, responded to the challenge by completing three consecutive swing passes to running backs Shiro and Walker. An MC offsides penalty made it first and ten Majors at the Choctaw 27. A run by LeJeune and another pinpoint Cox pass took the ball to the 12-yard line with 16 seconds left in the contest.

Mississippi College called two timeouts in an attempt to "ice" kicker Derrick McNeal, but as he had predicted the day before the game, his 29-yard field goal try sailed right between the uprights. An ecstatic group of Majors shouted with joy, hugged each other, and congratulated themselves as if they had won a national championship. Across the way, shell-shocked Choctaw players stood in motionless, stunned silence. And although the tom tom had for the first time grown silent in the home-side stands, sheer bedlam prevailed on the Millsaps side as the scoreboard flashed the improbable score—Millsaps 20 Mississippi College 19!

"I love it," exclaimed former Millsaps quarterback Byrd Hillman on the Major sideline as jubilant players hugged and congratulated each other beside him. "This is so huge!"

After order was restored, reserve Choctaw quarterback Ben Reed threw up a couple of desperation passes, but the effort was in vain. The Millsaps Majors had won what many would consider to be the greatest game of the series; and certainly one which equaled any contest played in the long and distinguished history of the series.

"It's everything we dreamed of," said athletic director Ron Jurney. "What an effort by our kids. A lot of people said we couldn't do it, but. . ."

"I wasn't one of them," interrupted an ecstatic Paul Benton. "And I'm glad to say I told you so."

After receiving congratulations from Coach Johnny Mills and Dr. Van Quick at midfield, Bob Tyler, who had coached under Bear Bryant and Johnny Vaught, and had led Mississippi State to its second bowl victory in thirty-five years, told the media members surrounding him that, "This was my best win ever! This was tremendous. I'm not a genius, and it wasn't because of a plan. These kids kept fighting and fighting. They fought 'em all the way. They believed they were going to win."

Several yards away, Marty Frascogna greeted his good friend, a very disconsolate Payton Perrett, at midfield. "Are you okay?" Frascogna asked as he noticed the patch covering Perrett's left eye.

"I'll be all right," Perrett replied. "Y'all played a great game, Marty."

"You too, Payton. It was a battle to the end."

"It was great being a part of it," said the Choctaw quarterback. "Congratulations on the win."

Moments later, in a triumphant Millsaps locker room, Coach Tyler's son Breck, who had played receiver for both Mississippi State and Ole Miss, agreed that the win was his father's "greatest victory as a coach. It was such a team effort," the younger Tyler exclaimed, "the students, alumni, fans and the players. . . .A total team effort."

The elder Tyler held the Backyard Brawl trophy aloft as cheers resounded throughout the Major locker room. "I thought of sixty-nine good things to say," the coach declared, "but I can't remember a single one. There's so much to say and I can't say it all. But I will say this—it's going to be a great 360 days!"

Assistant coach Shay Taylor reminded the team that they couldn't celebrate too much with a big game awaiting them the next weekend. "The next game with Austin College is the biggest game on our schedule now," he warned, "but gosh darn it, let's have a big time tonight!"

"This is the biggest win in Millsaps College history," announced A.D. Ron Jurney to another round of cheers.

"When we renewed this series," said former President George Harmon, "I knew we could do it."

After alumnus Wayne Ferrell thanked Mike Frascogna and the Sports Council for setting up the game, Frascogna replied by challenging the team to keep the winning spirit alive. "The difference between last season's 2-8 record," he said, "and beating Mississippi College this year is that you refused to die. And you'll get that Division III National Championship if you just don't ever die."

In response, Coach Tyler led the team in a chant, saying, "We will not die, we will not die."

When asked how he felt about kicking the winning field goal, Derrick McNeal said, "We said nine months ago and again last night that a last minute kick wouldn't be good for them [MC] and it wasn't. But I couldn't have done it without the team. It was a real team effort."

Another gleeful Millsaps player sought out alumnus Paul Benton, and shook the Majors' benefactor's hand. "Thanks a million," was all he said.

Up in the stands, Joe Whitwell, whose fumble forty years ago had set up a Choctaw touchdown en route to an MC victory in the series' final game, stared at the stadium scoreboard and shook his head in amazement. "What a game," he told his wife Marguerite. "I figured that Millsaps would give them a run for their money, but I never thought that it would end this way. What a way to end the game. I didn't know revenge could be so sweet after 40 years!"

Outside the Choctaw locker room, Coach John Smith, who had caught a touchdown pass to lead the Choctaws to victory in the 1959 MC/Millsaps game, was adjusting to the idea of losing to his longtime archrival. "We didn't play well and didn't really get after it," he said sorrowfully. "But," he added with a wan smile, struggling mightily to find a silver lining on a very dark cloud, "It was a great way to kick start the rivalry."

To the Division III record crowd of 12,200 fans who saw the 2000 Millsaps/MC Backyard Brawl, "a great way to kick start the rivalry" seemed the understatement of the new century. The greatest game in the history of an eighty-year old series had been a titanic struggle from the start, and had ultimately been decided by a 29-yard field goal in the waning seconds of the fourth quarter. Best of all, it would go down as one of those games that could never have been so memorable if it had been played for money or even for national acclaim. It was played by young men who had labored for days on end during the hottest Mississippi summer on record, and when the gun sounded, had spent every ounce of courage, endurance and fortitude they could muster, solely for love of the game.

EPILOGUE

The 2000 Backyard Brawl had certainly seen its share of stars. Payton Perrett gave an outstanding effort in a losing cause; the sophomore quarterback completed 18 of 30 passes for 199 yards and two touchdowns to become the most effective offensive player in the game. Joe Bayone led the MC defenders with 9 tackles, six for a loss, and also recovered a key Millsaps fumble. Major quarterback Allen Cox gave the game's gutsiest performance as he engineered the winning drive despite a severely hobbled leg. Linebacker William Jorden held the Choctaw offense at bay all night, and kicker Derrick McNeal won the game with two clutch field goals. Names like Perrett, Frascogna, Cox, Bayone, McNeal, Tyler and Mills would forever be mentioned in the same breath as Hale, Holloman, McAfee, McIntosh, Robinson, Bartling, Davis and McPhail. But the star of the game was the whole Millsaps squad, which held together in the face of superior talent where a lesser team would have folded like a tent.

The bold letters on the front page of the next day's *Clarion-Ledger* told astonished sports fans all about the upset—"Millsaps beats MC. . . after forty years." The front page of the Sports section said it another way—"Millsaps stuns MC 20-19." Major head coach Bob Tyler was quoted in the article as declaring the win the greatest of his career. His players were no less exultant in their comments to the press.

"We play for the love of the game," said fullback Matt Walker. "We put all our heart into the game. It's a great feeling. We gave it all we had."

"I didn't get nervous," said kicker Derrick McNeal in reference to his last second field goal effort. "I wanted to do it for my teammates."

"Everyone counted us out," Marty Frascogna added, "but we scratched and clawed and won. We won. Believe it. It happened."

Millsaps's upset of Mississippi College was so stunning that not everyone really believed that it had actually happened. One such disbeliever apparently was Michael Martin, a writer for the Jackson newspaper, *Planet Weekly*. Martin's September 6 article about the previous weekend's football games inexplicably read: "Mississippi College is better than Millsaps; they gotta be— 42-17." If one sportswriter couldn't believe his eyes, he certainly wasn't the Lone Ranger. The only ones who had really expected the Majors to whip the Chocs had been the never-say-die Majors themselves.

Which made the *Purple and White*'s reporting of the game all the more intriguing. Instead of running the news of the victory on the front page, as they had done whenever the Majors had defeated the Chocs in the twentieth century, the *P & W* ran the game story on the back page, under the simple headline, "VICTORY!" The front page article, as it turned out, condemned Millsaps students for placing offensive banners on their floats in the pre-game parade, banners such as "The Only Good Choctaw Is A Dead Choctaw."

Without even knowing they had done so, the *Purple and White* had revealed that a sincere change of heart had occurred at Millsaps and Mississippi College. Forty years earlier, students at both schools had allowed their passion for athletic competition to override their collective judgment, with the result that some of their fellows were seriously injured, and the schools were forced to cancel the longstanding series.

But now, a half-century later, both schools had earned glowing reputations as two of the best colleges in America, and had put all things athletic in their proper subordinate place. Consequently, it was now possible to renew the football series and play a game more exciting than any that had ever been played before, without resort to life-threatening violence.

There were many reasons for these changes, such as more enlightened student bodies and more insistent peacekeeping administrative leadership. And in an era where college football coaches routinely broke the rules in order to win at all costs, athletic directors and coaches at Millsaps and Mississippi College— men like Mike Jones and Ron Jurney, Johnny Mills and Bob

Tyler, Ron Gray and John Smith—brought a perspective to the game that other college coaches would do well to emulate.

However, it fell to *P & W* sportswriters Christopher Hedglin and Jeff Mitchell to make the best explanation as to why Millsaps/MC football had become such a delightful experience. In their post game article, they reminded everyone that, "Football players at Millsaps and Mississippi College are not on athletic scholarship. They are not on television every Saturday. Ninety-nine percent of the time they are not going to play football after their senior year is done. They are true student athletes: they study hard and they play hard. They play not for the attention, they play for the love of the game."

BIBLIOGRAPHY

The sources which I have utilized for information for this book include:

BOOKS, JOURNALS, AND TREATISES

Fraiser, Jim, *Mississippi River Country Tales*, Pelican Publishing Co., 2000.

Goodman, Marguerite, *History of Millsaps College*, Millsaps College Archives, 1972.

Harmon, George, *Millsaps College: Determining the Agenda*, The Newcomen Society of the United States, 1985.

The Journal of Mississippi History, Mississippi Department of Archives and History.

Leggett, John, *History of Millsaps Football*, The Ross H. Moore Faculty Papers, Millsaps College Archives, 1984.

Martin, Charles, *Notes on the Beginning of Choctaw Athletics*, Special Collection, Mississippi College, 1996.

McLemore, Richard, *A History of Mississippi Baptists, 1780-1970*, Mississippi Baptist Convention Board, 1971.

Sansing, David, *Making Haste Slowly*, University Press of Mississippi, 1990.

Weathersby, William, *History of Mississippi College*, Publications of the Mississippi Historical Society, 1925.

NEWSPAPERS

The Clarion-Ledger
The Daily Mississippian
The Delta Democrat Times
The Jackson Daily News
The Mississippi Collegian
The Northside Sun
The Planet Weekly
The Purple and White
The State Times

Jim Fraiser is the Director of Legal Defense for the Mississippi Band of Choctaw Indians. This is his fourth book. He also serves as a contributing writer for the Emmerich newspapers, the *Clarion-Ledger, Biloxi Sun Herald,* and *Northeast Mississippi Daily Journal.* He lives in Jackson with his wife Carole and daughters Lucy and Mary Adelyn.